MICHOACÁN AND EDEN

MICHOACÁN AND EDEN

*Vasco de Quiroga and
the Evangelization of Western Mexico*

BERNARDINO VERÁSTIQUE

UNIVERSITY OF TEXAS PRESS

The frontispiece and figures 1, 2, 3, 5, 6, 8, 9, and 10 are by Alfredo B. Cruz, adapted from the Codex C-IV-5 in the Real Biblioteca de El Escorial, Madrid, as found in *The Chronicles of Michoacán*, translated by Eugene R. Craine and Reginald C. Reindorp, University of Oklahoma Press, 1970. The map, Figure 4 (Santiago de Compostela), and Figure 7 (Vasco de Quiroga) are by Alfredo B. Cruz.

Part of Chapter 6 originally appeared as "The Millennial Kingdom in Mexico," *Harvard Divinity Bulletin* 22, no. 1 (1992): 6–9.

Frontispiece. A Purhépecha high priest and elders contemplate an ominous comet that appeared in the heavens prior to the arrival of the Spaniards.

COPYRIGHT © 2000 by the UNIVERSITY OF TEXAS PRESS

Printed in the United States of America

First edition, 2000

Requests for permission to reproduce material from this work should be sent to Permissions, University of Texas Press, Box 7819, Austin, TX 78713-7819.

♾ The paper used in this book meets the minimum requirements of ANSI/ NISO Z39.48-1992 (R1997) (Permanence of Paper).

Verástique, Bernardino.
    Michoacán and Eden : Vasco de Quiroga and the evangelization of western Mexico / Bernardino Verástique. — 1st ed.
        p.   cm.
    Includes bibliographical references and index.
    ISBN 0-292-78737-5 (cloth: alk. paper). — ISBN 0-292-78738-3 (pbk: alk. paper).
    1. Tarasco Indians—History—16th century.   2. Tarasco Indians—Religion.
3. Tarasco Indians—Missions—Mexico—Michoacán de Ocampo.   4. Indians, Treatment of—Mexico—Michoacán de Ocampo.   5. Quiroga, Vasco de, 1470– 1565.   6. Catholic Church—Missions—Mexico—Michoacán de Ocampo.
7. Michoacán de Ocampo (Mexico)—Church history.   8. Michoacán de Ocampo (Mexico)—History—16th century.   I. Title.
F1221.T3V47   2000
972'.3702—dc21   99-21505

You said that our gods are not true gods.

Calm and amiable,

consider, oh Lords, whatever is best.

We cannot be tranquil,

and yet we certainly do not believe;

we do not accept your teachings as truth,

even though this may offend you.

—from testimony by the *tlamatinime,* the Náhuatl wise men,
to the Franciscan friars in México-Tenochtitlán, 1524

CONTENTS

ILLUSTRATIONS

ACKNOWLEDGMENTS

I wish to acknowledge the debt that I owe to the many participants in this work. First, I would like to thank Dr. John B. Carman and his wife, Ineke, who helped me in uncountable ways during my tenure at the Center for the Study of World Religions at Harvard University. A special *abrazo* goes out to Dr. John Womack Jr. for taking me under his wing and for inspiring and teaching me about the history of Mexico. I am indebted to Dr. Clarissa Atkinson, who not only made the early phase of my study possible but also served as a reader of the manuscript. I am grateful for the support and sacrifices of my parents, Ben and Beatrice Verástique, *en paz descansen,* and I thank my family and friends for their patience during the time it took me to complete this project. Finally, I would like to thank my *padre espiritual,* the late Andrés Segura Granados, for those precious moments spent together discussing the indigenous traditions of Mexico. I cannot adequately express my appreciation for their support.

INTRODUCTION

In 1519 the Spanish governor of Cuba, Diego Velásquez, commissioned a military expedition to the mainland of Mexico. Its task was to search for gold and to secure slaves. Velásquez appointed Hernán Cortés, a young nobleman and member of the Santiago de Cuba town council, to command the expeditionary force. However, rather than following Velásquez's orders to establish a trading port on the Mexican east coast, Cortés instead led his troops into the mountainous interior, where they waged an assault on the wealthy urban cultures of the Mesoamerican highlands. On August 23, 1521, after a ferocious four-month siege, the Aztec emperor, Cuauhtemoctzin, surrendered the island capital of Tenochtitlán to Cortés and his Tlaxcalan allies. With the most powerful indigenous state in ruins, Cortés then turned his armies westward, toward the second most powerful Amerindian state, the Purhépecha kingdom of Michoacán.

The accommodation of the indigenous people of Michoacán to the subsequent military and spiritual conquest of western Mexico is the topic of the present study. This book focuses on the role of the famous judge and bishop Don Vasco de Quiroga (1477/8–1565) in the evangelization of the Purhépecha. Vasco de Quiroga was the first bishop of Michoacán, serving from 1535 to his death in 1565. During his tenure, he was known for his sometimes violent authoritarianism as well as his Franciscan-like compassion for the native people. In his diocese, he promoted a policy of congregating the Purhépecha into Amerindian *pueblos* (towns), where the mendicant friars could more easily teach them the fundamental beliefs of Christianity and the values of Spanish culture. Quiroga drew his organizational model for the *pueblos* from two primary sources: the ancient Judeo-Christian myth of Eden and Plato's idea of the republic as a perfect commonwealth governed by intellectuals.

In order to realize his vision of a Christian utopia, Quiroga patronized the construction of three *pueblos*—each of which included a hospital—the great cathedral of Santa Ana, and many churches and schools. He also established the Colegio de San Nicolás Obispo. Quiroga believed that the towns' residents should adhere to the principles of simple living, hard work, rigorous religious devotion, and universal education in farming and crafts. The stated goal of his plan was to lessen human misery. Nonetheless, the forcible congregation of the Amerindians left them vulnerable to the virulent epidemics that swept through Michoacán during Quiroga's residency.

To this day Quiroga is a controversial figure in the historiography of Mexico, for conflicting accounts of his life abound. The Mexican historian Aguayo Spencer regards him as a *taumaturgo* (miracle worker). Quiroga's earliest biographer, Juan José Moreno, portrays Quiroga as the "best man who has lived in these blessed places of Michoacán." Enrique Cárdenas de la Peña argues that Don Vasco laid the foundations of what would later become the Mexican social security system; he calls Quiroga "the Apostle of the New World." The Jesuit Paul Callens describes the bishop as a great reformer. Benjamin Jarnes, Paul Lietz, and Nicolás León also depict Quiroga as a positive historical figure, offering little critical interpretation of his life and actions. Silvio Zavala, who focuses on Quiroga's *pueblo*-hospitals, exaggerates the influence of Thomas More's book *Utopia* on the bishop. Lewis Hanke and Fintan B. Warren assume that because Quiroga was a Renaissance humanist, he must be considered a social liberal and defender of Amerindian rationality and culture. But if the latter were completely true, then Quiroga's rigid stance against the religious and secular forces that opposed him would be hard to understand. Moreover, if the bishop were a liberal and a pluralist, he surely would have sided with Bartolomé de Las Casas in the jurisdictional conflicts between church and state in the Americas. However, as Marcel Bataillon has pointed out, Quiroga publicly opposed Las Casas and defended the *encomenderos* and the *encomienda* system in New Spain.[1]

With regard to the apparent contradictions concerning the historical legacy of Don Vasco de Quiroga, the present study offers the following thesis: that these contradictions are due to the continual transmission of misinformation concerning the "New World" and to historical interpretations shaped by the authors' own prejudices and worldviews. Although this book most likely will not be free of all such errors, it aims to elucidate the subject from a variety of disciplinary perspectives, seeking thereby to arrive at a more accurate view of the conquest of Michoacán.

The subject of Mesoamerica's encounter with Catholic Spain has excited the imaginations of historians for nearly five hundred years now. A unifying theme in the vast historiography of the conquest has come to be known, tragically, as "the problem of the Indian." According to the Mexican historian Edmundo O'Gorman, the central problems for scholars of Mexico have been how to comprehend the Mexican historical past as a continuum and how to allow for the idea of uniqueness in Mexico's autochthonous, colonial, and nationalist periods. O'Gorman states that scholars must contend with the difficulty of accounting for one Mexico among the many Mexicos. Problems concerning the Amerindians most likely arise from scholars' inability, or downright refusal, to acknowledge how their own worldviews retrospectively legitimate specific systems of exploitation in the New World. After examining the conceptions of history and the past that were manifested in the conquest, the historian Enrique Florescano asserts that "in this era there was no dominant interpretation of history; rather, multiple interpretations of the past co-existed, produced by diverse sectors of the population, and each one of them was nourished by different concepts of time and the past."[2]

The Amerindian question is so controversial within the borders of Mexico that scholars have been incapable of identifying the merits of the Christianization or evangelization project. The claim of Spanish Catholicism to a "spiritual conquest" has appeared to nullify the Amerindians' gods. Needless to say, in a *mestizo* (mixed-blood) society, this problem is intensified and manifests itself in self-hatred, alienation, and feelings of illegitimacy.

The debate over the motives of the conquest has so inflamed the European imagination that the result has been a historiography of stereotypes and speculative excesses. As Benjamin Keen has noted, until his death Columbus believed that the Native Americans were Orientals. Peter Mártir de Anglería argued that the Amerindians were descendants of the lost tribe of Israel. The European conquerors believed that the New World cultures had to conform to the ontological parameters of the Book of Genesis. This judgment resulted in outlandish explanations of the Amerindians' place in the scheme of Judeo-Christian cosmology. In the first half of the sixteenth century the question of the nature of the Amerindians led to a prolonged theological debate concerning their humanity. If the Spanish theologians had been able to prove that the Amerindians were inhuman, then there would have been no need to baptize them, and they could have been legitimately classified as slaves. In a famous moment in this great debate concerning the humanity of the Amerindians, Juan Ginés de Sepúlveda stated at the University of Valladolid that certain Amerindian customs proved that "they be neither bears nor monkeys nor are they without the power of reason, that is to say, they are not animals; but men albeit imperfect."[3]

The sixteenth-century controversy concerning the Amerindians' status sometimes manifested the Spaniards' racism, as in the case of such early chroniclers as Gómara and Oviedo, who defended the brutality of the conquest as necessary in dealing with a barbaric people. Even pro-Amerindian mendicants such as Motolinía, Sahagún, Durán, and Mendieta described the American aborigines as either angels or beasts, steeped in ignorance and superstition.[4]

After 1767 and the expulsion from the Americas of the Society of Jesus, there arose a nostalgic literature that compared the Mesoamerican civilizations with the classical civilizations of Greece and Rome. This triumphalist strategy was employed by New World *mestizos* to counter the Spanish Creoles' pretensions to racial and cultural superiority. Both Francisco Javier Clavijero and Pedro José Márquez could be included in the vanguard of this important group of writers. In Clavijero's words, by glorifying Mesoamerican civilization he hoped "to restore the truth to its splendor, truth obscured by an incredible multitude of writers on America."[5]

The debate over the humanity of the Amerindians often demonstrated Europe's preoccupation with the justification of its own worldview. For instance, we see that Voltaire, who supported the idea of an enlightened aristocracy, praised the Aztecs because he believed their system of kingship resembled that of the French monarchy. In contrast, Montesquieu and Raynal, avowed enemies of the monarchy, criticized the Aztec rulers as irresponsible tyrants. And the idea of the "noble savage" (that the native people of the Americas led uncorrupted, naturally virtuous lives) has its source in the romantic writings and visual art of Europe.[6]

The Native American did not fare much better in the early twentieth century. Noted anthropologists like Edward Tylor and Lewis Morgan employed popular Darwinian theories of biological determinism and evolution to postulate that the Amerindian was a being who had lost out in the struggle for existence. Tylor and Morgan regarded Native Americans in the grand evolutionary structure as biological and cultural deviants whose worth for scholars resided in their value as research subjects. Thus the native people were viewed as specimens to be described and then assigned a lowly place in the hierarchy of evolution.[7]

Aside from a few fine studies, in the contemporary period the Amerindian continues to be classified as a "savage mind" or a kind of Paleolithic survivor in a hostile postmodern world. Perhaps the continuous web of misunderstandings that have shaped "white and Indian" relations can be explained by the simple political fact that Amerindians have been the losers in the battle for land, a battle that began in the sixteenth century and continues to this day.

In addition to the debate about the nature of the Amerindians, this study also is concerned necessarily with the idea of cultural synthesis. Thus it explores the meeting and eventual blending of the Purhépecha and Spanish cultures in Michoacán. An important assumption of my analysis is that a basic characteristic of a culture is its symbolic construction of boundaries, both internal and external. In other words, a culture's core identity is encapsulated in its perception of differences: differences within the culture, such as varying caste and class statuses, and differences between it and surrounding cultures. A community and its members thus define themselves in relation to significant others. For example, the Purhépecha elites saw themselves as the heirs of the Toltec kings and believed that they had a sacred entitlement to the land, which they held was given to them by divine beings. They distinguished their social and political autonomy in relation to their bitter enemies—their Aztec cousins and the fierce Chichimec nomads to the north. The Spanish after their arrival categorized the Purhépecha as *indios;* hence the Purhépecha's autonomous identity came to depend on their opposition to the Spanish perception of them as a subcaste. Likewise, the formation of the Spanish *cristiano* identity was characterized by the prolonged process of cultural differentiation called the Reconquista. The *cristianos* ultimately defined their cultural boundaries in terms of their religious differences with Iberian Muslims and Jews.[8] My objective in viewing the people and events in Michoacán in such a way is to highlight the cultural contours, or worldviews, that each party brought with it to the encounter. By employing this approach, I hope to demonstrate that the Purhépecha and Spanish responses and accommodations to one another were based in complex historical experiences and in presuppositions concerning their respective cosmologies.

I have organized the present study into eight chapters. The first two chapters investigate the rise to political and cultural dominance of the Purhépecha-Chichimec clans in western Mexico. Chapter 1 begins with a discussion of the geography of Michoacán and proceeds to an interpretation of the cultural traditions prevalent before the ascendancy of the Purhépecha aristocracy in the late thirteenth century. Chapter 2 presents an analysis of Purhépecha religion.

Here I demonstrate that the Purhépecha religion exhibits a dualistic theology that is common to all Mesoamerican religious thought. Chapters 3 and 4 evaluate the history and culture of Spain on the eve of the Conquest of Mexico. They delineate the many cultural influences and heterodox ideas that merged in the peninsula to form the militant ideology of Reconquista Spain. In the remaining four chapters, I focus on Don Vasco de Quiroga. Chapter 5 examines the violent decade of the 1520s in Mexico and the reasons surrounding Quiroga's appointment, and Chapter 6 studies the evangelization of Michoacán and the consolidation of Quiroga's diocese in the period of 1533 to 1565. Chapter 7 analyzes Bishop Quiroga's longest written work, *Información en derecho*, while Chapter 8 investigates Quiroga's utopian experiment in the town of Santa Fe de la Laguna. I conclude with an epilogue comparing the conquest of Michoacán to similar political and religious efforts to subjugate the Amerindians in other locations of New Spain.

MICHOACÁN AND EDEN

The modern state of Michoacán and its sixteenth-century boundary

ONE

The Purhépecha-Chichimec of Michoacán

One fundamental error in reconstructing the history of the Conquest of Mexico is the assumption that a monolithic Christianity encountered a generically uniform Amerindian culture. This misunderstanding has contributed to a vast literature on the successes and failures of the Christian evangelization of Mexico. Yet though Mexico today must be considered a Catholic country, in some areas of both the remote highlands and the sprawling metropolis of Mexico City the pre-Columbian religion is still very much alive. Thus it seems that the evangelization was both a success and a failure. In the sixteenth century two unique understandings of transcendence—Christian and pre-Columbian—are wedded in what appears to have been, at different times in the history of Mexico, a somewhat unstable marriage. The crucial period of the first encounter between the Purhépecha people of Michoacán and the Castilian conquistadors is the focus of this investigation. I hope that in reconstructing the religious ideals and conflicts of the age, I might better understand the contours of my own history and faith.

THE GEOGRAPHICAL LANDSCAPE

The modern state of Michoacán preserves the territorial integrity of the pre-Columbian kingdom of the Purhépecha-Chichimec. The maintenance of the boundaries of the Purhépecha-Chichimec kingdom was ensured by Don Vasco de Quiroga in 1538 when he established the Bishopric of Michoacán. Immediately preceding the conquest, the Purhépecha controlled about seventy thousand square kilometers. This area included lands that are now part of the modern states of Guerrero, Guanajuato, and Querétaro. Several cultures lived in this zone, among them the Teco, Matlaltzinca, and Otomí. According to Cook and Borah's monumental work, *The Indian Population of Central Mexico, 1531–1610*, the zone contained between one and one-half million and two million inhabitants.[1]

A formidable barrier in comprehending the history of the people of Michoacán is overcome when we understand the relationship between the region's people and the rugged landscape. Michoacán's spectacular natural beauty is the result of thousands of years of volcanic intensity and erosion, which created the great mountain ranges of the Pacific. Five major geological features characterize the area: the coastal plains of the Pacific; the Sierra Madre del Sur, which slices the region from north to south; the steep volcanic transversal that runs east to west across the upper portion of the state; the great Lerma River basin, which opens the northeastern portion of the region to the verdant grasslands of the Bajío; and the immense Balsas River system in the south.[2]

The mountainous terrain has resulted in the compartmentalization of the region into various climactic zones. The south (with the exception of the Balsas River depression) has a rainy season. The steppe area, where the Balsas and Tepalcatepec Rivers meet, is a dry, hot land that is known in Spanish as the *tierra caliente*. The *tierra fría* (cold country), which is higher than the Sierra Madre and lower than the highest volcanoes, is a temperate area that has a rainy season throughout the year.

Woven throughout the state's northern volcanic region is a system of landlocked highland lakes. Lakes Pátzcuaro, Cuitzeo, and Zirahuén in the northeast, as well as Lake Chapala in the northwest, historically have been the most dense centers of population. This is undoubtedly due to the abundance of fresh water and land for irrigation, and to the plentiful supply of fish, fowl, and forest game that can sustain fairly large settlements.

Mountains and the trees that covered them played a vital role in the lives of the pre-Columbian people of Michoacán. The mountains were not only the abode of the gods but also the site of the clouds that filled the lake. Trees provided food and fire for household hearths, and their leaves were cooked and used as medicine. Wood was also essential for transportation, since it was used to build lake canoes. *The Chronicles of Michoacán* states that the coniferous trees of the high sierras were the source of fuel for the fires burning perpetually in the Purhépecha temples. The forest's economic significance is evident in the fact that wood was a basic tribute commodity expected by the Purhépecha ruler, the *cazonci*.[3]

THE CULTURAL LANDSCAPE

The first people entered the Americas during the upper Paleolithic period, possibly as early as 40,000 B.C., traveling across a land bridge that joined Asia with the Western Hemisphere. Gradually exploring the Pacific coastline and the deep gorges cut by the Columbia River, clans of hunter-gatherers made their way to Mesoamerica, where the climate was more amiable and game was abundant. Many thousands of years passed before the various hunting groups developed distinctive cultural characteristics.

In order to gain an understanding of the processes that led to the growth of the complex society of the Purhépecha state, it is helpful to examine briefly the origins of both agriculture and settled village life in Mesoamerica.[4] The archaeological record shows that beginning roughly in 7000 B.C., hunter-gatherers in Mesoamerica began to locate themselves in small, sedentary villages. The settlement patterns of the first villages tended to be dispersed in the lowlands and nucleated in the highlands. The appearance of the earliest villages occurred simultaneously with the domestication of wild plants used for both sustenance and medicine. As the archaeologist Kent Flannery has noted, the hunter-gatherers of central Mexico

> *survived on the basis of a collecting strategy with many alternate moves and alternate food sources, depending on whether the rains came too soon or too late, the spring was too cool or too hot, the deer were in the valleys or up in the forests, the pinyon nut crop was heavy or meager. Finally, by 5000 B.C. one of their ultimate strategies became the artificial increase of certain edible plants by selection and planting. Beans, squashes, pumpkins, amaranths, chilis, tomatoes, avocados (and perhaps even prickly pear, maguey, and a whole series of semitropical fruits for which we have only Indian names) came under cultivation not long after this date. But the most important of these was maize or Indian corn.*[5]

With the studies conducted in the Tehuacán Valley of central Mexico, directed by the archaeologist Richard MacNeish, we are able to reconstruct a picture of the relationship of agriculture to settlement patterns. MacNeish posits that over a long period of time the hunter-gatherers of the Tehuacán

Valley became intimately aware of the seasonal changes in their microenvironments. Their migrations thus came to depend on the availability of food and game in a particular season. One result of the constant migrations was that clans often returned to their old campsites. In the cleared fields of these campsites began the slow mutation of the plants and fruits that were to become staples for the Amerindians. This event was probably the beginning of a primitive horticulture and an ever-increasing manipulation of the environment in order to create food surpluses. The immediate result of food surpluses allowed the people of the Tehuacán Valley to remain in their villages year-round.[6] The discovery of the fruits of agriculture, then, over and above hunting and gathering, significantly influenced the development of village and cultural life in Mesoamerica.

MICHOACÁN FROM THE OLMECS TO THE TOLTECS

According to George Kubler, the archaeological history of western Mexico comprised four principal stages: the early Olmec period, which endured several centuries in the state of Guerrero, from 1500 B.C. to A.D. 1; a middle period (A.D. 1–900), during which formative styles were amplified in funeral pottery, particularly in the region of Colima, Jalisco, and Nayarit; the postclassic period (A.D. 900–1250), when Toltec and Mixtec ceremonial forms intruded into Michoacán and Sinaloa; and, lastly, the period A.D. 1250–1521, which coincided with the Purhépecha state and its influence upon the lake districts of Michoacán.[7]

The Olmecs were the first Mesoamericans to construct great ceremonial centers, build mural-size bas-reliefs, and geometrically locate stelae altars carved in stone. Olmec culture flourished from its center (in the present-day states of Veracruz and Tabasco) to Michoacán and from Guerrero to Costa Rica. The Olmecs were noted for the invention of symbols that remained in use in Mesoamerica for more than two thousand years, until the Spanish Conquest. In addition, they most probably invented not only a system of writing but also a highly perfected calendar.[8]

Several ancient sites in western Mexico attest to the Olmec presence there. The archaeological site of Capacha (1450 B.C.) on the Colima coast west of Michoacán exhibits definite Olmec pottery characteristics. The Gulf Coast style is also visible at Capacha in the number of seashells from the Caribbean found together with an Olmec version of Saint Andrew's cross. At the oldest site in Michoacán proper, El Opeño (1300 B.C.), located on a hillside near the village of Curuturan, nine westerly facing burial chambers laid out in two parallel lines were discovered. These chambers contained primitive Olmec-like figurines with black-bean eyes and heavy neck ornaments.[9] Located also in Michoacán is stirrup pottery of definite South American design. Jacques Soustelle contends that

> *The relationships between Mexico and Andean America are a proven fact as far as a relatively late period is concerned, at the turning point between the classic era and the post-classic phase, when South American metallurgy was introduced into Mexico, first of all in the regions of Oaxaca and Michoacán bordering the Pacific Ocean. . . . A systematic comparative study of the entire panorama from 1500 B.C. to 1000 B.C., in Mesoamerica and the Andes, embracing the two oldest civilizations, that of the Olmecs in the north, that of Chavin in the south, could cast new light on the origin and the relations of the high cultures of the two parts of the continents.*[10]

Along an arc running from the southern portion of the state of Nayarit through Jalisco, Colima, and westernmost Michoacán are found the tombs of the Chupicuaro culture (200 B.C.–A.D. 1). The tombs contain polychrome pottery, mosaic mirrors of pyrite, and conch-shell trumpets. Richard Adams speculates that these artifacts demonstrate the culture's early development of a complex ritual funerary tradition.[11] At Chupicuaro, near the Lerma River, the tombs are laid out in an elaborate geometric and astronomical arrangement; some forty-six dogs accompany their masters in the graves.[12] The Chupicuaro culture represents a ceramic tradition in full flower. Its appearance illustrates that as early as 200 B.C. the central Mexican culture had reached the periphery of the northeastern region of Michoacán.[13]

From A.D. 100 until A.D. 600, a new cultural synthesis dominated a vast area of central Mexico. It was centered at Teotihuacán in the northeastern corner of the valley of Anáhuac. The period of its dominance was characterized by a dramatic demographic increase in the highlands, including the lake area of Michoacán. This marked population increase was accompanied by the appearance of a highly complex socioeconomic structure. Based on religious rites, it was administered by a sophisticated caste of theocrats who acquired their power from their esoteric knowledge, their ability to organize massive workforces, and their control of agrarian surpluses.

Teotihuacán was not only a ceremonial center that drew pilgrims from great distances but also a great urban complex with huge marketplaces, where craftsmen could display and trade their wares. Population estimates for the city range from 50,000 to 120,000 inhabitants. It has been calculated that it would have taken a surrounding agricultural base of 150,000 to 400,000 acres to support a population of this size.[14]

The city was laid out along an east-to-west axis in conformity with the standard Mesoamerican practice of giving all public monuments a solar orientation. The great Pyramid of the Sun at Teotihuacán is testimony to the monumental scale of the pre-Columbian astral religion, for it measures 689 feet by 689 feet at the base and rises 210 feet high. Eric Wolf calculates that it took a highly organized workforce of ten thousand laborers twenty years to complete the massive structure.[15]

In Mexico the pyramid is an architectural symbolization of what Mircea Eliade calls the "cosmic mountain as sacred center." As a sacred mountain, the pyramid constitutes an *axis mundi* (world center). Phenomenologically, it is nature's closest link to the celestial realm above and the subterranean paradise below. It is an altar and is thus a place of transformation. The gods and the regenerative forces of nature are sustained through sacrifice on the pyramid. Ritual action and sacrifice ensure the continuity of human and cosmic life by maintaining the stability of the agrarian cycles.[16]

According to Laurette Sejourné, a central concept of the religion of Teotihuacán holds that the essence of life consists of two complementary forces. In order for life to continue and harmony to reign over the chaos of the cosmos, the polar forces must be bridged. This linking of forces was accomplished through ritual and sacrificial action. In the Mesoamerican practice of sacrifice, the priest sought to unite the dualisms of the cosmos by transforming the thing sacrificed into the pure light of the sun. Teotihuacán religion taught that luminous consciousness was generated within the human heart. Through the sacrificial act this luminous matter was transmuted into energy that served to sustain the solar deity. Referring to the numerous heart glyphs at Teotihuacán, Sejourné says that the process of breaking through to spiritual enlightenment and obtaining wisdom was extremely painful: "That is why the heart is always represented as wounded (in Teotihuacán), and why the drops issuing from it are so significant that they alone are a sufficient symbol for it."[17]

The religion of Teotihuacán elaborated the Olmec cultural patterns and became a primary model of Mesoamerican religiosity. Its rituals were characterized in particular by the grandeur of their outdoor pageantry. This immense scale of worship was continued until the arrival of the Spanish. Robert Ricard states that the Catholic friars recognized the advantages of preserving the ceremonialism of the indigenous rites: it not only maintained the enthusiasm of the Amerindians, who were accustomed to great outdoor religious dramas, but also enhanced their devotion to the Christian rites. Thus Catholic rituals approximated the spectacles of the old religion. This resulted in the architectural innovation of the open atrium chapel, which could accommodate large numbers of natives out-of-doors.[18]

In the eighth century A.D., Teotihuacán experienced a major disaster that resulted in its collapse. Although the exact cause of the city's collapse is unknown, three major explanations have been advanced. Some observers argue in favor of an ecological collapse, saying that the surrounding agricultural base could no longer support the overgrown urban complex. Other scholars hold that the development of a warrior class led to a shift in power and subsequently to civil strife. Finally, there is the invasion thesis, which claims that Teotihuacán's collapse was caused by massive migrations of less advanced tribes into the central valley of Mexico. Some evidence suggests that before the city was sacked, its theocratic rulers destroyed their own temples in order to prevent them from falling into the hands of plunderers. Perhaps the real reasons for the great city's collapse will never be known.[19]

Between A.D. 950 and A.D. 1150 the cultural center of gravity in Mesoamerica shifted northwest to the Toltec city-state of Tula. Tula, or Tollan, differed from Teotihuacán in that power was no longer invested in the priestly lords but was held by warrior overlords, petty nobles, civil servants, merchants, and artisans. Its warlike stone reliefs depicting jaguar and eagle warriors engaged in mortal combat attest to this shift. At Tula, the ideas of the warrior state and of combat as a ritualized manifestation of the cosmic struggle between the forces of light and darkness come into their own.

During this period Toltec merchants *(pochtecas)* expanded westward and north into the frontier of the arid basin known as the Gran Chichimec. By 1150 A.D. they had made contact with the people of Casas Grandes in Chihuahua. Using Chihuahua as a staging ground, the *pochtecas* launched expeditions into the Hohokam and Anasazi areas of the present states of Arizona and New Mexico, trading copper bells for turquoise, slaves, peyote, salt, and various other commodities. Cultural influences followed commerce. Murals from the Awatowi in the Hopi area reveal southwestern versions of the Mesoamerican rain god Tlaloc and of Quetzalcóatl associated with the planet Venus. Furthermore, the architecture of the buildings of Chaco Canyon is remarkably similar to that of Toltec monuments.[20]

In Michoacán the hallmark of Toltec influence was the Chacmul figure. The Chacmul is a freestanding stela commemorating the kings of Tula. Primarily an altar stone, it appears prominently on the *yácatas* (pyramids) of

Tzintzuntzan and Ihuatzio. It depicts a male human figure reclining on his back. The knees of the figure are bent and he is resting on his elbows; his hands cover his heart.

The Toltec empire centered at Tula was short-lived. According to Jorge Acosta, the city was subjected to relentless pillaging by fierce invaders, nomadic tribes from beyond the northern frontier. As evidence, Acosta points to the charred remains of Tula's great pyramids and palaces. The invading nomads succeeded in establishing small epigonic Toltec kingdoms as far south as Chichén Itzá in the Yucatan peninsula, and among the Quiché and Cakchiquel people of the Guatemalan highlands.

In western Mexico the destruction of Tula resulted in a similar process of regional development in the twelfth century. The Purhépecha, who had developed a sedentary culture of subsistence farming and fishing, came into contact with the Chichimecs, the more fierce nomadic people from the north. These Chichimecs—like their cousins the Metzica-Chichimec of Tenochtitlán, who adopted high culture from more advanced tribal groups in the central valley—proved to be highly resourceful. In a short time they became the recipients of the greater Mesoamerican cultural diffusion. The archaeological record in Michoacán attests to this diversity of cultural influences in the many artifacts found in the region from the Andean, Olmec, Chupicuaro, Teotihuacán, and Toltec cultures. The arrival of the Chichimecs in Michoacán and their subsequent acculturation form the essential historical parameters of this study.[21]

THE CHRONICLES OF MICHOACÁN

The primary source for retrieving the social history of the Purhépecha-Chichimec is the *Relación de Michoacán* manuscript, or, as it is known in English, *The Chronicles of Michoacán*.[22] The manuscript was dedicated to the first viceroy of New Spain (1535–1550), Don Antonio de Mendoza.[23] Like other Spanish chronicles written in this period, *The Chronicles of Michoacán* contains information about both the indigenous tribute systems and the sacred and profane histories of the newly conquered people. It was presented to Mendoza as a gift during his second visit to Tzintzuntzan, the capital of the Purhépecha kingdom, in 1541. This event is depicted in the first of the forty-four native-painted illustrations that accompany the text.

The Chronicles of Michoacán was first published in 1869 by Florencio Janer. A second edition appeared in Morelia in 1903. A modern edition, published in Madrid in 1956, included a facsimile reproduction of the original text held in the Escorial. And an English edition that was based on the 1903 Morelia edition was published in 1970.[24]

The authorship of *The Chronicles of Michoacán* is in dispute. The editors of the 1970 English edition, Eugene R. Craine and Reginald C. Reindorp, state that the text was compiled between 1539 and 1541, "presumably by Fray Martín de Coruña, who with five Franciscans went to Michoacán in the year 1525 or early 1526."[25] J. Benedict Warren, a preeminent scholar of western Mexico, believes the text was written by Fray Jerónimo de Alcalá with the help of three parties: the Purhépecha *cazonci* Tangaxoan II; Pedro Cuinierángari, Tangaxoan II's adopted brother; and native priestly informants. Fray Jerónimo was active in the region of Tzintzuntzan and Pátzcuaro between 1538 and 1541. He is described by both the Franciscan chronicler Muñoz and the Purhépecha nobleman Don Pedro Guaca as being fluent in the Purhépecha language. According to Warren, the omission of Fray Jerónimo's name from *The Chronicles of Michoacán* was due to the Franciscan religious order's tradition of humility.[26]

THE PURHÉPECHA-CHICHIMEC SYNTHESIS

In the late twelfth century, Chichimec tribes who called themselves Eneani, Uacúsecha, Vanacaze, Zacapu-hereti, and Quachpanme crossed the Lerma River into Michoacán and settled in a fertile valley near the present-day town of Zacapu. The entry of these nomadic hunters was facilitated by the fall of the Toltec garrisons at Tula and the political vacuum created in the region by the city's demise. The *Lienzo of Jucutacato*, discovered by Don Crescencio García de Cotija, is the only primary source that attempts to trace the migratory movement of the Chichimec tribes into Michoacán. The painted linen text depicts the epic pilgrimage of the Chichimecs and eight other tribal nations from a place called Aztlán (Place of the Seven Caves) to their new home in the Zacapu area.[27]

Once in Michoacán the Chichimec warriors began to intermarry with the Purhépecha villagers of the Lake Pátzcuaro region. Nonetheless, at the time of the conquest the Purhépecha-Chichimec were not a homogeneous people. Their civilization had experienced a long process of cultural intermingling much like that of the Metzica (Aztecs), whose nomadic culture had become fused with the cultures of the urbanized Tepanecs of Azcapotzalco and the Culhuas of Culhuacan and Texcoco.[28]

The Purhépecha language is a hybrid Mesoamerican language, the product of a wide-ranging process of linguistic borrowing and fusion. It has many loan words, for example, from Quechua, the language of Peru, and from Zuni, which is spoken in the southwestern United States.[29] The origins of the term *purhépecha* are unknown. Today the people living in the lake area call themselves Purhépecha. The first Spaniards to arrive referred to these people as *tarascos*, which in Spanish carries pejorative connotations of "loathsomeness" and "disgust." *The Chronicles of Michoacán* claims that the name "Tarascan" is a misnomer arising out of the first meeting of Spaniards and Purhépecha:

> *Before they left [Tzintzuntzan], the Spaniards asked the Cazonci for two Indian girls from among his relatives and took them along, lying with them along the road. The Indians who traveled with them called the Spaniards Tarascue, which in their language means son-in-law. Later, Spaniards began to apply this name to the Indians, but instead of calling them Tarascue, they called them Tarasco, which is the name they have now, and the women are called Tarascas. They are quite embarrassed by these names, saying that these names come from those first women taken by the Spaniards to Mexico City.*[30]

The word "Tarascan" developed out of this miscommunication. The Spaniards believed that the term referred to the Purhépecha people's tribal name. Later Spanish colonizers used the name *tarasco* generically to refer to all Amerindian people of Michoacán. In the same way, "Indian" or *indio* replaced the self-designated tribal names of the indigenous people of the Western Hemisphere.

Fray Bernardino de Sahagún suggests that the Tarascans took their name from a god called Tarás. However, there is little evidence of such a divinity in the Purhépecha pantheon, although there is a deity called Tharés Upeme (The Ancient Engenderer) who rules over the southern quadrant of the four directions. Hence either Sahagún was mistaken or he based his information on an unknown source.[31]

J. Benedict Warren believes that the closest approximation to a native name for the people of Michoacán is *purhépecha*. He states that the *Relación de Cuitzeo* maintains this name meant "working men" and was used by the people to identify themselves.[32] This hypothesis seems to have some credibility. Fray Maturino Gilberti, who wrote the first Purhépecha grammar, translates *purembe* (singular of *purhépecha*) with the Náhuatl word *macegual*, which means "commoner" or "laborer."[33]

The present study will use the term "Purhépecha-Chichimec," or simply "Purhépecha," to refer to those people who controlled the greater portion of western Mexico prior to its conquest by the Spaniards. "Chichimec," a

Náhuatl word, is translated as "people of the dog lineage." It was used by the central Mexicans to refer to all those seminomadic and nomadic groups that lived north of the Gran Chichimec frontier.

With regard to these ambiguities in nomenclature Eugene R. Craine and Reginald C. Reindorp comment that "Placing the Tarascans in time and in space gives one the strange feeling that history was marking time by waiting for one group of actors to exit, a process slowly taking place, and another group to enter. It is even stranger when one realizes that, for the most part, the actors were completely unaware of the others, and yet their destinies are linked."[34] What Reindorp and Craine do not account for, however, is how the geography of the region contributed to the autonomy and identity of the people of Michoacán. It is not so difficult to understand the isolation of tribal families if one considers the mountainous terrain of Michoacán. As the Spaniards moved from one valley to the next during the early conquest period they encountered radically differing cultures and languages. The friars noted that the cultural diversity among the natives was one of the main stumbling blocks in the translation of Christianity. It is important to remember that the Purhépecha-Chichimec had successfully maintained their autonomy along-side powerful neighbors like the Aztecs precisely because the pine-covered volcanoes of the region were natural fortresses shielding them in their micro-environments.

At the beginning of the sixteenth century the Purhépecha were not the only aboriginal group in Michoacán. There were also Matlaltzincas, an Otomian group of fierce fighters who had migrated north from the valley of Toluca in the 1400s. They were employed as mercenaries by both the Metzica-Tenochca (Aztecs) and the *cazonci*. The Matlaltzinca can still be found in Michoacán, principally in the towns of Zitácuaro and Susupoato. A group of Naguales (Tecos) settled around the Lake Pátzcuaro area and today constitute a large proportion of the populations of such towns as Águila, Contepec, Coahuayana, and Maravatio. From the latter group the Purhépecha king recruited translators for his negotiations with the Aztecs and Spanish.[35]

THE *CAZONCI* AND THE FOUNDING OF THE KINGDOM

The first Chichimec who entered Michoacán in the thirteenth century were led by the warrior-priest Hireticátame. They established themselves on the mountain known as Uirimguampexo, near the village of Zacapu. These nomadic people were drawn to the area by its natural beauty, fresh water, plentiful game, and abundance of timber on the mountaintops, which they used for their fire rituals. A fertile and verdant land, it contrasted sharply with the arid regions of the Gran Chichimec that they had recently left.

Based in the valley of Zacapu, Hireticátame began to exact tribute from the farmers and fishermen already settled in the region. According to *The Chronicles of Michoacán*, Hireticátame also led numerous military campaigns against the villages on the shores of Lake Pátzcuaro. Upon his death Hireticátame was succeeded by his son Sicuirancha, who created an island stronghold on Lake Zirahuén near the present-day town of Quiroga.[36]

A nephew of Sicuirancha established the model for the Purhépecha-Chichimec monarchy in the fourteenth century. The son of an island woman from Jaracuaro, he was the great *cazonci* Tariácuri. By this time, then, the Chichimec clans had established a dynastic succession based on blood relationships.[37]

Tariácuri's reign was characterized by numerous wars of expansion. These resulted from the *cazonci's* efforts to extend the frontiers of Purhépecha influence by building a well-trained army, which enabled him to subjugate the regional chieftains. His armies first moved against the people of the Lake Chapala district. They crossed into Jalisco and established several garrisons on the far western frontier. Tariácuri's most successful campaign cut a wedge across the Sierra Madre toward the south. In the *tierra caliente* (hot country) his troops crossed the Balsas River and took the northern portion of the state of Guerrero, incorporating the Náhuatl peoples into the empire. The military campaign added considerably to the *cazonci's* wealth and power, since the region was a major source of precious objects used in the religious cult, such as copper, gold, silver, cotton, the feathers of tropical birds, gum, *copal* incense, *cacao*, beeswax, and vegetable fats. The treasures obtained in the south also enhanced the king's power at home, since in his priest-king role he was considered the primary guardian of the cult. Symbolically, the conquest of new lands was a testament to the power of the Purhépecha tribal deity Curicáueri.

Little is known of Tariácuri's personality. Some information suggests that in expanding the Purhépecha state he exhibited Machiavellian behavior. Two incidents illustrate this hypothesis. The first is recounted in *The Chronicles of Michoacán*, when the *cazonci* ordered his own sons killed because they violated the rules of sobriety. In the second incident, Tariácuri spitefully moved against an old advisor, the *cacique* Zurumbán, when he discovered Zurumbán's plot to overthrow him.[38]

Zurumbán was a local chieftain in the lake area. Apparently, he and Naca, a trusted priest, devised a scheme to oust Tariácuri. Tariácuri discovered the plot, however, and killed the priest. He then ordered the priest's body cooked and sent to Zurumbán with two of his agents, who were disguised as old men. The agents were to present the meat to Zurumbán and say it was deer meat. According to *The Chronicles of Michoacán*, "This was all according to custom, for when sacrificing anyone, these people would always divide the sacrificed one among the houses of the chief priest, and they would make the offering to the gods and eat the meat."[39]

When the *cazonci*'s agents arrived at Zurumbán's house the important men and women of the village were gathered outside. The "old men" presented the meat to the *cacique*, telling him the flesh was the ritually purified corpse of one of Tariácuri's slaves. Zurumbán was flattered by the supposed gesture and ordered the meat cooked and put on gourd trays. The two impostors then quickly disappeared. After the meat was ingested another set of disguised messengers appeared in the village and informed the *cacique* of Tariácuri's trick. Zurumbán was frantic, for he realized that he had eaten his co-conspirator's flesh. *The Chronicles of Michoacán* ends the story with the following scene:

> *Zurumban stayed in the patio vomiting, and his women put their hands in their mouths trying to vomit the meat, but they could not because it was already settled. . . . Zurumban was very much ashamed over the trick that Tariácuri played on him.*[40]

Upon Tariácuri's death the kingdom was divided between his son Hiqugage, who received the town of Pátzcuaro and its tributary villages, and his two nephews Hiripan and Tangaxoan I, who were given the towns of Cuyacán and Tzintzuntzan respectively. Hiqugage and Hiripan eventually died without conceiving heirs.

In the fifteenth century the kingdom was united under Tzitzic Pandacuare, the son of Tangaxoan I. A skillful general, Tzitzic Pandacuare is noted for having conquered the southeastern sections of Jalisco and parts of Colima. His most significant military accomplishment was the defeat of the great Aztec emperor Axayácatl in the bloody war of 1469 to 1478, which was fought in mountain passes near the Valley of Toluca. The defeat of the powerful Aztec armies ensured the autonomy of the Purhépecha-Chichimec kingdom until the arrival of the Spaniards.

The enmity between the Purhépecha and Aztecs was never forgotten, however. When Cuauhtemoctzin, the last emperor of the Aztecs, sent his emissaries to the king of Michoacán, Tangaxoan II, to ask for help in defeating the Spaniards, the latter suspected an Aztec trick and thus did nothing to aid the desperate Mexicans. Perhaps the *cazonci* hoped the Spanish and Tlaxcalan

FIGURE 1.   The boy Tariácuri finds his mother and relatives

armies would neutralize the Aztecs' power. In any case, Tangaxoan II knew that if the Aztecs were defeated his best recourse would be to make a separate deal with the Spaniards. He eventually did so, since after the Aztec catastrophe and the fall of the great city of Tenochtitlán the Spanish missionaries and conquistadors—in search of souls and precious metals—turned their attention toward the Purhépecha. As we shall see, this deal had devastating consequences for the Purhépecha state.

PURHÉPECHA SOCIETY

The Chronicles of Michoacán contains little information concerning the life of the common people of Michoacán. It is primarily concerned with the ruling castes: the *cazonci* and his nobles, priests, and warriors. More than likely the common people of Michoacán lived as they do today in their towns and villages, beneath the yoke of state institutions, yet still with the hope of maintaining their particular ideal of a life free from outside influence.

The fundamental unit of Purhépecha society was the extended family. Religious and civil laws applied to the family, which formed the basic social unit of the larger cities and provinces as well as the *pueblos* and family-owned ranches *(rancherías)*. This was the case because appointment to certain government offices depended on kinship and on membership in the important clans.[41] All Purhépecha towns and villages were divided into extended family wards according to a quadripartite plan based on the four cardinal directions, much like the Aztec system of *calpullis*.

The Chronicles of Michoacán places a great deal of emphasis on the institution of marriage in Purhépecha culture. Six chapters (chapters 10 through 15 of Book 3) are dedicated to defining what constitutes a good marriage and to discussing conflicts resulting from infidelity and adultery. The laws concerning adultery were the most severe. Cases were brought before the high priest, the *petamiti*, who was empowered with administering justice. A husband who caught his wife with another man would split the ears of both culprits as a mark of their dishonor. Both women and men could be considered the instigators of infidelity, and marital indiscretions often resulted in death.

Several passages in *The Chronicles of Michoacán* state that a boy and girl had to belong to the same *barrio* (neighborhood) in order to marry.[42] Since the group living within a ward most likely consisted of persons of the same lineage, it is safe to say that as a rule marriages in Purhépecha society were endogamous.[43] This does not mean, however, that marriages outside the clan or familial ward were prohibited. Marriages were often arranged between aristocratic families in order to consolidate political agreements. Nonetheless, within the primary clans of Tzintzuntzan, the Uacúsecha and Vanacaze, the rule was marriage with a blood relation: "they married women of the lineage they belonged to themselves and lineages did not mix just as with the Jew."[44]

Thus there were two criteria for marriages: the territorial unit to which one belonged *(hayácuaro)* and one's family lineage *(sarucua)*. For the ordinary people of the provinces the territorial prerequisite was probably the norm. But for the Uacúsecha living in frontier garrison towns or serving in important offices in the provinces, the lineage requirement was most important. The *cazonci* was married to many women. His marriages were political to the extent that they solidified a network of political alliances and social responsibilities.

THE DOMINANT ELITE

Honor and respect were admired qualities in pre-Columbian Michoacán, and many wars were fought over them. Honoring the gods, the clan, the ancestors, and communal properties and respecting fishing, forest, and agrarian rights are virtues outlined in *The Chronicles of Michoacán*.[45] Pedro Carrasco supports this thesis with his argument that social mobility in Mesoamerica was linked to the honor attained in performing civic and religious duties within the clan and village structure.[46]

Within the dominant clans, individuals had three avenues of social mobility: the military structure, the priestly hierarchy, and the artisan or commercial castes. The extent to which the common people had access to these structures is not detailed in *The Chronicles of Michoacán*. Most likely they formed their own militias, participated in the market system, and were incorporated to some degree into the state cult as observers at religious ceremonies.

Purhépecha society might be best visualized as a pyramid. The Eneani, Uacúsecha, Vanacaze, Quachpanme, and Tzacapu-hireti clans formed the upper strata of society. The *cazonci* held the very highest position,[47] while beneath him were the high priests and inner advisors. The latter included the *angatácuri*, a governor who was often a senior elder; the captain general in charge of the army; the lords of the *ocanvecha*, who were the census takers in charge of demographics and tribute; the *achaecha*, the most loyal guardians of the royal houses and treasury; and the various lords in charge of warehouses and properties of the *cazonci*. They also included the nobility who supervised specific crafts like blanket-making, feather work, and pottery; the administrators who coordinated hunting; the nobles who tended the *cazonci*'s aviary and zoo; the lords who supervised fishing in the lake; the governors of the *pulque* taverns; and the nobles who maintained armaments, messenger services, and so forth.[48]

The provincial chieftains also formed part of the elite in Purhépecha society. Charged with the responsibility of good government in their respective regions, they were expected to maintain order and to participate in the election of a new *cazonci*. Each regional *cacique* had a war chief who lived in Tzintzuntzan for part of the year. The provincial chiefs were also required to provide the tribute essential for maintaining the religious cult in Tzintzuntzan, such as firewood, maize, and *copal* gum. In addition, they were responsible for the defense of the kingdom and the proper cultivation of the land. They were instructed by the *cazonci* to be generous with their people in order to avoid rebellion.

Indigenous noblewomen fared better in Purhépecha society than under Spanish rule. Purhépecha women often occupied important positions in society. Not only were there female priests, but women also held significant administrative positions in the palace complex. For example, the *cazonci*'s household was administered primarily by women. The importance of women also can be seen in the institution of the *guatapera*. The *guatapera* was a women's communal house where girls were trained in crafts, in the procedures of sumptuous religious rituals, and in the administration of the *cazonci*'s household.[49]

The girls who lived in the *guatapera* were called *guananchas*. They probably entered the *guatapera* after puberty. *Guananchas* were also thought of as the wives of the solar god, Curicáueri. As such they were contractually married off to consolidate key political alliances with regional *caciques* and important army officers. In the provinces the *guatapera* fell under the jurisdiction of the regional lords.

In the palace women lived semicloistered lives, although they did participate in the royal festivals. *The Chronicles of Michoacán* states that the *cazonci* had many wives as well as female slaves. The *cazonci*'s first wife was called the *yreri*, and she held a special position above other women. The chief female guardian of the palace was called the *guatáperi*. The *cazonci*'s wives were required to be absolutely dedicated to him and upon his death were expected to keep him company by committing ritual suicide.[50]

THE PRIESTLY CASTE

The Chronicles of Michoacán provides a detailed account of the priestly caste that served the state religion. The head of the Purhépecha religion was the *cazonci*. Considered a priest-king, he led the priestly order known as *axámencha*. The *cazonci* never acquired the attributes of a divine personage as did the Aztec emperors. *The Chronicles of Michoacán* states that "the God Curicaveri was King and the *Cazonci* his human representative, governor, and captain-

FIGURE 2. The *petamiti*, or high priest, designates a new leader

general in war."[51] Among his chief religious responsibilities were vigilance over the temple fires and the procurement of sacrificial victims through ritual warfare. The Purhépecha goal in war was unlike the modern objective of war—i.e., the annihilation of the enemy. It did not benefit the *cazonci* to destroy his tribute revenue. Thus the Purhépecha fought within the constraints of limited goals.

The *petamiti* was the chief high priest who ruled over all priestly orders. The principal administrator of justice, he was distinguished by the earthen jugs he wore around his neck, the gourd with inlaid turquoise that he carried on his back, and a long, pointed spear made of obsidian. The gourd symbolized the earthly community for whose well-being he bore responsibility, and the spear signified that he was the highest judge in the land.

Minor religious specialists, who were many, were called *curitiecha*. They performed the responsibilities of preachers and officiated at purification rites and marriage ceremonies. Other priests oversaw the collection of tribute that was paid in wood to the king. The *curipecha* were in charge of the sacred fires in the temples, constantly attending them and filling them with tobacco rolls and incense. The standard-bearers of the sacred icons that preceded the *cazonci*'s troops were known as the *tininiecha*, while the *pasantiecha* were trumpet players and sextons at the temples. The *opitiecha* were in charge of holding sacrificial victims over the altar stone. They were accompanied by the *quiquiecha*, who disposed of the corpses and hung the victims' skulls on long poles near the temples. Other priests were dedicated to specific gods and goddesses; these included the *vatarcha*, who attended the cult of the moon goddess Xarátanga. Lastly there were the *hiripacha*, a group of sorcerers and shamans who specialized in carrying out exorcisms, interpreting omens and dreams, and conducting divinatory rites.

The priests had very long hair. Adorning themselves by painting their bodies black, they also wore deer skins and feathers. Members of all of the priestly orders were allowed to marry. In addition, each temple had its particular priestly hierarchy. The people called the priests "grandfather," and their offices were inherited, so that a caste was well established by the time of the Spanish friars' arrival.[52]

Between the thirteenth and fifteenth centuries the fundamental characteristics of Purhépecha-Chichimec society were established. They included a dynastic tradition, a privileged caste of men and women, regional chieftains, and a priestly tradition. The dominant Chichimec clans at the top of the social system maintained their political control over a mass of peasant farmers, who were the backbone of the kingdom.

TWO

The Purhépecha
Religious Worldview

The Chichimec clans that entered Michoacán in the thirteenth century fused their tough, nomadic way of life with the culture of the farming people around Lake Pátzcuaro. The hunters from the north were a resourceful group and quickly appropriated the cultural heritage bequeathed to the region by the paradigmatic civilization of Teotihuacán and Tula. *The Chronicles of Michoacán* recounts how these people imagined themselves in relation to the sacred world around them. The Purhépecha-Chichimec believed that they lived in a precarious cosmos dominated by the struggles between order and chaos, and light and darkness.

The Purhépecha's sacred world was quite different from the Christian universe. Christianity characterized the human condition as a quest for the perfection of ultimate being and "godliness" in a world inclined toward evil. Both religious worldviews explained the cosmic drama using metaphors of light and darkness, life and death, wisdom and aberration, fertility and regeneration, discipline and excess. But only Christianity understood the cosmic struggle as constituting moral absolutes. Whether the Amerindians uniformly rejected Christianity's moral matrix in favor of their own concepts of social duty and human benevolence cannot be known. However, in her work on Nahua drama from the early contact period, Louise Burkhart asserts that the native authors of the earliest passion play literature finessed the issue of life as an individual moral struggle. She argues that the mendicants labored, "largely in vain," to impress Christian ideas of the moral self on their Nahua charges; nevertheless, the most systematically evangelized indigenous scholars of Tlaltelolco wrote texts that celebrated collective redemption.[1]

THE SACRED PRINCIPLE OF DUALITY

In the Mesoamerican cosmos all existence—including the parental deities, the many divine manifestations and lower intermediary spirits, and all of the forces and powers in nature as well as the spirits dwelling in the world of the dead—is subject to a sacred, dynamic dualism called Ometeotl. This dualism was also known as the "Self-Created," the "Generating Conceiving Cosmic Principle," "Lord of the Close Vicinity," "Invisible as the Night Wind-Origin," and "Foundation and Goal of All Things and Humanity."[2] The Purhépecha also called this dialectic dualism Awándaeri Ka Echéreri Cueráuperi (Creator of the Celestial Paradise and Earth), which they represented symbolically as a woman.[3]

In the Purhépecha culture zone today there is some confusion as to the sex of the dual god: "Most informants refer to Cueráuperi as male; others take the god to be female, ranking her with Mary, the mother of God."[4] This ambiguity probably exists because of the principle's androgynous character. The Purhépecha conceive of all beings as possessing complementary masculine and feminine energies. Each kind of energy contributes to a polarity that contains elements of the other, as in the Taoist concept of *yin* and *yang*. Thus dualism exists in all life as a harmonic synthesis rather than a tension of opposites.[5]

The dual nature of the godhead and the multiplicity of its manifest forms have produced some interesting interpretations of Mesoamerican religion. Louise Burkhart, for example, asserts that alignment with goodness and avoidance of evil was not the essential problem of human life in the Mesoamerican world: "Rather, one had to discover the proper balance between order and chaos. One had to establish and maintain the order, continuity, and stability necessary for social and cultural survival while capturing just enough fertilizing energy to ensure biological survival."[6] Alfonso Caso, in *La religión de los aztecas*, argues that the pre-Columbian vision of the cosmos revealed three sociocultural tendencies: a popular polytheism; a priestly stratum that strived to consolidate multiple gods into a single deity; and an ancient philosophical school that affirmed the existence of the dual cosmic principle.[7] It might be more useful, however, to consider Mesoamerican religion not only as polytheistic at the popular level but as also having a pantheistic tendency. In pantheism all phenomena have sacred efficacy. At heart, pantheistic systems move toward monistic concepts of God. Following this line of thinking, what we discover in Mesoamerican religion is that there is only one divine entity, whose composition and actions include all living beings in nature. Furthermore, monism is the universal law of duality. By viewing Mesoamerican religion as pantheistic, then, we can understand how the many gods and goddesses and mythic themes recur in pairs—as if two polar elements were needed to express the ultimate monism of existence.

In volume 1 of his work *México a través de los siglos*, Alfredo Chavero argues that for the archaic Mesoamericans the "gods were material; eternal fire was eternal matter; men were the sons of gods and had been created by their father the sun and their mother the earth; fatalism was their philosophy of life."[8] Miguel León-Portilla accurately points out, however, that Chavero's perspective contradicts the widely held thesis that the people of antiquity tended toward animism, or toward diverse metaphysical conceptions.[9] Jacques Soustelle suggests that Mesoamerican thought is distinguished by its tendency to bind together swarms of interrelated symbols. He states, "What really gives Mexican cosmological thought its own peculiar quality is this binding together of traditionally associated images. The world is a system of symbols—colors, time, the orientation of space, stars, gods, historical events—all having a certain interacting relationship. We are not faced with a long series of ratiocinations, but rather with a continuous and reciprocal complex of the various aspects of a whole."[10]

The Purhépecha idea of God might best be described as a pantheistic monism wherein the divine principle is manifest in multiple but complementary forms, including intermediary gods, ritual objects, cultural heroes, and the forces of nature. Within the continuous symbol system that expresses the wholeness of being, sacred personages and themes blend into one another. But only one primordial engenerative couple predominates: the Sun and the Earth. All other divine personages and sacred powers—the planets, stars, mountain spirits, plus humanity and the animal world—are manifestations of the union of this sacred duality. The dual god's male aspect (the Lord of Duality) and its female aspect (the Lady of Duality) are associated with sexual fertility and other regenerative powers. The lesser or intermediary divinities, the Tlaloques (known as the Tirípemes by the Purhépecha), are the offspring of the cosmic union of the Sun and Earth and themselves give birth to humanity.

In the Mesoamerican worldview, then, human beings evolve from the sacred dualism. Their being and genealogical descent can be traced back to the absolute reality that undergirds all existence. In this way, human beings directly participate in the cosmic energy of regeneration. In this context, sacrifice, and human sacrifice in particular, sustain the continuous canopy of sacred beings and relationships from which all life comes.[11]

The Purhépecha organized their cosmos into three realms: Auándaro, the celestial domain; Echerendo, the earthly sphere; and Cumiechúcuaro, the subterranean paradise. In the celestial sphere the God of Duality is manifest in the guise of a primordial planetary family, which includes the Sun, Curicáueri (Great Fire); the lunar mother, Xarátanga (Woman Who Appears on High); a male child or the planet Venus, Curita-caheri (Great Priest of Fire); and the daughter Earth, Cueráuperi (Woman Who Unties in the Womb). The planetary family also includes the Pleiades and the tri-star cluster of Aldebaran, Beta, and Gamma. The latter stars were considered solar manifestations of the heavenly patriarchs: the grandfather Sun, the father Sun, and the grandson Sun. They represented the triple division of the cosmos.[12]

Emerging from the primordial gods are five lesser divinities, the Tirípemes. These intermediary powers were the cosmic governors of the four cardinal regions and the center. In Mesoamerican thought the space of a cardinal direction is fused with a particular time period. Thus the four quarters of the universe correspond to four ages. The fifth direction in space, or center, is the point of synthesis, where time and space meet. The center is understood as the present age.[13]

Each of the four directions has its corresponding color, wind, cloud, bird, tree, and mountain. Mountains formed the natural boundaries of the sacred geography of Lake Pátzcuaro. The Purhépecha villages and ceremonial centers also conformed to this quadripartite pattern and had astronomical orientations. In this way, space and time, and human actions on Earth, were believed to be inseparable.

In Christianity, transcendent unity with God is achieved by negating one half of the good/evil dualism. Christians perfect themselves through acts of will, as well as through the desire for unity and immortality with the godhead. Hence they must choose good, or order, whose ultimate source is found in the transcendent world, over the evil, or chaos, implicit in earthly existence.

In contrast, given the dialectical structure of their cosmos, Amerindians were not able to choose order over chaos so as to experience the sacred. For in the Mesoamerican system chaos is not always detrimental to human existence. The mendicant friars disapproved of polygamy and ritual drunkenness among the natives, associating these behaviors with the chaos of the natural world and the beast-like tendencies of the human body. But the two activities were considered positive by the Amerindians, who believed that polygamy and ritual drunkenness could produce the balance necessary for individual survival. Thus taboos informed by a moral absolute were not imposed on the two forms of behavior.

Like their Spanish conqueror, the Mesoamericans believed in a post-mortem self or soul. The evidence for this statement is abundantly available in the *Vocabulario en lengua castellana y mexicana y mexicana y castellana* (1555), which contains numerous indigenous words to describe the Spanish terms for soul, *ánima* and *alma*. In Mesoamerican thought, unity with the divine world is achieved by harmonizing the implicit dualisms of human existence and by recognizing the great mystery of the sacred ordering principle. The most apparent manifestations of this belief were the ritual offerings made by the common folk and the priestly castes. These offerings included ceremonial human sacrifice, ritual warfare, flowers, turkeys, and amaranth breads formed into anthropomorphic shapes.[14] The aim of the sacrificial act was to unify the bipolar structures inherent in the cosmos. The Amerindians believed that the survival of the ancient God of Duality, and ultimately of their world, depended on sacrifice. The Purhépecha taught that a spark of the divine essence was enclosed within every human heart. It was logical, then, given their assumptions about the structure of the world, that they would sacrifice the thing they most valued. In doing so they involved themselves in cosmogonic themes that explained the meaning of regeneration and death, space and time, and body and soul.[15]

LAKE PÁTZCUARO: THE CENTER OF THE WORLD

The Purhépecha constructed a monumental urban complex at Lake Pátzcuaro, which they regarded as a sacred space. Mircea Eliade explains this archaic cultural phenomenon in terms of the symbolism of the center of the world. He contends that ancient cultures conceived of the center of the world as the place where all essential modes of being come together, where there is a direct link with the supernatural powers, and where passage between the mundane and transcendent worlds is possible. The symbolism of the center does not merely include ritual social dramas acted out in the landscape, because it also demonstrates long-established ways of being, ways of thinking about nature, and cultural adjustments to the land and environment.[16]

In the early sixteenth century the Lake Pátzcuaro landscape was filled with powerful natural and supernatural forces. Here Purhépecha myths and ideas of cosmic order were anthropomorphized in the geography of the surrounding terrain. The lake was organized around a central axis intersected by the multiple realms of the cosmos. The very center of the lake was considered to be the place where one could obtain the most direct contact with the sacred.[17] *The Chronicles of Michoacán* states that in the lake area and the provinces there were four sacred districts, each ruled by a Tirípeme (divine power). The Tirípemes were invoked through the mediation of the four brothers of the solar deity Curicáueri. Each Tirípeme had a cult center in the appropriate cardinal direction on the shoreline of the lake.

The eastern portion of the lake was ruled by the red Tirípeme-quarencha, whose cult center was in the town of Curinguaro-achurin. The western district was governed by the white Tirípeme-thupuren, with his center located in the town of Iramuco. The yellow Tirípeme-xungápeti had a shrine on the north side of the lake in the town of Pichataro. The black Tirípeme-caheri was venerated in the village of Pareo, on the lake's southern shore. Forming an *axis mundi*, the island of Pacanda united the mandala in the center of the lake.[18] Pacanda was dedicated to Chupi-tirípeme, a manifestation of the Purhépecha tribal god, Curicáueri, who was similar to Tlaloc, the ancient Olmec deity of rain and regeneration.[19]

Even though the people of Lake Pátzcuaro perceived themselves as surrounded by a sacred geography, they were not solely concerned with religious ceremonialism. By the time the Spanish appeared on the scene, the Purhépecha capital of Tzintzuntzan had developed great markets and had become the center of a large empire. Purhépecha society also manifested sophisticated avenues of political, social, and economic participation. Paul Wheatley, in the passage quoted below, helps us to understand the multiple functions of Mesoamerican ceremonial complexes such as Tzintzuntzan:

> *Beginning as little more than tribal shrines, in what may be regarded as their classic phases, these centers were elaborated into complexes of public ceremonial structures, usually massive and often extensive and including assemblages of such architectural items as pyramids, platforms, mounds, temples, palaces, terraces, staircases, courts, and stelae. Operationally they were instruments for the creation of political, social, economic, and sacred space, at the same time as they were symbols of cosmic, social, and moral order. Under the religious authority of organized priesthoods and divine monarchs, they elaborated the redistributive aspects of the economy to a position of institutionalized regional dominance, functioned as nodes in a web of administered (gift or treaty) trade, served as foci of craft specialization, and promoted the development of the exact and predictive sciences. Above all, they embodied the aspirations of brittle,*

pyramidal societies in which, typically, a sacerdotal elite, controlling a corps of officials and perhaps a pretorian guard, ruled over a broad understratum of peasantry.[20]

Tzintzuntzan, with its great pyramid of five round altar reliquaries, was such a ceremonial center. According to the mendicant friar Juan Baptista de Lagunas, "The name [Tzintzuntzan] came from the hummingbirds of the region, prized for their feathers, which were used in making pictures."[21] Most probably the city was dedicated to the solar god, because throughout Mesoamerica the hummingbird is one of the guises of the sun. For example, hummingbirds are found in the murals of Teotihuacán as pictographic symbols of the sun. And the Aztec tribal god is Huitzilopochtli (Hummingbird on the Left), who is himself a manifestation of the sun god Tonatiuh.[22]

Tzintzuntzan was the cultural center of the empire for a relatively short time. When Vasco de Quiroga asked to move his bishopric from Tzintzuntzan to Pátzcuaro in 1538, testimony was taken that stated that the capital had originally been in Pátzcuaro. This position is supported by the fact that the *cazonci* and nobles continued to maintain their primary houses in Pátzcuaro after the conquest.[23]

Pátzcuaro had been the original capital for both climatic and mythological reasons. With plenty of fresh water, the town also has a more agreeable climate, whereas Tzintzuntzan is hotter and nearer to the marshlands. Pátzcuaro was also important in Purhépecha mythology. The patron deity of Pátzcuaro is Curicáueri appearing as Chupi-tirípeme. The centrality of the latter in the lake's sacred geography suggests that Pátzcuaro once held the special position occupied by the island of Pacanda. This perspective is supported by testimony in *The Chronicles of Michoacán* that states that Pátzcuaro was the location of the gateway between the tripartite worlds of the cosmos.

At Pátzcuaro four huge stones known as *petázecua* were believed to be the primordial parents of the Purhépecha-Chichimec. These sacred stones guarded the passageway to the world of the dead that was located beneath the surface of the lake. The celestial domain of Auándaro was also accessible through the entryway. *The Chronicles of Michoacán* explains how the wandering Chichimec lords found the *petázecua*:

After they [the Chichimec] had established themselves in a district of Pátzcuaro called Tarimichundiro, they built their temples on the top of some very high rocks on a site called Petázecua. The temples were built there because their legends say that the God of the Inferno sends them those sites for the temples of the principal gods. Then moving on upstream they came to a place they had wanted to see. Although there was no road because of the dense forest of oak trees and dense thicket, they continued upstream, coming out at the spring (in the Bishop's patio), which is formed by water coming from Cuirisquataro, a place higher up on the hill where the big bell is located.

They descended to the house which is now in the hands of Don Pedro, governor of the city of Mechuacán, and down to a place which later was called Carop or Pátzcuaro. They went about looking for bodies of water there, and when they had seen them all, they said 'This is, without a doubt, Pátzcuaro. Let us go see the sites we have found for the temples,' and they went to the place where the cathedral was to be and there they found the previously mentioned high rocks called Petázecua, which means temple site. Nearby there was a high place which they climbed, and reaching the top, they found some stones as if to be sculptured into idols. This caused them to say: 'It is certainly here. Here these gods (the Petázecua) say that they are the gods of the Chichimecas, and this site is called Pátzcuaro. Look, there are four of these gods. . . . Let us clear this place.' Thus they counted the oaks and the trees there, saying that they had found the place their gods had singled out for them. Their ancestors had held this place in great veneration and they claimed that it was the seat of their God Curicaveri. The former Cazonci used to say that here and nowhere else was the door to heaven through which their gods came and went.[24]

Bishop Quiroga was shrewd enough to build his cathedral above the sacred *petázecua*, in effect preserving the sanctity of the geography for the Purhépecha. This act was in keeping with the Catholic practice of constructing churches over pagan temples as symbols of Christ's victory over the "infidels." In the passage quoted above, we see how the Franciscan chronicler is careful to note that the cathedral is victoriously imposed on the *petázecua*, the bishop's house is located over the spring, and the bell is atop the mountain. The stones, he says, stand "as if to be sculptured into idols."

THE PANTHEON

The center was a pervasive organizing principle in Purhépecha religion. It applied to their idea of time, as in the Mesoamerican calendar where four past ages, or suns, circumambulated the present age, or central fifth sun.[25] The spatial model of the center also served to organize the numerous deity clusters in the Amerindian pantheon, in addition to influencing architectural design and the collection of tribute.[26]

FIGURE 3.   Penitents in a cave

According to Laurette Sejourné, the spatial model of the center is very ancient in Mesoamerica and can be deciphered in the numerous quincunx figures of Teotihuacán. A quincunx is a four-sided figure with a central focus.
Sejourné contends that not only does the quincunx refer to the point where
heaven and earth meet, but it also represents the continuous process of trans-

figuration to which the creative union between matter and spirit is subjected in the human heart. For Sejourné this process is a struggle for inner purification and a striving for union with the divinity.[27] If the great pyramid at Tzintzuntzan were described with Sejourné's idea in mind, it becomes a sacred space where heaven meets the earth atop five reliquary altars, which represent the cardinal points of creation. Each altar is a point of transfiguration, where unity with the sacred cosmogonic forces maintaining existence is achieved.

An incredible array of deities inhabit the Purhépecha-Chichimec world. The deities are organized in groups of five, as in the five Tirípemes ruling the four cardinal directions and the center. The gods express major cultic themes such as cosmogony, creativity, fertility, regeneration, ritual warfare, and human sacrifice. In the pantheon's configuration, the numinous powers are portrayed materially as sacred pictographic symbols, which are venerated because they reveal the fundamental powers of the cosmos.

In ancient Mexico visual perception played an important role, similar to that of dogma in European Christianity. Visual perception defined orthodoxy and ontology. Since the Amerindians had not fully developed a script for writing, the communication of ideas about the gods developed around the visual and oral process of interpreting and reinterpreting complex hieroglyphs. In the pictographic books, monumental stelae, and ceramic works, the deities are visually located in their proper "time" and cardinal direction. They are further distinguished by their form and color. The god Curicáueri was represented, for example, as the sun, an eagle, or a great bonfire, while Chupi-tirípeme was depicted as blue rainwater, or as the stone in the temple of his cult at Tzacapu.[28]

The different forms and colors of the divine regalia identified particular sacred entities and conveyed specific meanings to the people. For example, a butterfly glyph was used in order to communicate the idea of the transformative power of the sun. If a butterfly were depicted above the head of an anthropomorphic figure, it represented Curita-caheri, the planet Venus as the messenger of the solar god (because Venus precedes the sun in the morning sky). The Venus-butterfly glyph thus visually communicated meanings related to the journey of the sun in the heavens. In this way Venus became the patron deity of pilgrims. Butterflies are also prominent on the chests of the Chacmul figures on the *yácatas* of Tzintzuntzan and Ihuatzio. Here, however, the meaning is connected to the transformative character of life as it relates to the drama of ritual sacrifice: the Chacmul is the messenger who lifts human hearts to the heavens to be used as divine nourishment.[29]

Through symbolic additions or deletions particular gods could be transformed into other divinities, rulers, or cultural heroes. For example, priests could be shaped into demigods. Often the divine images of conquered peoples were incorporated into the pantheon at Tzintzuntzan, adding to the sanctuary's power. The Purhépecha did not personify God as an absolute supernatural being as did the mendicants. This difference in conceptualizations of the divine led to many difficulties in translating Christianity. For example, the Spaniards used the term *Cueráuperi,* which refers to the Purhépecha earth goddess, to translate *dios* (god).[30]

Tutelary deities varied from village to village. The village tribal god is an ancient Mesoamerican phenomenon. When the migrating Chichimec nomads entered the valley of Tzacapu in the thirteenth century, their shaman priests carried representations of their sacred patron, Curicáueri, on their backs. *The Chronicles of Michoacán* outlines how this deity gained supremacy in the region:

> *The chief priest related this story. Our god, Curicaveri, began his seignory near the village of Zacapo Lacanendan. The ancestors of the Cazonci, in the end, came to conquer this land and were Masters of it. They extended their seignory and conquered the province which was first inhabited by the Mexican people, Quatatos, who spoke the same language, for it seems that other tribes had been here earlier. Each village had its chief, its people, and its own gods.*[31]

The *cazonci,* the earthly representative of Curicáueri, extended the lands of the primary Chichimec clans and hence the power of the Chichimec tribal god. In return, the divine patron showered blessings upon the people by providing an abundant harvest and a plentiful supply of fish and game and by making them a great people. The relationship between the supernatural and natural world was also dependent on the *cazonci*'s fidelity in maintaining the solar cult, through the care of the perpetually lit temple fires. At midnight the Purhépecha would light the sacred fires in their temples. The priests known as *thiumencha* (black squirrel) played gourd and shell trumpets from the highest points of the *yácatas* and contemplated the planets. The *hiripati* priests rolled up small balls of tobacco and threw them into the fire, uttering the following prayer:

> *Thou God of Fire who has appeared in the midst of the houses of the chief priests, perhaps there is no virtue in this wood which we have brought to the temples and in these fragrances which we have here to give to thee—receive them thou who art called primarily Morning of Gold and to thee Uredecuavecara, God*

*of the Morning Star, and to thou who hast the Reddish Face. See how contrite
the people are who have brought this wood for you.*[32]

The phrase "Morning of Gold" that appears here refers to the light of
Venus and the new sun. Venus was venerated throughout pre-Hispanic Mesoamerica. In the Náhuatl cultures Venus is known as Quetzalcóatl (Plumed
Serpent). In the Mayan cultures Venus is called Kukulkan, which is a Maya
translation of Quetzalcóatl. The widespread devotion to the morning star appears quite early in Teotihuacán and was disseminated throughout the city-
state's colonies. The Venus cult continued through the disruption caused by
the fall of the Toltecs and appears to have been brought to Michoacán with
the Chichimec, who called Venus Curita-caheri.

Curicáueri was also invoked in the guise of Curita-caheri. At times this
creates some confusion in distinguishing between the solar god and Venus.
This is due to the central role played by Venus, the messenger of the sun, in
Purhépecha religion. In the pictographs accompanying *The Chronicles of Michoacán*, Curita-caheri wears clay jugs around his neck. The jugs became a
symbol of the priests in their role as intermediary agents of the god. Plate 19
of *The Chronicles of Michoacán* shows a high priest administering justice. He
holds a spear and wears a necklace of clay vessels. Many examples of these
ceramic containers can still be seen in the Museum of Michoacán in Morelia.
José Corona Núñez states that the jugs are exact replicas of vessels found in
Peru, giving testimony to the ancient relationship between the two cultures.[33]

THE GODDESSES

The goddesses of the Purhépecha pantheon express the Purhépecha culture's
ideas of fertility. They also reflect themes of regeneration and abundance that
are characteristic of planting cultures. The divine women of the pantheon are
interpreted variously as the Earth-mother, the engenderer or giver of life, and
as the Moon-woman. The goddesses, who are usually costumed in rich vege-
tation, represent the female aspect of the dual cosmos.

The principal goddess is Cueráuperi. The mother of the terrestrial deities,
the powerful forces of nature, and the spirits of the underworld, she is the divine Earth herself. Cueráuperi lived in the eastern quadrant of Lake Pátzcuaro
near the hot springs of Araro. There she is said to have created four sacred
clouds that nourished the lands inhabited by the Purhépecha. Cueráuperi is
also the goddess of rain and the grandmother of the Moon, Xarátanga, who
is believed to have germinated the seeds of earthly life.[34]

The cult of Xarátanga (She Who Appears on High) was centered on the island of Xaráquaro, near the southern banks of Lake Pátzcuaro. The ancient island shrine predates the Chichimec intrusion. In this locale Xarátanga was worshipped as Acuitze-catápeme (Serpent Which Binds—perhaps a reference to the umbilical cord). According to José Corona Núñez, Xarátanga was appeased with offerings of *chía, chilis,* corn, and beans. The moon goddess was also carried into war as the Serpent Who Imprisons. She was the patroness of silver craftsmen, and women danced for her wearing wreaths of flowers. In Mesoamerica the snake is a feminine symbol because it crawls next to the earth and because the hissing sounds of rattlesnakes are associated with rainwater. In contrast, the serpent is a symbol of evil in the Christian cosmos, so that the friars immediately associated Xarátanga's cult with Satan worship.[35]

Uinturopati (Dressed in Corn Ears) was the Purhépecha corn goddess. She was linked to Xarátanga in her role as the goddess of sustenance. Like the five colored clouds, there were five colors of corn, each associated with a particular divine patroness. Pehuame was the grandmotherly goddess of childbirth and patroness of the sweat lodge *(hurínguequa).* Mauina was the goddess of love, and Auicanime the goddess of hunger and famines.[36]

Fertility and regeneration themes formed a significant part of the Purhépecha religious worldview. The people of Michoacán were primarily seed planters, fishermen, and hunters. They spent a great amount of time felling and hauling timber, which they used in building houses and canoes. They gathered natural products such as *piñón* nuts, *tunas* (fruits of the prickly pear cactus), clays for pottery, and an amazing variety of herbs that were used for teas and medicines. Above all, they tended the great fields of maize, squashes, and beans. The Purhépecha were thus absolutely dependent on climatic variations and on the lunar and solar cycles that determined the seasons. The problem of maintaining a fruitful alliance with the natural and supernatural forces, therefore, was a central issue in their culture's relationship with the gods.

Purhépecha social and religious values were closely linked to their agrarian festivals. Grotanelli writes of agrarian societies that "the ritual aspects of cultivation and the rhythmic periodicity of that economic form, in which periods of great abundance are followed by periods of scarcity, require strong differentiation in time and the concentric recurring periods of the days of the year. The yearly calendar of cultivators is thus a festive calendar."[37] Among the Purhépecha, planting and harvest practices revealed an egalitarian ideology of collective labor. This ethos manifested itself in festive consumption and hospitable generosity through redistribution of the crops. The agricultural ethos of the Purhépecha also reflected the state's values. By 1519 the Purhépecha state was a vertically structured system in which authority, status, and wealth were concentrated at the top. In this vertical social structure cooperation and solidarity were identified with the elite castes' ability to organize, determine, and distribute the annual production.[38]

Fertility and regeneration themes were also associated with the symbol of water. *The Chronicles of Michoacán* states that the Purhépecha believed that the earth was surrounded by water and that their current age had been preceded by a time of catastrophic floods. Furthermore, the sacred geography of Lake Pátzcuaro, which itself was considered a living being, was surrounded by a network of aquatic power spots. These included healing springs, magic waterfalls, and sacred rivers. The importance of water can also be seen in the belief that the spirits of people who drowned went directly to the subterranean paradise. Among the Purhépecha, water was a substance that both purified, as in the sweat lodge rituals, and terrified, by causing the lake to flood.

As a lake culture, the Purhépecha depended on seasonal rains that swept down from the high volcanoes to fill the lakes and nourish the fish, the aquatic fowl, and the crops. Chupi-tirípeme, the water deity, was enshrined on the *axis mundi* island of Pacanda.[39] Together with fire, earth, and air, water was considered one of the four elements necessary for the existence of life. Each of the earthly Tirípemes was identified with specific colors of clouds that streamed out of their respective domains in the quadripartitioned universe. *The Chronicles of Michoacán* tells us that on the Feast of Sicuindiro, the *huaripiupecha* priest would mark the chests of two slaves who were to be sacrificed. *Principales* who came to the feast were adorned as white, yellow, red, and black clouds:

> *They dance with . . . four priests . . . and they sacrifice the slaves who have been marked. When they take out the victims' heart, they perform customary ceremonies with them and while the hearts are still warm they are taken from the village of Cinapecuaro to the hot springs of the village of Araro, where they are thrown into a small hot spring and covered with boards. These springs give off a vapor of their own, and they say the clouds rise to give rain and that the goddess Cueravaperi is in charge.*[40]

The Sicuindiro sacrifice is a ritual act of reintegration in which blood, as a life-giving substance, is the rainwater of the body. Human life is returned to the goddess Cueráuperi because she creates the clouds and the rain, making the cycles of planting and harvest, and life and death, complete.

THE MYTH OF THE COSMIC BALLPLAYERS

The myth of the cosmic ballplayers is a Purhépecha creation myth. In it the primordial Sun, Cupantzieeri (Ballplayer), plays a sacred ball game known as *tlachtli* against the powerful night sky. The night sky is personified as the god Ahchuri-hierepe (Hastening Night). Ultimately Cupantzieeri loses the game to his dark adversary. As a consequence of losing the match, he is killed by Ahchuri-hierepe at a place named Xacona (House of the Night).[41]

In the narrative we learn that Cupantzieeri had a son who was called Sira-tatáperi. Sira-tatáperi was out hunting one day when he saw a large iguana. He took his bow and arrow and killed the mysterious creature. Then the iguana suddenly spoke to Sira-tatáperi:

> *"Don't shoot me and I'll tell you something. The one you now think is your father is not because your real father went to the house of the God Achurihirepe to conquer, and he was sacrificed there." When Siratatáperi heard this he went to the village of Xacona to get vengeance on his father's murderer. He excavated the place where his father was buried, exhumed him, and carried him on his back. Along the way there was a weed patch full of quail which took to flight. In order to shoot the quail he dropped his father, who turned into a deer with a mane on his neck and a long tail like those that come with the strange people.*[42]

The myth of the cosmic ballplayers has many levels of meaning. The setting Sun of the western sky is killed by the Hastening Night and so descends into the subterranean land of the dead. The regenerative Sun, Sira-tatáperi, rises in the east and conquers the night. He rescues the body of his father in the underworld, or the house of the night sky. The corpse of the old Sun is reborn in the form of a sacred deer with a mane, which forms a halo of light around the animal's head.

Eduard Seler interprets the primordial sun Cupantzieeri as a symbol of the Chichimec's primogenitors, who migrated from a place in the north called Aztlán. He suggests that "The metamorphosis of the hero into the animal, the *tuitze*, which resembles a deer, ties the myth to the Cuingo fiesta, the great fiesta which corresponds to the Mexican fiesta called Tlacaxipeualiztli, whose symbolism includes the rejuvenation of the sun, agricultural renovation, and the new year."[43] Seler translates Sira-tatáperi as "Principal Root," or "Trunk Which Sprouts from Human Beings Laterally." This phallic imagery also suggests the divine dualism as the creator of humanity, since the reborn Sun rejuvenates not only the solar cycle but also earthly life. The mythological *tuitze* is a primary symbol because it refers to the primordial creation and to the sacred ancestors whose sacrifices of flesh ensured the survival of human existence. When the Spaniards arrived in Michoacán they thought it humorous that the natives offered stewed turkey meat to their horses. If they had only known that the turkey was a sacred bird used in ritual sacrifice, they would have understood that Purhépecha were making offerings to the sacred *tuitze* and not to their horses.[44]

In the myth of the ballplayers the Sun is a crucial contestant in a cosmic battle. The Purhépecha's cosmos was the ball court whereon the great struggle between the solar and nocturnal forces was reenacted daily. The rejuvenation of the Sun explained the profound mysteries of continuity and fertility. It explained how new life sprouted from death. The ancient Sun was a huge celestial orb batted about the heavens by the dark, unpredictable powers of the cosmos. The myth reveals that for the Purhépecha the fifth age was surely a time of uncertainty and chaos, in which earthly existence required precaution and faithful adherence to the cult. Today in Michoacán vestiges of this ancient struggle can still be seen at dusk, when boys gather to bat around a fiery ball of maguey roots. The scurrying tongues and shadows of fire evoke an uneasiness in us as the fireball slowly disintegrates into the black field of night.

THREE

The Historical Landscape of Spain

In order to better understand Vasco de Quiroga and his work in Mexico it is necessary to comprehend the panorama of historical forces that influenced his formation. At the beginning of the sixteenth century Spain had just emerged from eight centuries of warfare against Islam. Behind the militant Christian imperialism of the sixteenth century, however, stood the diverse cultural history of the Iberian Peninsula and a vast field of heterogeneous experiences. Yet Spain's divergent historical experiences merged in this period, known as the Reconquista, to create a unified national identity.

In the long struggle for political dominance in the peninsula, the dispute quite naturally took on a transcendental character. Faced with the catastrophe of the Islamic advance, the Iberian Christians put their faith in the supernatural forces offered them within Catholicism. Thus they countered the exclusive Islamic affirmation of "there is no God but Allah" with their invocation of the Warrior Apostle, Santiago de Compostela. During the "Age of Discovery," then, what it meant to be Spanish and Catholic was bound to theological and ritual distinctions and to the Christian kingdoms' military response to Muslim aggression.

THE LAND OF IBERIA

The geography of Iberia is a landscape of remarkable complexity. The peninsula exhibits no uniform land mass as in France or Italy, where geological unity is relatively simple.[1] The Iberian Peninsula contains four principal regions: the northern highland zone, which consists of the Pyrenees Mountains and their westward extension, the Cantabrian Mountains; the central table-land, the Meseta; the mountains that stretch southeastward from Burgos to Valencia and the Mediterranean coast; and the plains of Andalucía, which lie between the southern barrier range and the central tableland.

The Pyrenees and the Cantabrian Mountains of the north and northwest are the backbone of the Basque provinces of Navarra, Asturias, and Galicia. The Pyrenees are laid out in an unbroken pattern from the Mediterranean to the Bay of Biscay, reaching a maximum height of 11,169 feet at the Pico de Aneto. The Spanish part of the range covers nearly 15,000 square miles. The topography of the mountains resembles the Alps, with narrow deep-cut valleys.

The Cantabrian slope lies mainly in the province of Galicia. It is a rugged green region that receives abundant moisture, where fast-moving rivulets descend abruptly to the Atlantic. The largest river of the northwest is the Miño, which starts at Lake Fuenmiña in the province of Lugo and, in the course of nearly 190 miles, drains the eastern half of Galicia. Between the western Pyrenees and the eastern termination of the Cantabrian Mountains stretches an area of small mountains and constricted river valleys that is the nucleus of the Basque homeland. Extending some 100 miles from east to west and approximately 50 miles from north to south, the region includes the hinterland of the coast between San Sebastián and Santander and lies in the provinces of Vizcaya, Guipúzcoa, Álava, and Santander. The Pyrenees provinces also include Navarra and Aragón, while on the east coast lies Cataluña with its elegant capital city of Barcelona.

The Meseta is the most prominent geographical structure in Spain. It is a vast central tableland that slopes gradually to the southwest, toward the coast of Portugal. The Meseta does not present a uniform landscape. During its long history, buckling and erosion divided it into a northern upland basin and a southern plateau that are called, respectively, Castilla Vieja and Castilla Nueva. The land mass is separated by an ominous diagonal fold of mountains. From behind these 9,000-foot mountains the northern Christian kingdoms withstood the onslaught of Islamic armies for more than eight hundred years.

The Ebro River and its basin collect the water drainage of approximately one-sixth of Spain, making it the greatest river of Iberia. It rises from the springs at the foot of Peñalabra some 3 miles west of Reinosa and flows southeast toward its delta in the province of Tarragona. During its 576-mile course, the river collects water from more than 222 tributaries. The wide curves and hilly topography of the great Ebro, however, do not facilitate commercial traffic into the interior of the peninsula. The river terrain actually isolates adjacent areas more than it links them together.

The Mediterranean side of the Ebro River basin is dominated almost exclusively by the barrier ranges that run north to south and parallel the coast. There are two primary ridges: one nearest the Mediterranean that produces a coastline of cliffs and sandy coves, and a second, more imposing interior line that climbs to 5,000 feet in the northeast. The southern barrier range, or Bética Cordillera, is a series of mountain ridges that separate upland valleys. The highest mountains in Spain, the Sierra Nevada, are found in the south and reach a height of almost 12,000 feet.

In the far south, the Plain of Andalucía is a triangular-shaped region lying between the Bética Cordillera and the Meseta. Strategically, it is the only significant lowland corridor that offers easy access to the interior of the peninsula. The Guadalquivir is the most important river in this area. The river and its tributaries divide and wander through a large marshy plain. At higher altitudes it flows through a semiarid sandy land.

THE HISTORICAL LANDSCAPE

The Iberian Peninsula's geographical diversity contributed to a complex pattern of sociopolitical regionalism, which prompted the Spanish historian Américo Castro to search for "an uninterrupted continuity" in the history of the Iberian people.[2] This section will outline the primary contours of Spanish history, in order to discover the continuities or patterns of which Castro speaks.

The emergence of the Spaniards as an identifiable culture group is a fairly recent phenomenon. Even as late as the eleventh century the name *spania* was applied to the territory occupied by the Muslims and not to the lands of the Christian kingdoms. The terms "Spanish" and "Hispanic" are inadequate to describe the dynamic synthesis to which these terms refer. Unlike the compartmentalized valley-to-valley isolation of the Mexican cultures, in the Iberian Peninsula's history a collage of cultures formed over time.

If we imagine ourselves as the spectators of a great historical drama who are viewing the development of the Spanish cultural identity, we see that representations of the Spaniards' earliest ancestors are found in the strange prehistoric cave paintings at Altamira. Those images, which date back to the Ice Age, are the first evidence of human settlement in Iberia. At that time, changes in the climate brought on by glacial movements scattered groups of settlers into the valleys. These hardy people lived by hunting and fishing and by collecting a variety of seeds and plants native to the mountain regions. At Altamira they took refuge from the harsh atmosphere in cavernous chambers in the mountainside.

Small-scale agriculture in the lowlands also developed during this period. The formation of village hamlets based on the cultivation of cereals and grains appeared on the archaeological horizon, as did the creation of megalithic monuments used in funerary rituals. Knowledge of copper and bronze reached the peninsula in the period 2000–1500 B.C., while iron artifacts date from 800 B.C.[3]

Semitic Phoenician seafaring merchants established the first trading towns along the eastern shore of the Mediterranean in 1500 B.C. Their second-generation descendants, the North African Carthaginians, settled along the coast by 1000 B.C. These settlers would come to dominate much of the peninsula in the following millennium. By 800 B.C., Greek colonies had sprouted up along the eastern coast of the Mediterranean, with the Greek settlers especially favoring the cultivation of Spanish olives and wine.[4] The Basque people moved into the northern provinces of the Iberian Peninsula around the same time. The reasons behind this migration remain a mystery. The nomadic Basques spent their days tending their flocks of sheep and goats. They had a patriarchal social structure and also an apparent need for warfare.[5] The dissemination of Basque culture to the south was checked in the fifth century B.C. by the arrival of a Celtic strain of Central Europeans. The Iberian Celts, like the Celts of France, were tribal nomads.

The Roman defeat of Hannibal in 206 B.C. brought an end to the Carthaginians' dominance of the peninsula. For the next three hundred years the Celts in the remote north and northwest sporadically resisted Roman rule. The rebellions ceased, however, after A.D. 133, and Spain became the Roman province of Iberia. Roman rule brought with it peace and stability, and Iberia experienced less war and political disturbance than any area in the empire.[6]

Roman culture flourished mainly in the older Carthaginian and Greek urban centers and in the trading towns along the Mediterranean coast, including those in the warmer southern provinces. Gade (Cádiz), Tarraco (Tarragona), Malaca (Málaga), and Barcino (Barcelona) were the principal Roman towns. Yet the Romans, who were not satisfied with merely occupying the trading ports, also built new cities. This tendency is demonstrated by the proliferation of Roman towns in the interior. As new urban centers became more prosperous, the old garrison towns disappeared.

Roman rule had lasting effects on the human geography of the peninsula. Latin, the language of Rome, not only unified the many cultures of the peninsula but also gave their people access to the greater Mediterranean world. The Romans implemented a legal and governmental system with a monopoly-oriented economy. Iberia's prosperity at this time was directly related to its participation in the Roman Empire's economic orb and particularly to trade with the more lucrative commercial centers in northern Europe. Later, throughout the long years of the Reconquista, the Spanish Christians would idealize the Roman period as a golden age of peace and prosperity.

Roman hegemony in Iberia was challenged and eclipsed by the invasion of the Visigothic tribes from north central Europe. In A.D. 409 invaders called Alans, Vandals, and Suevi swept across the Pyrenees. These nomads laid waste to the Roman garrison towns and flooded Iberia with settlers from a new culture group. Over the next two generations the Catalonian Visigoths crushed the rival Suevi and Alan bands and reduced the Vandals' territory to the southern part of the peninsula, in the land they called Al Andalus. The small number of invading Visigoths left intact the basic structure of Roman administration and culture in the peninsula. Gothic and Roman cultures fused with one another to create a new cultural synthesis.[7]

The Visigoths were not total strangers to Roman culture and ideology, for in their trek across Europe they had assimilated a brand of Aryan Christianity. Aryanism holds that the first and unique absolute principle of divinity is the Father. Christologically speaking, this perspective relegates Jesus to second place in the godhead. The Christian concept of a divine supreme monarch was particularly compatible with the Visigothic patriarchal system of petty kings. The Iberian Christians, however, considered Gothic-Aryan Christianity a heresy. Religious tensions between the two groups resulted in violence and widespread religious fanaticism. The period of Visigoth rule was characterized by frequent outbreaks of rivalries between Aryan Goths, Catholic Iberians, and Jews.[8] By the early eighth century a series of petty feuds had splintered the Visigothic ruling elite into a multitude of warring kingdoms.

At this juncture, Arab armies led by the chieftain Tariq crossed at Gibraltar from Morocco into southern Spain. The speed with which the Arab armies took possession of Iberia was greatly facilitated by the chaos inside the Visigoth kingdoms. Within two years of landing at Gibraltar, or Jebel Tariq (Place of the Hill), Islam could claim sovereignty over the whole of the central Meseta, the Ebro River valley, and parts of Galicia and León. In A.D. 720, the Islamic armies crossed the Pyrenees and spilled over into France. The Muslim advance was ultimately checked by Charles Martel at the Battle of Tours, saving the Franks from the occupation endured by the Iberians. The swiftness of the conquest of the Iberian Peninsula suggests that there was little cultural unity in Spain and that the subjugated Iberian minorities were ready for a change. North African Islamic culture was thus firmly planted on the southern side of the Pyrenees by the ninth century. The Islamic presence continued to be challenged from the highland areas of Galicia and the key Christian nucleus of Asturias.

The Christian response to Islamic victory took the form of a religious and military crusade called the Reconquista. From the Roman through Islamic periods, Catholicism had provided the Iberians with their only sense of cultural and historical continuity. Thus Catholicism gradually became synonymous with the Spanish cultural identity: to be a *cristiano* was to be Spanish, and vice versa. To be a *cristiano* was not, however, to be a pacifist as Jesus of Nazareth had taught, and warfare between the *cristianos* and Muslims became the predominant way of life, enduring for some eight hundred years.[9]

The Muslim occupation deeply affected the status quo in Iberia. In fact, even to characterize the Islamic presence as an occupation is questionable. Thirty-two generations of occupation translates into many lives and many lifetimes. During its eight hundred years of Islamic rule Spain became thoroughly Islamicized, and Islamic culture became an essential ingredient in the Spaniard's identity.

The Arab imposed himself on the Iberians as a tribute-receiving lord according to the oriental model of the sultan and his suzerain. A version of this model of land tenure would later be replicated by the conquistadors in the New World. The Islamic territories had a large and wealthy population, in contrast to the Christian kingdoms and northern Europe. This was due to the advanced agricultural system brought by the Muslims and to their broadly based craft industries. The Muslims constructed a series of small-scale irrigation channels that took advantage of the mountainous terrain. They also established a more equitable system of sharecropping based on the Arabian agrarian system, in which the harvest was equally divided between owners and peasants. This encouraged harder work and resulted in a greater yield in production, more so than in northern Europe, where peasants did not own what they cultivated.[10] Among the important crafts produced were textiles, paper, glassware, pottery, and steel for fine armor. In addition, the leather industry of Córdoba acquired a continent-wide reputation. Medieval Islamic Spain also developed a flourishing Mediterranean trade, and the appreciation for fine mozarabic craftsmanship opened markets in India and China.

The long process of acculturation to Islam is one of the most remarkable phenomena in all Spanish history. It was accomplished by means of cultural diffusion and conversion, not by a mass influx of Arabs. Great numbers of Iberian Christians did not convert to Islam (as did the New World populations to Christianity); rather, a gradual process occurred whereby Gothic Christians became culturally orientalized in all but their christocentric faith. Jews, being a "people of the Book" like the Muslims, were incorporated into important positions of learning and commerce under Islamic rule. Religious affiliation thus became the basis of cultural and caste identity and resulted in the phenomenon that Américo Castro has labeled as the culture of the three religious castes.[11]

Al Andalus (the Arabic term meaning "Hispania") was the cultural leader of Europe in the Middle Ages. Philosophy, grammar, poetry, music, physical and naval sciences, mathematics, alchemy, and architecture all reached their apex under Islamic guidance. The greatest intellectual achievement of Islamic Spain was its preservation and transmission of the works of classical antiquity, particularly the writings of the Greeks. At the beginning of the medieval period, many texts including those by Euclid could not be read in any language but Arabic. Arabic editions of classical texts as well as Greek, Latin, Persian, and Hindu works formed the standard university curriculum well into the sixteenth century. Foremost among these works was the Islamic translation of major works in both the Aristotelian tradition and Renaissance Platonism.[12]

SPANISH SOCIETY IN THE MIDDLE AGES

In the sixteenth century Spain developed an extremely complex society. The social organization of the Iberian *cristianos* in particular should be considered within the context of greater Roman Catholic Europe.[13] No categorical distinction between religious jurisdiction and the jurisdiction of the secular state existed then. The whole sociopolitical structure was subsumed under a public entity called the *res publica*. The model for this structure had been outlined by Saint Augustine in *City of God*, which entered Spanish intellectual circles through the works of Saint Isidore of Sevilla.[14]

According to Augustine, the republic, or township, consisted of a family of people with similar interests "suffering together the exigencies of life on the earth."[15] Conflict among the townsfolk was avoided by allotting "things equal and unequal, each to its own place."[16] The North African bishop believed that the republic must adhere to God's plan. He held that material or earthly life was too ephemeral to order itself and that only in the celestial afterlife could perfection be achieved. Those who did not choose God's plan were destined to burn eternally in the fires of hell, located within the bowels of the earth. Augustine's radical faith in God's providence caused him to emphasize justice as a kind of spiritual and civic virtue: "Justice was the sole end of human society, and government was simply applied justice."[17] The Spanish preoccupation with realizing the Augustinian ideal of justice was reflected in the formation of complicated legal codes. Law was considered a gift from God. Divine law was complemented by the positive law, *Mos* (sacred custom). *Lex* was the written law and was based on positive law.

Later Castilian jurists and theologians used the term *derecho* to mean unwritten law and *fuero* for the written law. The various Reconquista codes culminated in the monumental *Siete partidas* (Law of Seven Parts), compiled during the reign of Alfonso X. The quest for absolute and perfect Christian justice, along with the spiritual goal of universal human equality, made Spanish law a collection of complicated ethical prescriptions. These precepts were designed as guidelines that informed moral conduct rather than behavior per se.

Spanish society by the late Middle Ages can be visualized as a vertical hierarchy of castes. Each social group's designated status was based on the general society's perception of the value and function of the service performed by the group. Moreover, rank was accompanied by an ornate set of privileges and immunities.[18]

There were three orders or castes among the *cristianos:* the clergy, the nobility, and the commoners. The clergy had two components, the seculars and the regular clergy. The seculars included the ecclesiastical hierarchy, archbishop, bishop, provincial, prior, parish priest, deaconate, and so forth. They administered the sacraments and had direct charge over the souls of their flock. The regulars included the Cistercian and Benedictine monks who entered the peninsula in the early Reconquista period. The mendicants, or begging friars—the Dominicans, Augustinians, and Franciscans who arrived in the thirteenth century—also were considered regulars. The regular orders differed from the secular clergy in that they took vows of poverty, chastity, and obedience and, in theory, could not earn wages or own property.

The clergy's primary purpose was to prepare Christian society for salvation. Salvation was understood as deliverance from the limitations of the human condition and the evil inherent in mundane life. It also included the divine promise of immortality, to be realized at the end of time. Because of the importance of this responsibility, the clergy were granted special social privileges. For example, they were exempt from certain tithes. The most important exemption was from the *pecho* (personal tax). The clergy could own estates, urban properties, conventual houses, and the specific endowments bequeathed by the faithful without paying taxes. They also administered a network of charities that could not be taxed.

The nobility, which constituted the second order of the republic, primarily consisted of the old Visigothic lords. During the Reconquista the nobility's ranks were augmented by a group of lesser nobles called *hidalgos* (sons of prominent persons). *Hidalgos* had to be publicly recognized before achieving this status. *Caballeros* were also noblemen; they were knights who served the king in wartime.[19] The noble caste was primarily identified by its ability to fight. Nobles enjoyed special privileges in return for protecting society: they were exempted from paying the *pecho*, they had to be tried before their peers, they could not be imprisoned, and their property could not be confiscated.

Members of the upper nobility included *optimates, grandes señores,* and *magnates.* They also were invested with the lordship of their *señorío,* a privilege that gave them the right to hold certain government offices, to enact laws, and to exercise legal jurisdiction. The *señores* had exclusive control over coining money, collecting taxes, and raising levies. Ultimate lordship resided with the king, and *señorío,* furthermore, was not bestowed in perpetuity. It ended with the death of a great lord. This resulted in endless disputes over the inheritance of titles and property.

The commoners made up the third caste in Spanish society. They bore the weight of the royal prerogative and the social groups above them in the hierarchy. They provided the goods and labor services required by the republic. In the Reconquista period commoners were agricultural workers of status varying from free peasants to serfs. With urbanization there arose a new category of commoners known as *vecinos* (townsfolk), which included merchants, craftsmen, artists, and, in general, all people of fixed residence. The *vecinos* were subject to royal and upper-caste jurisdiction, and they had to pay taxes. By the sixteenth century, many towns on the Mediterranean coast contained powerful groups of *vecinos.* Ranked behind the kingdom and country in medieval Spain, the municipality was characterized by a densely populated nucleus and an agrarian hinterland. A town council, or *cabildo,* exercised jurisdiction over the township. Both the *cabildo* and the *vecinos* could own property. The civic identity of the burgers was built on this structural relationship.

Iberia was also home to people who did not belong to the Christian social order: namely, the two large quasi-independent populations of Muslims and Jews. Interestingly, the Catholic monarchs recognized the cultural and economic importance of these populations and so did not want to restrict their contribution to the realm: "By the terms of the negotiated surrenders, the *pactos protectores,* the Christian victors permitted the vanquished Moors to retain their faith and property as long as they accepted the dominion of the Christian princes and paid tribute to them."[20] Many Muslim lords rejected this offer, but large numbers of tradesmen accepted, forming a new group that became known as the *mudéjares*. The Jews were subject to the same restrictions mandated after the victory of Ferdinand and Isabella. Many of them chose to remain in their ancestral homes as *conversos* (new Christians). Both Muslims and Jews performed valuable tasks in a land top-heavy with warriors and also represented a tremendous surplus of capital that could be taxed by Christian lords.[21]

The one experience common to all people of sixteenth-century Spain was participation in the exclusively Christian-dominated social order. In this structure the monarch was the greatest of the lords. During the Reconquista the king was usually selected from among the nobility. It gradually became the custom, however, to elect the king from within the same family; thus the tradition of dynastic succession was established. The codification of the *Siete partidas* legalized the practice, and claims of divine authority advanced by the upper clergy reinforced the concept. The church had long held that spiritual stability was predicated on social order.

The king had both public and private duties. As a public figure he adjudicated conflicts through legal decrees that he "held" in his custody. As a private citizen he governed his family patrimony. The monarch "held" the title to all land, water, and mineral rights; filled public offices; and delegated patrimony. The crown also possessed the privileges of *regalías* (the royal prerogative). This included the right to intervene in ecclesiastical affairs, since the monarch was lord protector of the church. As such he claimed the right to establish sees and monasteries and to name prelates. The monarch also could convoke church councils, judge episcopal disputes, and censor various decrees. The papacy naturally disputed the religious pretensions of the Spanish monarch, but from a weak position, especially after the Islamic invasion. The crisis in Spain after the Islamic invasion left the church dependent on the protection of the Christian knights. Therefore, at the beginning of the sixteenth century, Iberian Catholicism was essentially a Spanish institution greatly influenced by a warrior caste of upper nobility.

SANTIAGO DE COMPOSTELA

The merger of religious and military ideals into the ideology of patriotic Catholicism can be traced to the ninth-century goal of regaining Christian political independence. The historian Stanley Payne contends that this goal

FIGURE 4. Santiago de Compostela

was fueled by a kind of neo-Gothic romanticism: Even as early as 760, after the increased Christian immigration into Asturias and the first generation of counterattacks, there were glimmerings of the "neo-Gothic" idea of restoring the independent Hispano-Christian monarchy of the Visigoths. This concept also identified the political and military mission of the society with its beliefs, and by the ninth century, chronicles would speak of religious strife with the Muslims as the main motive of the frontier struggle.[22]

The political and military mission of the Christian kings found an appropriate spiritual ally in the figure of Santiago de Compostela. Faith in the power of the Catholic saint united the northern kingdoms into a single military force. In fact, some scholars argue that the history of Spain would not have taken the direction it took without the belief that the body of Santiago was in repose in the chapel at Compostela *(campus stellas)*.[23] Américo Castro reinforces this perspective when he writes, "Faith in the physical presence of the Apostle gave spiritual support to those who fought against the Moors."[24]

According to popular tradition, Santiago, or Saint James, was the blood brother and apostle of Jesus of Nazareth. After the Christ's death and resurrection Saint James went to preach the gospel in Iberia. However, there is little information on his activities in the peninsula. Upon his return to the Holy Land a few years later he died a martyr's death in Jerusalem when his throat was cut. Eventually Santiago's body was transported back to Spain by his disciples. After nearly eight hundred years had passed, the apostle's body was miraculously discovered in Galicia.

Alfonso the Chaste took full political advantage of the discovery of the apostle's corpse in his efforts to build a Christian resistance movement. Santiago elevated the morale of the *cristiano* minorities, who found themselves subjugated to Islamic overlords. And in Santiago the Christian knights saw a powerful religious symbol that they could invoke in their time of need.

In the Middle Ages, Compostela was considered the third most sacred site in Christendom, after Jerusalem and Rome. Its importance is reflected in the growth of the town of Compostela under Bishop Diego Gelmírez (1100–1139). Prior to the twelfth century there were only isolated villages in the area. But in the Middle Ages the town and sanctuary became part of a huge pilgrimage network. A complex economic and communications system was developed around the sanctuary in order to sustain the many pilgrims who visited the shrine.

The pilgrimage route stretched the length of the *via francigen*, which started in northern Europe. The Benedictine monks at the monastery in

Cluny promoted Compostela in northern Europe, printing religious pamphlets and distributing information about hospices located along the way to the shrine. The many pilgrims coming to the sanctuary from northern Europe contributed to the area's thorough Europeanization. The influx of devotees also promoted a substantial economic and cultural interchange with the north. More significantly, the eleventh-century Europeanization created a sense of spiritual renewal and unity within the Catholic world. By the late Middle Ages, Compostela had become a sacred precinct of great prestige presided over by a militant spiritual patron, who had proven credentials in the defeat of the foreign "infidel."

Papal authority also was reintroduced to Spain through southern France. The Cluniac monks, who entered Castilla and León during the last part of the eleventh century, were spokesmen for the pontiff. They were concerned with purifying the moral life of the Spanish clergy. In addition, Romanization brought to Iberia the Roman Church's fascination with icons, such as the cult of relics and images of saints, theretofore little practiced in the peninsula. The pilgrimage center of Santiago thus promoted the spiritual and economic revitalization of Spanish Catholicism.[25]

Visually, Santiago de Compostela is pictured as a *caballero*, a noble medieval warrior. Dressed in full armor, he carries a raised sword and rides a white warhorse. Other images of Saint James show him as bearing a remarkable likeness to the Christ. In this Christlike guise he carries a pilgrim's staff and the Holy Scriptures. The identification of Santiago with the Christ is visible on the standard of an equestrian figure that is carved into the great cathedral at Compostela. The standard, which reads *Sanctus Jacobus Apostolus Christi*, suggests that Santiago occupies the place next to the prophet Jacob and the Christ. Américo Castro posits that there are two images of Santiago at Compostela: the learned, orthodox Saint James the Apostle, and Saint James the Moorslayer. Both images were used by the Asturian monarchs to feed the religious imaginations of the Iberian Christians.[26]

The devotees of the Warrior Apostle embodied all the characteristics of a fighting clergy. In twelfth-century Spanish history the powerful quasi-religious military orders of Calatrava, Santiago, and Alcántara occupy the foreground. These military orders took religious vows of poverty, celibacy, and obedience and received combat training. There was no contradiction between ascetic discipline and warfare. The Muslims had a similar institution called the *ribat*. The *ribat* was a hermitage where holy men *(almorávides)* alternated between asceticism and warfare. What occurred in the highly Islamicized *cristiano* cultures might be understood as part of a process of psychological and cultural borrowing; i.e., the Christian military orders imitated the model of the *ribat*. The fighting orders also may have been the prototype for "the future permanent army of Ferdinand and Isabella."[27]

In the peninsula the relations between the Christian north and the Islamic south were characterized by prolonged warfare with obvious devotional themes. The acts of pilgrimage and devotion to Santiago de Compostela reinforced the faith and unity of the Christian community and countered the religious fervor generated by the Muslims in their pilgrimages to Mecca.

Another aspect of Santiago can be seen in his guise of Saint James the Moorslayer, or Santiago Matamoros, in which he is transformed into a combative supernatural force. The poem *El Cid* illustrates this phenomenon: "The Moors shout: Mohammed! And the Christian: Santiago."[28] In the *Poema de Fernán González*, the Count of Castilla calls on the saintly Moorslayer to help him defeat the Islamic chieftain Almanzor: "There will the Apostle Santiago be called, Christ will send his servant to protect us, with such aid Almanzor will be stopped."[29]

In Santiago religious and military ideals are synthesized into a militant patriotic ideology. Santiago becomes a symbol for the "holy war" that Spanish Christians are willing to wage against the Moors. Saint James of the Gospels is transformed into the spiritual advisor of the military orders long before the orders had any kind of legal recognition.[30] Even bishops and abbots took up the sword under Santiago's protection and led military campaigns.

Santiago de Compostela was the spiritual patron foremost in the formation of the Spanish identity. He united the Christian kingdoms by providing a common enemy and a common goal. Ultimately this would reach a zenith in the sixteenth century in the idea that the Spaniards were the new "chosen people." Interestingly, at the same time, the militant ideology within Catholicism was attacked by an Erasmian spirit of renovation. The new ingredients of Hapsburg imperialism and the "discovery" of the Americas culminated in a full-blown Spanish nationalism. The latter was characterized by a long international rivalry with the forces of the Protestant Reformation and the Ottoman Empire. During an age of spiritual reform and internationalism the Inquisition developed, with absolute religious unity and exclusiveness as its hallmarks. While the intellectual forces of Spanish Catholicism flourished well into the beginning of the seventeenth century, they also grew increasingly rigid.[31]

FOUR

Religion in Spain on the Eve of the Conquest

By the late fifteenth century Roman Catholicism had become the spiritual and philosophical foundation of Spanish culture. The aggressive zeal of the medieval faith, which had propelled the Iberians through the long struggle of repossessing the land, erupted in a tempest of religious passion. The militancy of Iberian Christianity would have long-lasting implications for the people of the "New World."

The political unification of the peninsula under the Catholic monarchs Ferdinand and Isabella was not duplicated in religious culture. A powerful orthodox church was arrayed alongside a variety of heretical groups and religious ideas. This theological diversity may be attributed to four factors. First, a sense of regionalism persisted in the peninsula. Second, the reform of the regular orders in the late fifteenth century heightened the popular religious consciousness, which in turn led to a reevaluation of the faith. Third, there was an expanded dialogue concerning the personal strategies of piety, primarily within the middle and upper strata of society, communicated through devotional books written in the vernacular. And lastly, Spanish religion was strongly influenced by the international religious milieu of the period, especially the Protestant Reformation and the encounter by the Europeans with the vast New World.

RELATIONS BETWEEN CHURCH AND STATE

During the latter part of the fourteenth century the blending of religious and political ideals revived the spirit of the Crusades against Islam. In October

1469 Isabella, heiress to the throne of Castilla, married Ferdinand, the son of John II of Aragón. According to John Lynch, the marriage was hardly a love match, even though "the nineteen-year-old bride, plain and not strikingly feminine, grew fond enough of her husband to be jealous of his numerous infidelities."[1] Although the monarchs were blood relations, they married without papal approval. Nevertheless, a sense of boundless optimism spread throughout the peninsula.

The union of the major kingdoms of Castilla and Aragón created a formidable military block, adding to the efforts of the renewed Christian crusade. In 1482 the Catholic monarchs began a long and bitter war against the Sultanate of Granada. The result of this campaign was the surrender of Granada; on January 2, 1492, the Catholic monarchs entered the Alhambra in triumph. The fall of Granada and the closing of the frontier unleashed the forces of expansion that had been bogged down in the wars against the Muslims. Spain at last was on the threshold of a great colonial empire.

With the Muslims in check, the monarchs turned their attention to the Spanish Jews. On March 30, 1492, a royal edict was issued stating that the Jews had four months in which to become Christians or leave the kingdom. Out of approximately 200,000 Jews in Spain at this time, nearly 150,000 migrated to Portugal.[2] With the subjugation of the Muslims and the forced exile of the Jews, Christian Spain was finally united, thus becoming more powerful than any country in Europe.

The Spanish church remained the sole independent institution that could rival the state. The wealth and power of the ecclesiastical establishment posed a serious threat to the extension of the royal patronage system into the newly reclaimed territories. The monarchs' apprehension about church power may have been exaggerated, however. Catholicism in Spain was far from homogeneous. The cultural regionalism of the peninsula promoted both theological and liturgical diversity. Furthermore, as Lynch states, "Like the crown the church had lost prestige and property in the civil wars of the mid–fifteenth century, in which the most powerful members had participated on one side or the other for reasons that had little to do with religion."[3]

The church was essentially a feudal structure, politically and culturally particularized. And it was difficult for the Catholic monarchs to purge the regionalisms prevalent in Spain. Even the royal kingdoms of Aragón and Castilla were not combined into one kingdom but remained autonomous sovereign states until after Isabella's death. The superficial unity of the church, therefore, resulted in a royal policy of firm discipline and rigid orthodoxy. Ferdinand and Isabella rationalized that the policy was necessary because of the "degenerate" state of a religion long influenced by both Judaism and Islam.[4] The monarchs' plans for reforming the church were part of a well-conceived plan that included the subjugation of the three estates to royal control.

In 1478 a radical reform of the clergy was begun under the supervision of Isabella's confessor, the Franciscan provincial Cardinal Jiménez de Cisneros. Cisneros was one of the outstanding figures of the Spanish imperial age. With Isabella's support, he eagerly embarked on a program to curb the worldly excesses of the clergy. At this time concubinage was so rampant among the rural clergy that when Cisneros outlawed this practice physical violence erupted, and "a number of friars emigrated to Morocco and converted to Islam, rather than give up their women."[5] A vital requirement in Cisneros's reform included the fulfillment of pastoral duties. His program also provided for reeducating the clergy in order to raise their intellectual caliber.

In 1478 the pope authorized the establishment of the Holy Office of the Inquisition. It was designed to purge the Spanish church of crypto-Judaism.[6] Later, after the 1520s and Luther's challenge in northern Europe, the target of the Inquisition was widened to include Moorish converts, Illuminist mystics, Erasmians, and Protestants. The reform of the clergy and the institution of the Inquisition ensured, at least publicly, a unified church. Clerical abuses had become so ingrained through generations of practice, however, that they did not disappear overnight. A half-century later a more uniform reform of the clergy was initiated by the Counter Reformation.[7]

A unique aspect of church-state relations in sixteenth-century Spain was the level of influence exercised by the crown upon the ecclesiastical establishment. The Spanish church was in fact governed by the Spanish crown. Royal patronage of the Catholic Church had originally been granted by Pope Innocent VIII to Ferdinand and Isabella in 1486 as a reward for their defeat of the Muslims. Eventually Ferdinand further consolidated his position and gained more patronage concessions from successive popes. In 1508, in the papal bull *Universalis Ecclesiae Regimini,* Julius II granted Ferdinand full rights of patronage in the Indies. The crown enjoyed this privilege for nearly three hundred years of the colonial period, to its great benefit; as Shields states, "The importance of this single arrangement in the creation and consolidation of empire is inestimable."[8]

Royal privilege gave the Spanish crown the right to exercise a vast range of functions in Spain and in the colonies, especially with regard to church administration and finance. This not only included the appointment of all clerics but also meant that the monarch could determine church policy, designate parish boundaries, collect tithes, and call church councils and synods. The monarch served as the absolute liaison between the upper clergy in Spain and the Pope in Rome. Thus, at the time of the conquest, Catholicism in Spain could truly be called a Spanish institution. In Michoacán, as in all of the New World, the state of the church and the spiritual and material welfare of the Amerindian vassals also fell under the auspices of the *patronato real.*

POPULAR RELIGION IN THE COUNTRYSIDE

The religious product exported to New Spain through royal patronage was a specifically Iberian brand of devotional Catholicism. In it were blended a variety of pagan, Christian, Jewish, Islamic, and other medieval traits. In Spain it represented the pious practices of the common people of the towns and villages, of both the mountainous countryside and the tableland.

Local or popular religion exhibited a broad differentiation at the beginning of the sixteenth century. Its particular character was connected to the development of ritually complex localized cults and the appearance of regional shrines, village patron saints, and other liturgical regionalisms. This style of piety, mostly propagated by the Franciscan mendicants, paid special devotional attention to the images of the suffering Christ, the Crucifixion, and the Passion. Although the Virgin Mary was a major object of shrine devotion, it was in her role as La Dolorosa, the sorrowful mother of the crucified Christ, that she was most often venerated.[9]

In his book *Local Religion in Sixteenth-Century Spain,* William Christian provides a clear picture of this diverse devotional panorama. His analysis is based on responses to a questionnaire sent out by Philip II in 1575 and 1580 to the towns and villages of Castilla Nueva. The survey reveals a landscape dotted with holy sites, chapels, and shrines. It indicates a strong belief in the efficacy of miracles and indulgences and demonstrates an ardent devotion to the Crucifixion, La Dolorosa, and the saints. The religion thus depicted is not the religion of the Scholastic theologians but is instead geared to farmers and herdsmen, and to those people most subject to the powers of nature.[10] Analyzing the survey responses, Christian identifies four devotional tendencies in the countryside: a devotion to patron saints and their relics, a devotion to particular cultic images, shrine worship dedicated to the Virgin Mary in her many guises, and devotional practices directed to the crucified Christ.[11]

In early Christianity, devotion to the saints began when the faithful congregated to commemorate the death of a local martyr or bishop. This practice eventually developed into the traditional celebration of the saint's feast day. Saintly corpses soon became the locus of popular veneration, because people believed that possession of the bones of holy men and women had a magical salvific power. Consequently, the church required that the corporal relics of the saints be sealed within the altars of the temples. Indulgences, or the priestly absolution of transcendental punishment in exchange for money or other material forms of penance, was closely linked to the veneration of the relics of saints. By the beginning of the sixteenth century the sale of indulgences had become so abused that the practice rivaled currency in its popularity and material value.[12]

A second form of piety practiced in Castilla Nueva was the contemplation of sacred icons. Visual images such as statues, paintings, crucifixes, sacred clothing, and so forth provided a greater flexibility for devotees than did the bones of saints. They were more mobile and so could be transported from village to village. More importantly, since the images were not bound to the cathedral building, they could be tended to and virtually "owned" by the villagers. This development resulted in a new locus of sacredness.

Soon veneration of the images of patron saints formed the heart of the liturgical cycle of village life. Some images had greater significance than others: "More important were the images of those saints whose cult had its origins in collective vows (*promesas*) made by the villagers in times of crisis, such as epidemics, drought, or other disasters."[13] Each disaster required a specialized protector whose aid the villagers could enlist. Saint Sebastián was invoked for pestilence, Saint Gregory of Nazianzus for vine worm, Saint Agatha for hail, and so forth. In this way image worship brought together villagers and created a sacred network of shrines, shrine keepers, and fiestas, all geared to protect the village from the harmful forces in nature.

A third kind of devotion was associated with the shrines of the Virgin Mary. Victor and Edith Turner contend that the earliest Marian devotion in Spain was probably connected to the commemoration of her assumption.[14] As late as the twelfth century there were four Marian feast days: the Purification (February 2), the Annunciation (March 25), the Assumption (August 15), and the Nativity (September 8). The mendicants became devotees of the Virgin after the twelfth century. William Christian states that Marian piety represented an attempt by the mendicants to universalize devotion and to counteract the particularism of the patron saints. He argues that the friars hoped to create a situation that placed less emphasis on the power of relics. If this was the case, then the mendicant promotion of Marian devotion represented a move toward greater orthodoxy. Mendicant aims were quickly compromised, however, by the strength of popular devotion. Devotion to the Virgin soon took on the style of the cult of the saints:

> *One of the reasons for the enormous proliferation of Marian shrines in central and southern Spain from the twelfth century on was the vacuum left by the Moorish occupation: after the reconquest, there were simply not enough shrines of saintly relics to reconsecrate the territory. Here, 'invention' of Marian relics was secondary to apparitions and discoveries of images. The belief in the As-sumption of the Virgin meant that she could reappear to selected mortals less problematically than a devoutly dismembered saint. As far as the discovery of images was concerned, the common tradition was that these were ancient stat-ues hurriedly hidden as the Moors advanced, then unearthed one by one as the reconquest rolled them back.*[15]

In this fashion, devotion to the Virgin Mary in her many guises became a wider practice than petitions to the saints, who were considered more spe-cialized healers. Marian shrines were usually situated near caves, waterfalls, or springs; under a holy tree; or on a mountain. Symbolically, the shrines collapsed the differences between the Mother of God, the Mother of the Christ, and Mother Nature. The Virgin Mary's identification with the fer-tility of nature represented a reassertion of the goddess worship of pre-Christian Iberia.[16]

A fourth characteristic of local religion centered on the figure of the cruci-fied Christ. This form of veneration reached its zenith with the great pagean-tries of the *cofradías*, or confraternities. The shift to a christocentric cult was influenced by the early Renaissance emphasis on the accessibility and human-ity of Jesus of Nazareth. Jesus Christ's humanity found vivid expression in the art and iconographic realism of the later Middle Ages. The themes of divine suffering and loving forgiveness surrounding the Passion story were central symbols in the period. One of the earliest Christ images was the San Salvador of Oviedo. Other popular images of Christ that acquired powerful reputa-tions were located at Burgos, Orense, Valencia, and Sevilla.[17]

The appearance of shrines dedicated to the veneration of the crucified Christ coincided with the rise of the flagellant processions of the *cofradías*. This naturally led to an increased number of religious confraternities and sodalities: "As many as one hundred different confraternities might be found in certain cities of no more than ten thousand population, an average of one confraternity for every one hundred people."[18] The confraternities' func-tions included a broad range of liturgical and philanthropic activities. In the dramatic processional reenactment of the Passion, the *cofradía* member gained spiritual rewards through participation in the divine suffering.

Vivid representations of the bloodied body of Christ being scourged and carrying the cross thus joined the images of the Crucifixion scene in the folk religion of the Spanish countryside. Of the sacred imagery produced in this period, only Mary as the Mother of God and Mary as Mother Nature, together with the crucified Christ, came to assume a major role in the Americas. Though the saints were imported to New Spain, their meaning had little to do with their European namesakes. The European saints did not become the objects of an extensive cult among the Amerindians. Although many Amerindian villages today venerate their local patron saint, the saint is theirs by invention. In Mexico, San Juan is not merely the evangelist, he is also the ruler of the eastern quadrant. Owned by the village of San Juan, he is San Juan de los Lagos.[19]

THE ALUMBRADOS

Spanish culture in the sixteenth century revealed a heightened religiosity that cannot be ascribed merely to imperial policies, social advances, or ceremonial forms. For what was at stake for the spiritual master represented a new experience of God and a new brand of piety. It stressed each person's direct experience of the divinity through a systematized physical and psychological contemplation. The Alumbrado, or Illuminist, movement was not confined to one social stratum or particular group in Spanish society. It was a heterogeneous phenomenon that produced a galaxy of spiritual masters. The leaders of this religious movement reflected the greater European concern for the spiritual cleansing of Christianity.[20]

It is not within the parameters of this essay to examine in depth the vast mystical literature of sixteenth-century Spain. My intent is to illustrate the general characteristics of the movement, especially within the mendicant ranks. The late-fifteenth-century reforms of Cardinal Cisneros and the greater European reevaluation of Christian piety led to the inclusion in the Illuminist ranks of such noted Franciscan mystics as Francisco de Osuna (1497–1542), Bernardino de Laredo (1482–1540), San Pedro de Alcántara (1499–1562), Diego Estrella (1524–1578), and Juan de los Ángeles (1536–1609). The Dominican and Carmelite Illuminists included Luis de Granada (1504–1588), Santa Teresa de Jesús (1515–1582), and San Juan de la Cruz (1542–1591). The Augustinians could claim Hernando de Zárate (d. 1592),

Alonso de Orozco (1500–1591), and the great writer of the Spanish golden age Luis de León (1528–1591).[21]

Marcel Bataillon and Américo Castro both have affirmed that a great number of the Alumbrados (enflamed ones) were originally Jewish *conversos*.[22] These Alumbrados espoused an intellectualized form of inner-focused religion known as *recogimiento* (recollection) or *abandono* (abandonment), which stressed the personal illumination received through mental contemplation of the love of God. *Alumbrismo* was eventually considered a heresy by orthodox Catholicism. Even so, it continued to flourish throughout the sixteenth century in Spain. The existence of two great Spanish saints, Santa Teresa de Jesús and San Juan de la Cruz, attests to the success of the movement.

The Alumbrados had little to do with the northern European reform movement. Nevertheless, they were persecuted by the Spanish Inquisition from 1525 onward. The Inquisition's autos-da-fe were likely inspired by racism and by "old Christian" jealousies of the *conversos'* newly acquired power as "new Christians." While they were still Jews the *conversos* were barred from holding any office within the Catholic Church or civil structure. After their conversion, however, these legal restraints were removed. Ironically, their new position afforded them the right to enter the clergy; Bataillon states that the Spanish Franciscans were densely populated with "new Christians." After the Inquisition trials of the 1520s the government instituted the *limpieza de sangre* (purity of the blood) statutes, whereby any person of Jewish or Moorish descent was forbidden from entering corporations, craft and religious guilds, state offices, and other social organizations. By the 1540s the descendants of the Jews and Moors, though thoroughly Spanish in culture, were forbidden to enroll in the universities.[23]

According to Illuminist thought, it was possible through physical and mental techniques to achieve a state of this-worldly spiritual perfection. This position challenged the traditional view of the sacraments as necessary instruments employed in the perfection and salvation of the practitioner. The Illuminists believed that there was no need to perform the external religious works regulated by the orthodox church. They held that praying the rosary, enacting penances, prostrations before sacred images, signs of the cross, and attending mass were not necessary. God could only be found internally in the profound depths of the human heart and mind.

Bataillon defines Illuminism as an "interiorized Christianity with a live feeling of Grace" that circumambulates certain methods and formulas.[24] The debate about how to achieve this feeling of Grace was the most characteristic aspect of the movement. It unfolded along two rival lines of thinking focused on, respectively, recollection and abandonment.

The recollectionist tendency found its richest expression in the writings of the Franciscan cleric Francisco de Osuna. Osuna was raised sixty miles from Sevilla. He went to Africa with his father and witnessed the siege of Tripoli in 1510, and later attended the University of Salamanca and served in the novitiate in Sevilla. In 1530 he was elected Franciscan Commissary General of New Spain, a post that because of ill health he never assumed. From 1532 on, throughout the remaining years of his life, he traveled in France, Holland, and Spain.[25]

In his manual of contemplative techniques, *El tercer abecedario espiritual* (The third spiritual alphabet), 1527, Osuna writes, "The cause which chiefly moved me to write this book was to bring to the general notice of all this exercise of recollection to show all how they may reach the universal Lord, who wills to be served of all with all to have friendship."[26] Osuna did not wish the book to be an elitist work reserved only for monks. In this respect his work reflected the broader perspective on humanity that characterized Renaissance thought.

Osuna's text portrays the soul's search for God through the trial and error of contemplative prayer. The pursuit of God's essence requires an unlearning and a learning of the personality. It especially demands mental detachment from the material fascinations of the mind and the body. The detachment of the practitioner called for by Osuna is so radical that all thoughts of the world must be put aside.

The technique of spiritual detachment was accompanied by a rigorous asceticism. Osuna states that the technique of recollection results in an emptying of the self, so that "God fills up the heart." The heart is the prime vehicle for experiencing God, because the external senses interfere with the internal disposition to know and to ultimately be one with God. Unlike his apprentice, Santa Teresa de Jesús, Osuna did not see mystic contemplation as a series of halting stages. Instead, he warns that often those who think they are on the path of perfection actually are being fooled by their own imaginations. Osuna's writings were very popular among the "discalced" mendicants. The term "discalced" (shoeless) refers to special sandal-clad groups of monks and nuns who practiced recollective prayer and an exacting asceticism.

The most famous Illuminist was Santa Teresa de Jesús. Teresa, who was born into a *converso* household in the town of Ávila, lost her mother when she was twelve years old. As a young girl she read a great deal about the lives of the saints and also about chivalry. One of her earliest dreams was of joining a crusade to the Holy Land and dying a martyr at the hands of the Moors. At the age of twenty Teresa entered the Carmelite convent of the Incarnation at Ávila, where for thirty-five years she lived in anonymity. But suddenly in 1555, while entering the oratory for prayer, she testified that she saw the wounded body of Christ, who had come to reveal the meaning of the Crucifixion. Because of this episode she began studying Augustine and meditating with the help of Osuna's *Tercer abecedario.* Teresa's experience resulted in her reform of the Carmelite order. During the remainder of her life she worked outside of the convent among the poor and founded thirty-two religious houses.[27]

A key concept borrowed by Teresa from Osuna is the "prayer of quiet," which appears in her work *Las moradas* (The interior castles). Teresa defines the prayer of quiet as the state where the physical senses are entirely inactive, especially as they relate to the phenomenal world. She describes the soul as touching and embracing the supernatural realm by way of the mind. In this psychological state the faculties of the soul are drawn closer to divine perfection through a series of mental stages. On the journey to God, however, the will is the most important human faculty because it is occupied in the dialectic struggle to be one with God. Teresa writes, "There are many souls who reach the state of the Prayer of Quiet, but few pass beyond it, and this very often for lack of instruction. . . . [T]he Prayer of Quiet is but a tiny spark *(centellica)* from God's fire."[28] According to Teresa, the resulting experience of living grace is

> *a glorious folly, a celestial frenzy, where true knowledge is learned, it is a most delightful way to enjoy the soul. It is a sleep of the faculties, which are neither wholly lost, nor yet (does one) understand how they work. In that state the soul does not know what to do, for it does not know if it speaks or is silent, it laughs and weeps. I clearly understand that (in the state) there was not complete union of all the faculties . . . yet truly they are almost in complete union, only not so wholly engulfed that they cannot work.*[29]

For Teresa, quiet recollection is the gateway to the mystical experience of God. It is the point where the soul leaves the mental and physical attractions of the mundane world, which have become distractions from the higher experiential spheres.

The abandonist faction of the Illuminist movement described contemplation of the godhead as a surrender of the soul to God. They taught that it was essential for the practitioner to realize that the senses were exterior aspects of human beings. All thoughts had to be discarded, so that one could be in the quiet space of the soul with God. Marcel Bataillon postulates that the *aban-doneros* and the *recogimienteros* both advocated an internal form of meditative piety. Their principal difference developed around the idea of whether to pray with the eyes open or the eyes closed, as taught by the Franciscans.[30]

The practices of the Spanish *beatas* also can be grouped alongside the diverse religious expressions of the period. The *beatas* were charismatic laywomen famous for their mystical illumination through the agency of the Holy Spirit. They maintained an intimate connection to the mendicant orders in their role as spiritual guides. The more famous of these women were the Beata of Piedrahita, who belonged to the Third Order of Saint Dominic; Isabel de la Cruz, a Third Order Franciscan; María Cazalla, whose brother was the Franciscan bishop Juan de Cazalla and Cisneros's chaplain; and Francisca Hernández, who was well known within the intellectual circles at the University of Alcalá through the Franciscan Bernardino de Tovar, the brother of Juan de Vergara and her devotee. (Cardinal Cisneros had hired Vergara to be the director of the Complutensian Bible project.)

The *beatas* were spiritual and physical healers who based their cures on their love of God. Often regarded as scandalous, they caused an uproar in the cities because of the charismatic appeal they held for young male mendicants. For example, up until 1519 Francisca Hernández was devotedly pursued by three socially prominent gentlemen: the *morisco converso*, the Franciscan Bernardino Tovar; the Franciscan Gil López; and Antonio de Medrano. According to Marcel Bataillon, Francisca's passionate public greetings as well as her sexual intimidation of Medrano caused tremendous social turbulence in Valladolid.[31]

The contemplative piety movement had widespread popular appeal in the early years of the sixteenth century. For the Illuminist, possession of the beloved godhead was the highest of all possible human experiences. Both the *recogimiento* and *abandono* techniques stressed the individual's direct access to the divine, and understanding the intricacies of the human mind was necessary for the union experience. The most difficult act for the practitioner was to surrender the mind, body, and soul to the all-encompassing love of an invisible God. This difficult action had its rewards for the practitioner: the Illuminists believed that it was possible to order one's life to such a degree that it became impossible to sin. The accusation that the traditional church promoted ritual idolatry was heard consistently from Illuminists, beginning with Osuna and continuing with Santa Teresa, and including Juan de los Ángeles at the end of the century. This intensely active militant fervor, seen primarily within the mendicant ranks, would fuel the evangelization of New Spain.

ERASMIAN HUMANISM IN SPAIN

In the first quarter of the sixteenth century, the mystical ideals of the Alumbrados converged with the ideals of a Christian humanism that was inspired by Erasmus of Rotterdam (1469–1536). The entry of Erasmus's work into the religious landscape of Spain marked a new phase in the Spanish Renaissance. To a great extent this entry had been well prepared by Cardinal Cisneros's clerical reforms and the founding in 1498 of the University of Alcalá. Cisneros hoped that his university would be the location of the new learning movement inspired by humanist scholarship. This movement entailed rigorous ecclesiastical training, which eventually would prepare a core of intellectually elite mendicants for the arduous task of evangelizing Mexico.

Traditionally portrayed as the most significant intellectual and social movement of the European Renaissance, humanism had its nucleus in Italy and the Low Countries of northern Europe. Now, the term "humanism" in its present usage can mean any kind of concern with human values. This widening of the definition in modernity has caused much confusion. In the modern sense of the word, a great variety of thinkers—religious, antireligious, scientific-Marxian, or anti-scientific socialist—can claim to be humanist.[32] In the Renaissance, however, the term "humanism" was used in much the same way as the word "humanities" is used today. Literally referring to the intellectual discipline called *studia humanitatis*, it consisted of "a clearly defined cycle of scholarly disciplines, namely grammar, rhetoric, history, poetry and moral philosophy, . . . [with] the study of each of these subjects . . . understood to include the reading and interpretation of its standard ancient writers in Latin and to a lesser extent in Greek."[33] Unlike the "higher" theological impulses of Illuminist mysticism, in humanism the focus is more on humanity. The Renaissance historian Paul Kristeller describes this characteristic as "not as such a philosophical tendency or system, but rather a cultural and educational program."[34]

Renaissance humanism was elitist to the extent that it was an overwhelmingly intellectual discourse. No common philosophical doctrine can be found for the humanist project except a belief in the renewed value of humanity and the revival of ancient learning, both understood within the Christian cosmology. Yet developing social programs to perfect humanity according to Christian and classical ideals did not mean that all humanists were necessarily humanitarian. Few became social workers for the needy. The plan for educating and perfecting humanity, according to the guidelines of a classical curriculum and the ideals of a "purified" Christianity, represented a broad cultural and literary movement that was not exclusively philosophical or religious.

In *Erasmo y España* Marcel Bataillon demonstrates that a virtual Erasmian frenzy swept through Spain in the first quarter of the sixteenth century.[35] Erasmus's appeal was facilitated by the atmosphere of learning created by Jiménez de Cisneros. Cisneros is an immense figure in both the religious and secular history of Spain. He renounced a life as a Spiritual Franciscan recluse in order to become Isabella's religious confessor in 1492. He was provincial of the Franciscans in Castilla, archbishop of Toledo, and, beginning in 1495, primate of Spain. In 1507 Cisneros assumed the post of inquisitor general and twice functioned as regent of the kingdom. Thanks to his efforts to ensure that clerics were persons of virtue and learning, an unprecedented number of men and women entered religious orders in the latter part of the fifteenth century. Moreover, the Franciscan and Dominican houses in Spain became far superior to their counterparts in northern Europe.[36]

Cisneros was a man of vision and zeal who was deeply influenced by the ideal of a reformed Christianity achieved by way of the "new learning" practices of humanist scholarship. In order to accomplish his reforms, he put together a series of political alliances, first with Isabella and then with the young prince Charles of Hapsburg. These alliances bridged the interests of church and state; Cisneros joined royal patrimony and the goals of the Catholic Church.

In 1498 Cisneros founded the University of Alcalá. It was intended as a model educational institution where clerics could be taught the new techniques of scholarship. In order to accomplish this task, Cisneros assembled Europe's leading scholars to work on a major translation of the Christian Bible. The *conversos* Alfonso de Zamora, Pablo Coronel, and Alfonso de Alcalá were put in charge of the Chaldean and Hebrew manuscripts. Demetrio Ducas, from Crete, and the Spaniards Hernán Núñez, Juan de Vergara, Diego López de Estúñiga, and Antonio Nebrija translated the Greek texts.

The Complutensian Polyglot Bible consisted of five volumes printed synoptically in the original languages together with the Latin Vulgate. It was a massive feat of organization and scholarship. The Polyglot was printed in 1517, the year Luther nailed his "Ninety-five Theses" to the chapel door at the University of Wittenberg and the year of Cisneros's death. With the publication at Alcalá the Bible became more accessible to the clergy and the laity in Spain, taking some of the sting out of later Protestant criticism.[37]

Cisneros invited Desiderius Erasmus to join the faculty of Alcalá in 1516, after the publication of his translation of the New Testament. Erasmus was without a doubt one of the preeminent intellectual figures of the sixteenth century. In describing him Peter Gay writes, "Erasmus was a true classical spirit in his search for clarity and simplicity, a modern in his complexity, an ancestor of the Enlightenment in his critical temper and pacific cosmopolitanism."[38] Erasmus's lifetime goal was to employ humanism in the service of religion. He felt that the classical methods of humanism could facilitate the discovery of the original revelation of the Holy Scriptures. He believed that in order to realize the original biblical ontology, a more scientific and scholarly approach to the text was required.

Erasmus's formative years, 1475 to 1484, were spent with the Brothers of the Common Life at the monastery at Deventer. Here he was introduced to the methods of humanist scholarship by Alexander Hegius. He was also taught the methods of the *devotia moderna*, which emphasized the imitation of the life of Christ.[39] Erasmus was already popular among intellectual circles in Alcalá at the time of Cisneros's invitation. Although he never accepted the academic position at Alcalá, he wrote, "I owe more to Spain than to my own country, or any other."[40] By 1522 the most powerful ecclesiastics in Spain supported Erasmus's intellectual project. For example, both Alfonso de Fonseca, the archbishop of Toledo, and Alfonso Manrique, the archbishop of Sevilla and inquisitor general, were his allies and financial patrons.

Erasmus's book *Enchiridion militis Cristiani* (Manual of a Christian knight) was especially popular in Spain. Written in 1503, it was dedicated to Archbishop Alfonso Manrique. By this time Erasmus was already forty years old and had spent seventeen years at the monastery at Steyn. Steyn had been a negative experience for Erasmus. He felt that the friars were more concerned with their ritual obligations and other such formalities than in what he believed was the spiritual message of the New Testament.[41]

The Enchiridion is important because it outlines the goals of Erasmus's thought. Erasmus conceived of the work as a kind of lay guide to Scripture. He tells us that it was composed for a soldier who feared "the superstitious kind of religion," which was "a sort of Judaism" that would ultimately teach the Christian "not to love but fear."[42] Erasmus describes his task as providing "in a concise fashion some method of living which might help (a Christian) achieve a character acceptable to Christ."[43] Through the militant metaphor of "a soldier of Christ," *The Enchiridion* develops the attractive thesis of a reformed piety accomplished through education. Erasmus called this thesis his *philosophia Christi*. He argued that medieval Christianity must be changed through a reexamination of the writings of the Fathers and the Holy Scriptures. Only through imitating the spiritual message of the Christ could salvation be achieved. It is remarkable how suited the soldier metaphor was to the temperament of the Spanish faith.

Two themes are developed in the book. First, the Christian soldier must protect himself with a powerful weapon: that is, a personal understanding of the Scriptures. And secondly, true religion is an internal process, consisting of a heartfelt love for God and neighbor. Erasmus contends that religion does not consist of venerating external forms and images. It is not, he says, the illusory materialism of the clerics: "No worship of Mary is more gracious than if you imitate Mary's humility. No devotion to the saints is more acceptable and more proper than if you strive to express their virtue. And although an example of universal piety be sought most fittingly from the Christ, yet if the worship of Christ in his saints delights you very much, imitate Christ in the saints. If this happens, I will not disapprove those things which are now done in public."[44]

Another feature that appealed to Spanish readers was Erasmus's emphasis on Saint Paul's idea of the mystical body of Christ. In *The Enchiridion* Erasmus insists that the Christian knight must understand that he is a brother to his neighbor and a member of the universal body whose head is Christ. He rebukes the knight and sharply remarks, "Your brother needs your help, but you meanwhile mumble your little prayers to God, pretending not to see your brother's need."[45] Erasmus implores the reader to recognize "your brother in the Lord, coheirs with you in Christ, a member of the same body, redeemed by the same blood, a comrade in the common faith, called to the same grace and happiness in the future life."[46] This appeal for religious universalism was particularly well received by the imperial and triumphalist elements in Catholic Spain. Ironically, the same idea ultimately led Erasmus to a position of political pacifism. And it was Erasmus's cosmopolitanism and internationalism that moved him to decline Cisneros's invitation to teach at Alcalá.

Erasmus's anticlerical statement that most clerics "stay as far away from religion as possible" evoked quite a stir when *The Enchiridion* appeared in Spanish in 1527. Manrique convoked an Inquisition court in 1527 to judge the work. Six weeks later the court had failed to reach a consensus. Manrique, Erasmus's patron, then ruled in favor of the publication and forbade further attacks on Erasmus.[47]

In the late 1520s, however, there was a conservative reactionary response to Erasmus's liberal ideas. This was due in part to the rightly perceived threat of the northern European Protestant reformers. In 1529 Alfonso de Valdés wrote two treatises attacking clerical abuses. He also criticized the sack of Rome by Charles of Hapsburg as the result of papal perversity. Around the same time, Alfonso's brother, Juan de Valdés, published an essay attacking Erasmus's critics as hypocritical Christians. In June, Charles V, who was himself influenced by an entourage of liberal Flemish intellectuals, left Spain for Italy. During the emperor's absence Juan de Valdés was convicted by the Inquisition and forced to leave the country. In 1533 the pro-Erasmian ally Archbishop Manrique was removed from the post of inquisitor general.

By the mid-1530s the Inquisition had successfully established a connection in the minds of the public between Erasmus and the heresy of Martin Luther. This led to the suppression of Erasmian ideas in the peninsula and to the repression of his supporters. The *converso* Juan de Vergara was imprisoned in 1533. Pedro Lerma, the Erasmian chancellor of Alcalá, was forced to resign in 1537. Cardinal Manrique, the last upper-clergy supporter of Erasmus, died in 1538. By 1540, then, Erasmian humanism in Spain was considered heretical and hence on its way to extinction. Having quieted the Erasmian intellectuals, the Spanish Inquisition and the church in Rome set about to consolidate their respective authority through the mechanism of the Counter Reformation.

Erasmus's critique of the religious materialism of medieval Christianity, his faith in the Holy Scriptures, and his emphasis on the power and universality all intellects achieved through their participation in the mystical body of Christ greatly influenced the translation of Christianity to Mexico. The great mendicant ethnographies of the native cultures were compiled in order to translate the Bible into the Amerindian languages. Pedro de Gante, who set the model for New World evangelization, wrote two works, the *Doctrina breve* and *Doctrina cristiana*, both of which contain passages from *The Enchiridion*. The Franciscan archbishop of Mexico City, Juan de Zumárraga, was very much influenced by Erasmus's ideas of a renovated interiorized Christianity and the return to a Christlike piety. Zumárraga also favored the classical curriculum over scholastic training for instructing the Amerindians. The New Spain mendicant ideology "was in accord with the Spanish tendency to temper Erasmian insistence on the godlike nature of man with the more traditionally Christian view of the corruption of man offered by Augustine."[48] In Mexico, Erasmus's program was viewed as a modern methodology to be employed in converting the Amerindians. However, his ideas of Christian universalism were suppressed when they clashed with Spanish economic interests as well as the mendicant aim of theocratic rule.

FIVE

The Conquest of Michoacán and the Appointment of Vasco de Quiroga

In 1519 Diego Velásquez, governor of Cuba, planned an expedition to the mainland of Mexico. The expedition was charged with searching for gold, securing slaves, and establishing a trading port on the Mexican coast. Hernán Cortés, a town councilman and *encomendero*, was appointed commander of the operation. Instead of establishing a coastal trading port, however, Cortés led a sortie into the interior, where he encountered the wealthy urban cultures of central Mexico. On August 23, 1521, after a fierce four-month siege, the last Aztec king, Cuauhtemoctzin, surrendered the great city of Tenochtitlán to Cortés and his Amerindian allies. With the most powerful pre-Columbian society in check, Cortés turned westward, toward the kingdom of Michoacán.

The first Spaniard to step foot in Michoacán was Francisco Montaño, who arrived there in 1521. In July 1522 the *cazonci* of Michoacán peaceably received a force led by Cristóbal de Olid. In 1524 Cortés distributed the towns and villages of Michoacán to his captains, reserving for himself the capital city of Tzintzuntzan, its dependencies, and the mining region to the south. And the Franciscans began their evangelization efforts in 1525, while the Augustinians followed suit in 1533.

The 1520s was thus a brutally violent decade in Michoacán, resulting from multilayered conflicts between the native rulers, the Spanish *encomenderos*, the mendicant orders, and the new bishop, Vasco de Quiroga. During this period the Purhépecha lost their identity as Purhépecha-Chichimec and came to be thought of, generically, as *indios*. This radical transformation of the Purhépecha's identity was caused by a number of factors, primarily their enslavement and the devastation of their population by the endemic diseases brought by the Spaniards. The decade ended with the Purhépecha's most serious crisis: the assassination of the *cazonci* in 1530.

OMENS OF THE SPANISH INVASION

The traditional manner in which the Purhépecha experienced their world was violently altered in the crucial years between the fall of Tenochtitlán in 1521 and the arrival of Vasco de Quiroga and the second Audiencia in 1530. *The Chronicles of Michoacán* relates the stories of a number of omens that purportedly foretold the Spanish invasion. As early as four years prior to the appearance of the conquerors, Purhépecha sages began to wonder about the mysterious deterioration of their temples. Astronomers who had sighted two ominous comets crossing the heavens over Lake Pátzcuaro warned their leaders of the imminent demise of the kingdom. One priest even dreamed that he saw fully armored Spanish warhorses charging across the land.

The most detailed prediction was provided by a woman in the household of the *cacique* of Ucareo. This woman informed the Purhépecha sages that she had been physically transported to the celestial paradise by the goddess Cueráuperi, who had appeared to her in the guise of an eagle. In paradise, she witnessed the divine assembly of the Purhépecha pantheon. *The Chronicles of Michoacán* preserves the woman's vision as follows:

> *She saw the gods seated there, painted and wearing wreaths of colored cotton on their heads, some wore headbands, others clover-leaf wreaths, a few had temples on the crowns of their heads, and others were dressed in many other ways. They also had many kinds of wine, both white and red, made from maguey, cherries and honey. They had gifts, many of fruit, which they were taking to another god called Curicaveri, who was the messenger of the gods and whom they all called Grandfather. To the woman it seemed that they were all in a very large house and the eagle (who took her there) told her to be seated and she would hear everything that was said.*[1]

At the meeting the deity Tiripanienquarencha informs the assembly of the ancient deities' offense against the mother goddess Cueráuperi. He warns them that the penalty for this offense is the total destruction of their world, explaining that the gods and people of the earth must die so that new divinities can be born. The survivors of this cataclysmic event will then be responsible for beginning the new world. This was ordered, says the deity, when the world was created in primordial time. The apocalypse is announced with the following command:

> *Break all those jugs for it shall not be from here on, as it has been up to now when we were very prosperous. Break all the wine tubs everywhere, leave off the sacrifice of men and bring no more offerings with you because from now on it is not to be that way. No more kettle drums are to be sounded, split them asunder. There will be no more temples or fireplaces, nor will any more smoke rise, everything shall become a desert because other men are coming to earth. They will spare no end of the earth, to the Left Hand (west) and to the Right (east), and everywhere all the way to the edge of the sea and beyond. And you, woman, who are pretending not to hear us, publish this and make it known to Zuangua the King, who is in charge of all of us.*[2]

For the Purhépecha, the appearance of a group of Aztec emissaries in Tzintzuntzan was the first sign of the Spaniards' arrival. The Metzica-Tenochca had come to ask the Purhépecha king for his help in combating the conquistadors, who had surrounded their besieged capital at Tenochtitlán. The sixteenth-century Franciscan chronicler Gerónimo de Mendieta contends that the Aztec mission arrived in Tzintzuntzan in October 1519.[3]

The eighteenth-century chronologist Fray Pablo Beaumont, in his work *Crónica de Michoacán*, states that the *cazonci* Zuangua agreed to Moctecuhzoma's request for military aid. However, Beaumont continues, the *cazonci* changed his mind after learning of the Spaniards' military strength. It appears that with both his own sages and the gods predicting the victory and rule of the "new men from the east," Zuangua believed it would be futile to resist the Spaniards.[4] And while the Aztecs and the Purhépecha were first cousins—since both groups had migrated together to the area in the late thirteenth century—they were also bitter enemies. Thus suspicion of Moctecuhzoma's motives may have played a significant role in the *cazonci*'s decision to refuse the Aztec leader's petition.

In addition, according to *The Chronicles of Michoacán*, the *cazonci* sent a Purhépecha delegation to the Aztec capital to get a firsthand account of the embattled city. Upon their return they told the king that they had climbed a prominent hill near Texcoco where they had a good view of the city. The delegation testified that the island city was surrounded by Spanish brigantines, which constantly bombarded the great urban neighborhoods. Although the Aztec emissaries showed the Purhépecha a battle plan of how the two kingdoms could defeat the Spaniards, the *cazonci* was still hesitant to ally himself

FIGURE 5.   Moctecuhzoma's ambassadors plead for help

with his old enemies. In the manuscript he is depicted as attributing the Aztecs' predicament to the fact that they had not maintained the discipline of the sacred temple fires; he says that the Aztecs had merely sung songs to their gods.[5] The *cazonci* did not know that the delegation had also brought back an enemy that was more lethal than the conquistadors—namely, smallpox. The

Amerindians had no immunity to this European disease, and Zuangua himself soon died from the illness.[6]

Zuangua's son, Tzintzicha Tangaxoan II, succeeded him as *cazonci*. But shortly after his installation a serious quarrel broke out between him and his three brothers, Tirimarasco, Azinche, and Cuini. *The Chronicles of Michoacán* states that the quarrel concerned certain "ambitious" women who were sexually involved with the brothers. The women were charged with wanting to usurp the authority of the new *cazonci*. Under the advice of the king's war chief, Timas, Tangaxoan II had the women and his brothers killed. The conflicts stemming from the assassinations contributed to the political confusion when the Spanish arrived.[7]

There is some confusion about the identity of the first Spanish visitors to Michoacán. According to J. Benedict Warren, the chronicler Cervantes de Salazar contends that a soldier named Porrillas first visited Michoacán with a group of Matlaltzincas, who came from an area near the present city of Morelia. The brothers Juan de Herrera and Pedro Hernández, in an inquiry in 1541, testified that they had visited the town of Taximaroa with Porrillas. However, neither episode is mentioned in the *Letters from Mexico.*[8] Cortés does state, in the *Third Letter of Relation*, that he met with a Purhépecha delegation and asked if there was a passage through Michoacán to the Pacific. He relates that on that occasion he ordered a military show of cannon fire and cavalry charges to impress the native delegation. Cortés further states that after this event he sent a small expeditionary force of four Spaniards, led by Francisco Montaño, back to Michoacán with the emissaries.[9]

The first encounters between the Purhépecha and the Spaniards left lasting impressions on both parties. At first the Purhépecha misjudged the Spaniards. They believed that the Spaniards, like the Aztecs, might have been Toltec lords recently returned to earth to reclaim their heritage. But the level of military atrocities and the fact that the Spaniards could be wounded and killed soon convinced them otherwise. For their part, the early Spanish military expeditions verified that Michoacán was a densely populated and rich land, with resources well worth exploiting.

CRISTÓBAL DE OLID'S EXPEDITION, 1522–1524

Less than a year after the fall of Tenochtitlán, Cortés sent a large army to Michoacán, ostensibly to establish a Spanish colony in the kingdom. The soldier-chronicler Bernal Díaz del Castillo suggests that Cortés had other motives. Díaz del Castillo asserts that Cortés hoped to rid himself of the officers in his camp who were complaining about the amount of treasure he had personally claimed. In dividing the booty of war, Cortés usually reserved the richest land for himself. This complaint resulted in a series of violent feuds among the conquerors that brought New Spain to the brink of disintegration by the late 1520s.[10]

The military force left Tenochtitlán in July 1522 with Cortés's old friend Cristóbal de Olid in charge.[11] According to Warren, between two hundred to three hundred Spaniards and more than five thousand Amerindian allies, mainly Tlaxcalans, made up the force. *The Chronicles of Michoacán* verifies the large Amerindian contingency, saying that the Tlaxcalan force was led by many native lords. The army arrived at the fortress town of Tajimaroa on July 17 during the rainy season.[12]

The Spanish-Tlaxcalan military intrusion into Michoacán naturally terrified the young *cazonci*. *The Chronicles of Michoacán* informs us that the king, confused about the invasion, was on the verge of panic and thus sought advice from his council of elders. The council decided to assemble a large force of allied tribes including Matlaltzincas, Otomís, Huetamas, Cuitlatecas, Escamoechas, and Chichimecs. They all agreed that the army should position itself near the outskirts of Tzintzuntzan and that the entrance to the city should be fortified. The nobleman Cuinierángari, known later by his Christian name Don Pedro, was assigned to meet the Spanish-Tlaxcalan army to ascertain its intent.

When Cuinierángari arrived in the enemy encampment he recited the *cazonci*'s instructions: "Go to, receive the gods, see if it is true that they are coming; perhaps it is a lie, perhaps they came only as far as the river then turned back because it is the rainy season. Go, see, and report back to me, and if they have come, let them come at once to the city."[13] Olid feared he was being set up for an ambush. He ordered the Purhépecha envoy to return to Tzintzuntzan and to arrange a meeting with the king near the town of Quangaceo. Olid also stated that the Purhépecha king should bring a large tribute payment of gold and silver.

While in the Spanish encampment, the Purhépecha delegation witnessed the celebration of a Roman Catholic mass. Cuinierángari, or Don Pedro, relates that the natives tried to make sense of the Roman rite according to the categories of their own worldview. He describes the celebrant friar as staring and whispering into a cup filled with red liquid. Don Pedro and his companions believed that the priest was performing some kind of divinatory rite:

"[The priest] must be a medicine man . . . who looks in the water and reads the future. They also thought that in this way the Spaniards would know that they wanted to make war on them, and they began to fear." [14]

By the time Don Pedro returned to Tzintzuntzan, fear and confusion reigned in the city. The war chief Timas, who had promoted Tzintzicha Tangaxoan II to his position as king, advised Tzintzicha that as king he was doomed to face the invader's wrath. He told the *cazonci* that his only solution was to drown himself in Lake Pátzcuaro. Timas instructed the king to kill himself by putting copper weights around his neck, so that he might quickly sink to the bottom of the lake. According to Purhépecha religious thought, a person who drowned went directly to the subterranean paradise where they existed peacefully in eternity. Tzintzicha Tangaxoan II had hoped that Don Pedro would bring back an alternative to Timas's suggestion. But he abandoned Tzintzuntzan before Don Pedro arrived and fled to Uruapan.

When Olid heard that the *cazonci* had left Tzintzuntzan he ordered the army to march upon the Purhépecha capital. The people who lived in the "land of the hummingbirds" offered little resistance to the Spanish warriors, peacefully inviting them into their city. As the Spaniards entered the great plazas of the pyramids they were horrified to see the temples awash with the blood of recent human and animal sacrifices, performed in hopes of averting the crisis.

The Chronicles of Michoacán declares that the Spanish-Tlaxcalan armies looted the temples and destroyed the sacred image of Curita-caheri, with the Purhépecha looking on in horror at the desecration of the god's image and his temple. The people asked themselves why this humiliation and violence had not brought down the wrath of their gods, but the sky over Lake Pátzcuaro remained silent. The destruction predicted by the woman of Ucareo had finally come to pass.

Captain Olid was in Michoacán for four months. During that time the people of Tzintzuntzan were subjected to tremendous pressures, for they had to feed both the Spaniards' lust for precious metals and the huge army they had brought with them. Each day thus required an enormous exertion of human labor and the preparation of vast quantities of food. [15] J. Benedict Warren provides a systematized account of the first major plunder of Michoacán in *The Conquest of Michoacán*. [16]

Along with the human suffering produced by the Spanish invasion of Michoacán, new political alignments were created. Don Pedro emerged from the conflict as an important power broker. He had been the major intermediary between the *cazonci*, Olid, and Cortés. After the invasion he helped to consolidate the *cazonci*'s authority by having the war chief Timas killed; he also had put to death all the elders who had suggested that the *cazonci* drown himself. Don Pedro would later become an ally of Vasco de Quiroga as well as an important informant in the compilation of *The Chronicles of Michoacán*. The text's narratives of his service illustrate how he shrewdly helped to preserve the native power structure and survive the Spanish subjugation. J. Benedict Warren posits that Don Pedro became the *cazonci*'s "hatchet man." [17]

ANTONIO DE CARAVAJAL'S TRIBUTE SURVEY

In 1523 Cortés asked Antonio de Caravajal to make ready a small military expedition to survey the tribute system of the *cazonci*. Cortés, wanting a precise idea of the king's assets, assigned Caravajal to compile a list of the main towns in the province and the agrarian villages that were subject to them. The documents of Caravajal's survey were essential to Cortés's subsequent distribution of the first *encomiendas* in Michoacán. In the fragments of the report found by J. Benedict Warren, five major towns *(cabeceras)* and their tributary villages were identified; these included Comanja, Uruapan, Turicato, Huaniqueo, and Erongarícuaro.[18]

Cortés awarded *encomienda* grants to the officers serving in the inner core of the army, particularly to those men who had been with him since landing at San Juan de Ulua. Diego Hernández Nieto received half of Turicato, while Rodrigo de Albornoz took the major town of Matalcingo and its subject villages of Uritla, Irapeo, Moquenza, Totula, Coyuzla, Necotan, Maratuhaco, Vichitepeque, and Maritaro. Gonzalo de Salazar received Tajimaroa and its subject towns. Domingo de Medina was awarded half of Tancítaro, and Juan de Albornoz was given the town of Jacona and the villages under its jurisdiction. Francisco de Villegas received the important town of Uruapan and its subject hamlets. Finally, Cortés himself took the silver-mining zones in the south along with Tzintzuntzan.[19] Warren states that Cortés used the distribution of *encomiendas* to bribe Rodrigo de Albornoz and Gonzalo de Salazar, both royal treasury officials who had criticized him for withholding the royal fifth.[20]

Between 1524 and 1526 Cortés was in the Honduras attempting to suppress an insurrection led by his former ally, Cristóbal de Olid. Upon returning to Mexico City on May 24, 1526, he found that a power shift in the politics of the city had taken place. Historians attribute this shift to the fact that, in the distribution of the New World booty, Cortés had given preference to his original army officers. A political coup was then instigated by the reinforcement army led by Pánfilo Narváez. The second wave of conquistadors thus joined the interim governors—the treasurer, Alonso de Estrada; the accountant, Rodrigo de Albornoz; the inspector, Peralmíndez Chirinos; and the factor, Gonzalo de Salazar—in usurping Cortés's authority. The anti-Cortés faction went so far as to spread the false rumor of Cortés's death and to hold a public funeral.[21]

During Cortés's absence from the central valley the Amerindians had borne the burden of the Spaniards' greed and the political squabbles in the capital. The narratives of the period convey the image of an atmosphere of chaos, plunder, and anarchy. The crown attempted to resolve the confusion and chaos by the appointment of a new governor, Luis Ponce de León. Ponce de León was already an elderly man, however, and he died shortly after his arrival in the Mexican capital. His death only added to the discord. Yet Cortés's letter to Charles V of September 11, 1526, offered a relatively optimistic interpretation of current events:

> *The country is somewhat fatigued by the recent disturbances, but with the friendship and good treatment of the Indians, which I always strive to maintain, it will be restored. God willing, for the Indians, although they have necessarily received some vexations from our people because of the change of masters, are multiplying and increasing so rapidly that it seems that there are more natives now than when I came first came to these parts. The religious are doing much good, especially among the children of the caciques. The Christian religion is being so well planted that your Majesty owes many thanks to God for it.*[22]

Cortés's positive evaluation of the situation in New Spain did not reflect the intense rivalry and violence occurring in 1526.

In 1527 gold was discovered in the jagged terrain of western Michoacán known as the Motín. Shortly thereafter a full-scale rebellion of the Náhuatl-speaking people in the region broke out. Pedro Sánchez Farfán led a pacification force to the region. But the Náhuatl tribes proved to be quite vehement in their resistance to the Spanish-Amerindian army.

The gold strikes in western Michoacán were a further hardship to the *cazonci* and the Amerindian economic infrastructure. The *cazonci*'s tribute *pueblos* were expected to furnish laborers for the mines and were also responsible for feeding mine workers and livestock and clothing the Spanish-Amerindian army that guarded the mines. Over and above these obligations, the townsfolk were expected to contribute to the support of the native nobility. Increased interest in mining in western Michoacán also resulted in a frenzied invasion of adventurers and fortune seekers. Francisco de Torres, who was in western Mexico at the time, describes the atmosphere of violence as follows: "At that time they (the Amerindians) killed many Spaniards who were travelling through towards the said towns of Colima and Zacatula, and in many parts of it we Spaniards needed to keep watch because many towns were in a state of war and rebellion, as they were when the treasurer Alonso de Estrada, who was governor at the time, sent a captain who was named Garrovero to Motín."[23] The chaos caused by gold speculators resulted in the visitation of the royal representative Juan de Ortega in the late spring of 1528. Ortega's visit was partly a judicial visit and partly a military venture to put down the rebellion.

The indiscriminate violence inflicted on the Amerindians had convinced them that the Spaniards were not divine beings; subsequent Spanish atrocities were thus met with violent resistance. In 1527 Ortega reported that between sixty and seventy Spaniards were killed in the conflicts. The Purhépecha were particularly dismayed by the ransacking and desecration of their temples and burial tombs. Ortega had fueled the conquistadors' greed by stating that any Spaniard might take the treasures they found in the temples provided that they pay the royal fifth. During his tenure in the province Ortega also initiated the loathsome practice of branding slaves in the face.[24]

Meanwhile, in Sevilla the Council of the Indies began to receive reports of the serious situation developing in New Spain. The crown was concerned that the Amerindian populations on the mainland would be devastated, as they had been on the Caribbean Islands. There was also the more immediate problem that a general civil war might break out at any moment, led by conquistadors who hoped to establish their own fiefdoms far away from Spain.

The crown's answer was to appoint a court of royal representatives called the first Audiencia to the colony. The Audiencia was instructed to assemble the important political players in Mexico City and to reestablish the crown's authority amidst the chaos. The council members included the bishops of Tlaxcala and Mexico, the prior of the Dominican order, the prior of the Franciscan order, three representatives from each mendicant order, the president of the Audiencia, and the royal judges (*oidores*) of the Audiencia. Their specific duties included the following:

These men were to consider ways of reducing the native population to Christianity as soon as possible and of distributing the land and Indians among the conquerors in an equitable fashion. A second instruction . . . provided that all encomiendas *becoming vacant during the investigation of the council were to be given preferably to married men, as it was thought they would remain longer and treat the Indians better, and (there was) a long instruction . . . forbidding the Indians to have arms or horses.*[25]

By the eve of the arrival of Beltrán Nuño de Guzmán, the president of the first Audiencia, the people of Michoacán had endured a prolonged period of plunder, ecological disruption, readjustment, and, finally, open conflict with the Spaniards. Their fear that the conquistadors would refuse to respect them as human beings had quickly become a bitter reality.

THE CONQUEROR BELTRÁN NUÑO DE GUZMÁN, 1528–1530

The crown and the Council of the Indies believed Beltrán Nuño de Guzmán to be a tough strong-willed man and a capable lawyer. Both assumed that Guzmán had the kind of "law and order" personality required for ending the anarchy in New Spain. The traits that appeared to be lawfulness and orderliness, however, were actually ruthlessness and obstinacy. In hindsight it is obvious that the government in Spain had no idea of the character of the man whom they had appointed as president of the Audiencia.

Sparse information exists about Guzmán's life before he reached Mexico. He was born into a noble family in Guadalajara, Spain, in the late 1480s or early 1490s. Like Cortés he was trained in law but never received a degree. Some evidence suggests that Guzmán was a royal bodyguard in the court of Charles V. His loyal service to the crown eventually won him the governorship of the kingdom of Pánuco, north of Veracruz, Mexico. Here Guzmán acquired the reputation of a ruthless ruler because of his brutal suppression of an Otomí rebellion. During his tenure in Pánuco he systematically enslaved the natives, branding men, women, and children in the face. He also loaded entire village populations onto Spanish ships and sold them to sugar planters in the Caribbean Islands in exchange for cattle and horses.[26]

Guzmán assumed office as president of the first Audiencia on November 13, 1528. Along with Guzmán, the Audiencia members consisted of Alonso de Parada, Francisco Maldonado, Juan Ortiz de Matienzo, and Diego Delgadillo. Parada and Maldonado died mysteriously within two weeks of their arrival in Mexico City.

Guzmán governed New Spain as he had ruled Pánuco. He sold Amerindians into slavery, ransacked their temples searching for treasure, exacted heavy tribute payments from the *caciques*, and kidnapped women. Guzmán's cruelty was not limited to the native population, however. At times he was equally spiteful with his fellow countrymen. For example, he confiscated the *encomiendas* that Cortés had given to his closest captains and redistributed them to his own cronies. Furthermore, he boldly sealed the ports on the mainland so that no adverse information could reach Spain.

Upon his arrival in Mexico City, Guzmán had attracted the company of a thug and vulgarian named García de Pilar. Pilar was one of the few Spaniards who had "gone native." Fluent in Náhuatl, he brazenly walked around Mexico City dressed in a loincloth and sporting feathers in his hair. J. Benedict Warren describes Pilar and Guzmán as "self-seeking leeches" who sucked up the indigenous population's wealth for their own benefit.[27] The bishop-elect of Mexico City, the Franciscan Juan de Zumárraga, anathematized Pilar, saying that his "tongue should be taken out and cut off, so that he would no longer speak with it the great evils that he does speak."[28] Zumárraga protested to Guzmán about having such a degenerate person in the employ of the royal court, but Guzmán responded that, like the bishop, Pilar was also a servant of the crown. Guzmán actually ignored the protestations of Zumárraga because he believed that Zumárraga's status as bishop-elect weakened his authority.

Guzmán's major error in this episode was to underestimate Zumárraga's personal and spiritual tenacity. The Franciscan proved to be a formidable adversary. Zumárraga and Guzmán came into direct conflict over the question of their judicial authority. Zumárraga had been appointed protector of the Indians and inquisitor of New Spain by the crown; both of these positions carried a judicial function and responsibility. In Mexico City, Zumárraga initiated court proceedings to hear Amerindian complaints about Spanish atrocities. These activities overlapped with the civil jurisdiction of the Audiencia, however. The resulting jurisdictional ambiguity was the primary reason for his frequent and violent clashes with the *oidores*.

The conflicts over jurisdiction reached a climax in early 1529. By this time Guzmán's negative responses and outright hostility to the plight of the Amerindians resulted in open warfare with the Franciscan order. At stake was Zumárraga's title of "Protector of the Indians." The tensions became so strained that Guzmán issued a decree forbidding, under pain of arrest and imprisonment, that redress be sought by appealing to the spiritual authorities. A delegation of Franciscans and Dominicans discussed the matter with Guzmán, but to no avail.

In April 1529 a delegation of *caciques* from Huejotzingo arrived in Mexico

City to speak with Zumárraga about Spanish abuses. Huejotzingo was an *encomienda* of Cortés. The guardian of the monastery there was the famous Franciscan Motolinía, one of the first missionaries to arrive in New Spain. The Huejotzingo ambassadors told the bishop of their suffering and asserted that their plight was due to the unjust tribute they were commanded to pay Pilar and Guzmán. They accused Pilar of skimming goods from their payments before the tribute reached Guzmán.

The bishop-elect told the Huejotzingos that he would intervene in their behalf. When Zumárraga presented the charges to the Audiencia, Guzmán answered that his orders must be obeyed, even if it meant the death of Huejotzingos. Guzmán also warned Zumárraga that if he persisted in defending the natives he would encounter a fate similar to that of the bishop of Zamora. Zumárraga understood the threat, knowing the bishop of Zamora had been hanged by the civil authorities during the War of the Communes in Spain. Guzmán further instructed the *alguacil*, the constable Pedro Núñez, to go to Huejotzingo, arrest the *caciques*, and bring them to Mexico City. In the meantime Zumárraga had his servants warn the Huejotzingo elders, who then took refuge in Motolinía's monastery. Fray Motolinía strictly forbade the *alguacil* to enter the friary under penalty of excommunication.[29]

The tension between the *oidores* and mendicant clergy climaxed on Pentecost Sunday. During high mass the Franciscan priest Francisco Antonio Ortiz was publicly critical of the Audiencia in his sermon. In the presence of Archbishop Zumárraga and Bishop Julián Garcés of Tlaxcala, Guzmán stood up and violently interrupted the sermon. The *oidor* Delgadillo then ordered the local constable to drag the priest from the pulpit. The next day Zumárraga excommunicated the members of the first Audiencia. He sent his personal agent to inform them of this action and announced that the royal judges were restricted from attending mass until they begged for absolution. The *oidores* responded by issuing a decree to exile Zumárraga's messenger from all territories of Charles V. The agent heard that he was about to be arrested and took refuge in a church, but the Audiencia ordered his food supply cut off. Zumárraga again intervened and persuaded the *oidores* to publicly repent at the convent of San Francisco, and the incident was temporarily resolved.[30]

The peace between Guzmán and Zumárraga was short-lived, however. Not long after the Huejotzingo incident Guzmán ordered a Franciscan chapel destroyed and a magnificent house built on the site. During its construction he forced the natives to work nonstop with no compensation. When Zumárraga challenged Guzmán on this issue, Guzmán laughed in the Franciscan's face.[31]

The rivalry and open hostility between the civil and church authorities was not the only conflict brewing in the colony. A conflict within the religious orders themselves was also escalating. The Franciscans, who first arrived in 1523 and 1524, had selected the best locations to build their monasteries and convents. The friars had usually chosen *cabeceras*, or major towns, with large aboriginal populations in rich agricultural zones. This did not seem quite equitable to the Dominicans, who arrived two years later in 1526. Nor did it please the Augustinians, who arrived in 1533. The Franciscan domination of the large population centers proved to be an ongoing source of conflict between the orders. When Zumárraga gallantly took a stance against Guzmán, the Dominican vicar Vicente de Santa María opposed him on the grounds that the Spaniards had always treated the Amerindians well.[32]

Furthermore, there was little harmony inside the Franciscan ranks. In August 1529 the Franciscan Juan de Paredes filed charges against his fellow friars Luis de Fuensalida, Francisco Jiménez, Pedro de Gante, and Toribio de Motolinía, claiming that they had conspired with the natives to overthrow the civil government.[33] As Robert Ricard states, the chaos in New Spain thus stemmed from "difficulties within the Orders and between the Orders, difficulties within the episcopate and the secular clergy, and difficulties with the civil authorities, and, along with these internal difficulties, the stubbornness of the pagan religions and superstitions."[34]

THE ASSASSINATION OF TZINTZICHA TANGAXOAN II

The year 1529 was critical in the life of the young *cazonci* Tzintzicha Tangaxoan II. At the time of the Spaniards' move into Michoacán, the kingdom was politically unstable due to the *cazonci*'s recent purges. Although the *cazonci* was the most powerful Amerindian leader alive in 1529, he found himself in the precarious position of having to welcome the very men who would later sentence him to death.

Tzintzicha's first encounter with Guzmán occurred when the *oidor* ordered the *principales* from each kingdom to pay homage to the first Audiencia in Mexico City. Zumárraga wrote to the crown concerning the meeting:

(A)s they (the lords) would arrive, the said Pilar would make long discourses to them secretly in the house of the President; and therefore I believe, and do so affirm to Your Majesty, that the purpose was not so that they should come to holy Baptism. And it is believed and has been seen that the lords did not come empty-handed, and there was not wanting one of them who did not come with

his offering, and with these presents the will to covetousness was opened even further.[35]

The *cazonci* did not personally respond to Guzmán's request; instead, he sent a Náhuatl interpreter to Mexico City with several gifts. Since the king had visited Cortés in Mexico City on three previous occasions, Tzintzicha likely believed that he had already made a sufficient diplomatic gesture to the Spaniards. Guzmán was not persuaded by the gifts, however, and he ordered Antonio de Godoy to bring the *cazonci* to Mexico City.

The Chronicles of Michoacán affirms that the *cazonci* arrived in México-Tenochtitlán in the spring of 1529. On that occasion the Purhépecha leader presented Guzmán with twenty silver plates and many gold ingots. But the treasure did not please the president of the Audiencia. Guzmán asked Tzintzicha, "How is it that you have come here empty handed?" The *cazonci* responded, "Lord we did not bring you anything because we left in a hurry."[36] Zumárraga testified that the small amount of treasure enraged Guzmán, and he instructed his guard to imprison the *cazonci* until he received more gold. The ransom was eventually paid, and the *cazonci* was back in Michoacán by May.[37]

Meanwhile, Guzmán and the Audiencia decided to mobilize a large army for a treasure-hunting expedition to the land of the Chichimec. This territory, located north of Michoacán, would later be called Nueva Galicia. It took eight months of threats and intimidation for Guzmán to assemble a huge army of 150 cavalrymen, 200 foot soldiers, and between 10,000 and 12,000 Amerindian allies.[38]

In August 1529 the *cazonci* was again summoned by Guzmán. Tzintzicha was informed of Guzmán's upcoming expedition and ordered to collect large quantities of weapons, clothing, and food for Guzmán's army. He also was instructed to bring Guzmán more treasures of gold and silver. (The Purhépecha would bear the full impact of the expedition, because Michoacán was used as a staging ground for Guzmán's assault on the Chichimec frontier.)

The *cazonci* was imprisoned in Guzmán's house from August until late December 1529. He was tortured, shackled about the ankles, and confined to his room until his release on Christmas Day. Shortly thereafter Guzmán and his army left Mexico City from the neighborhood of Tacubaya. Zumárraga reported that the troops departed with great fanfare, even though many of the Spanish officers were pressured by Guzmán to join the expeditionary force. The *cazonci* had gone to Tzintzuntzan ahead of the army in order to prepare the heavy levy required by Guzmán.

Less than a week after Guzmán arrived in Tzintzuntzan, he imprisoned the *cazonci*. Guzmán charged Tzintzicha with obstructing the *encomenderos'* work and therefore the Spanish exploitation of the region. The Spanish *encomenderos* living in the kingdom had actually furnished Guzmán with the complaint. Guzmán's ally, García de Pilar, said that Guzmán arrested the *cazonci* because the king neither furnished the *oidor* with enough gold nor gave him all the expected army supplies.[39]

Guzmán ordered that a court be organized to hear the dubious charges against the *cazonci*. As the proceedings progressed many indigenous people were tortured and forced to accuse Tzintzicha of various crimes. During the trial the *cazonci* was stripped naked, then bound and tortured for about fifteen days, according to Pilar. The humiliation and interrogation of the Purhépecha king centered on four accusations: that he had planned to ambush Spaniards traveling in Michoacán; that he had withheld tribute payments in gold from the Audiencia; that he was a sodomizer; and that he had secretly retained and venerated images of the Purhépecha gods.

On January 29 Guzmán again assembled his army for the march to the land of the Chichimec. The army's ranks had been swollen by some eight thousand Purhépecha warriors. The force headed north, following the Lerma River. Guzmán took the *cazonci* along with him in chains. After two weeks of marching, the *cazonci's* trial continued on the banks of the rapid-moving river. *The Chronicles of Michoacán* reports that many Purhépecha who had been tortured testified against the *cazonci*, along with several *encomenderos*. On February 14, 1530, Guzmán pronounced his sentence:

> *I find that I must condemn, and I do condemn, the said Cazonci, named Don Francisco, to the penalty for the crime that he had thus committed, and I condemn him that he shall be taken from the prison where he is, his hands and feet being tied, with a rope around his neck, and with the voice of a crier to make known his crime, and he shall be put into a pannier, if one can be had, and, tied at the tail of a nag, he shall be dragged around the place where the camp is situated, and he shall be taken to the side of the ford of this river and there he shall be tied to a timber and burned in living flames until he dies naturally and becomes dust. And if the said Cazonci should wish to die as a Christian, since he has received the water of baptism, even though after he received it he went back to commit idolatry as is evident and apparent from his confession and this trial, I command that before he is burned, he shall be given the garrote at the neck so that the said Cazonci shall die and be separated from the*

FIGURE 6.   The *cazonci* and lords attempt suicide by drowning

living spirit, and afterward let him be thrown into the fire and burned, as has
been said. And because it is presumed that the natives of the said province will
take the ashes of his body and will carry them off to commit idolatry with them,
from which God Our Lord will be ill-served, I command that the ashes that
remain from his body and flesh shall be thrown into this said river in such a
way that they cannot be had. And, moreover, I condemn the said Cazonci to

the loss of all his goods, and I adjudicate them to the chamber and treasury of His Majesty and to the cost justly made in this lawsuit, the assessment of which I reserve to myself. And judging it to be thus, by this my definitive sentence I pronounce and command it through these writs.[40]

The execution of Tzintzicha Tangaxoan II that was then carried out hurled the Purhépecha people into chaos. Guzmán had finally achieved his goal of eliminating the uncooperative native ruler and also had obtained absolute control of Tzintzicha's assets. This crucial event marks the rupture between the autonomous Purhépecha kingdom in Michoacán and the beginning of total Spanish control. Ironically, however, Guzmán was unaware that he had ensured the spiritual happiness of the *cazonci* by throwing his ashes in the sacred waters of the Lerma.

THE ECOLOGICAL COLLAPSE

The effects of the Spanish conquest and the early colonization efforts were particularly severe in Michoacán. Because of the *cazonci's* peaceful capitulation, however, the region managed to escape the particular ravages inflicted on the central valley. Three factors contributed to the severe loss of life in Michoacán: warfare, ecological collapse, and the loss of life resulting from forced labor in the *encomienda* system.

The territory controlled by the Purhépecha was approximately seventy thousand square kilometers. From the demographic information compiled by Cook and Borah it can be estimated that in 1520 this zone contained approximately 1,500,000 or 2,000,000 people. According to Mendieta and Núñez, the Purhépecha constituted about ten percent of this total, or 200,000 people, mainly living in the lacustrine area and the highland valleys.

Between 1520 and 1565 the population of Michoacán was reduced to about thirty percent of its preconquest total. Thus in only forty-five years nearly 600,000 people died in Michoacán. The death rate in the whole of New Spain at this time was equally devastating. From 1492 to 1568 the population from the Isthmus of Tehuantepec to the Gran Chichimec in northern Mexico fell from 25,000,000 inhabitants to around 3,000,000. By 1630 only 750,000 indigenous inhabitants remained—a mere three percent of the preconquest total.[41]

The horrendous loss of life did not occur at the same rate at every location.

Low-lying tropical areas along the Pacific and Gulf coasts were the hardest hit. The cooler highland areas retained their populations for a longer time. Nicolás Sánchez-Albornoz comments that the population collapse in the Americas is a phenomenon "without parallel in the modern history of the world's population. Europeans colonized other continents—Africa and Asia —in the nineteenth century, but contact with the inhabitants there never brought a decrease in the indigenous population nearly so disastrous as it had in America." [42]

Bartolomé de Las Casas, author of the impassioned *Breve relación de la destrucción de las Indias*—which was translated into several languages in the sixteenth century—testified that the population decline was primarily due to the violence inflicted upon the Amerindians. This violence was particularly intense when it came to plunder, rape, forced labor, and the confiscation of food. [43] Yet the population decline was not only due to warfare. The wars of conquest were violent but not long-lasting. The Aztec capital fell after less than a year of siege, for example. Therefore, the tremendous loss of life must be due to more extensive and far-reaching sources.

Historians have struggled to imagine such a catastrophe. In *Plagues and Peoples* McNeill points to the Amerindians' biological isolation and their contraction of endemic diseases of European and African origins as the source of the demographic collapse. Typhus, malaria, mumps, and smallpox and measles, the two great early killers, ravaged the indigenous populations. [44] Concurrent with the invasion of conquistadors and microorganisms, an invasion of ungulate mammals occurred. Francois Chevalier asserts in *Land and Society in Colonial Mexico: The Great Hacienda* that the multiplication and virtual explosion in the number of livestock on the fertile grasslands of New Spain, as well as the gradual introduction of new agricultural items aimed primarily for European consumption—such as wheat, barley, and sugar— played a significant role in the demographic catastrophe.

In the chapter entitled "The Preponderance of Cattle Raising," Chevalier explains how livestock herds expanded in the favorable climate of central Mexico. From 1538 toward the end of the century, the horse, mule, sheep, swine, and cattle herds multiplied at a fantastic rate, spilling out of the central plateau into Michoacán and the shrub-covered Bajío. By mid-century the specialized industries of stock raising and precious metals had become New Spain's primary economic resources. [45] But the herds competed with the embattled Amerindian populations for food resources. Moreover, the massive mobilization of native corvée laborers and their forced conscription as auxiliaries in the army also contributed to the rapid demographic decline.

FORCED LABOR AND THE *ENCOMIENDA* SYSTEM

Under the *encomienda* system groups of Amerindian families—usually the inhabitants of a village or town, or a group of towns—were entrusted to the charge of Spanish colonists or clerics, who thus "held" these people in *encomienda*. Throughout an *encomendero*'s lifetime he was entitled to exact both commodities and labor as a tribute from the families and towns that had been granted to him. In return for the royal grant, the *encomendero* was obligated to provide military protection and a good Christian education for his charges. Hence the primary objective of the *encomienda* system was twofold: to Christianize and educate the indigenous peoples according to the guidelines of a European worldview, and to provide the holder with an unpaid labor force. The crown's rationale was that "civilizing" the Amerindians would encourage orderly behavior and good industry, while also satisfying the needs of *hidalgos* who thought of themselves as warriors and not workers.

The colonial historian Charles Gibson claims that the history of the *encomienda* system in fact accelerated the decline in native population.[46] He points to the system's cruel and exploitative measures as major factors in the loss of life. The forced grouping of Amerindian laborers in the silver mines and on the construction sites of Spanish towns and baroque church buildings quickly took its toll on the native population. In Michoacán the *encomienda* arrangement compounded the social and ecological collapse, particularly in the rich silver mines near Tamazula and Zacatecas.[47] According to Gibson, however, "When the human resources were depleted, *encomienda* necessarily declined. The result in the late sixteenth century was a pattern of institutional decay."[48]

Lesley Byrd Simpson states that in *encomienda* relations, the Spanish conqueror found himself in the position of "having serfs to do his bidding and support him in the pleasant life of a quasimilitary parasite."[49] Today's *campesino* (peasant) societies of rural Mexico have developed directly out of the *encomienda*'s emphasis on the personal relationships between a Caucasian European elite and an Amerindian or *mestizo* townsfolk. In these relationships the conquered obey and do not ordain. George Foster describes this social dynamic among the contemporary peasant farmers of Tzintzuntzan: "They do not command. They wait to be told, but they do not make major decisions themselves. They are at the ends of the lines of communication and authority that radiate from the cities. Before injustice, the arbitrary, and the incomprehensible they must be passive acceptors, for they lack the power and knowledge to be otherwise."[50]

The *encomienda* grant was also fertile ground for bribery and corruption. In fact, land swapping for political favors resulted in a situation in which each new political authority would try to consolidate his position by assigning *encomiendas* to his supporters, at the expense of opposing political interests in the colony. This activity was made all the easier because none of the governors seems to have kept an official register of grants of *encomienda* as a general administrative practice. Thus it continued to be a rule that the only proofs that a person had to his right of *encomienda* were his *cédula* (award letter) of the grant and the testimony of friends.[51]

The transformation of Purhépecha society was the result of an extensive military invasion mounted by the Spanish and their Amerindian allies. It was also due to vast ecological changes in the land and its people that resulted in the decimation of the Amerindian populations. Forced labor, especially in the silver mines, and the severe tribute system of the conquistadors similarly imposed extreme pressures on Purhépecha society. With the destruction of the indigenous nobility, the temple complexes, and ritual centers came a gradual whittling away of the Purhépecha's collective memory, making local or regional memory more and more prominent. This resulted in the alteration of Michoacán from an independent indigenous kingdom to a collection of farming communities. This city-village tension has caused the *campesino* to develop a quasi-independent social order based on personal action and responsibility within the village-town framework. Furthermore, the demise of the native nobility and their replacement with Spanish overlords resulted in the development of an elite group of people whose wealth and status was determined by their blood and by their entitlement to the labor services of the Amerindian populations. This social arrangement was dominant in Michoacán until the end of the sixteenth century; in some cases it lasted well into the seventeenth and eighteenth century under the *hacienda* system.[52]

DON VASCO DE QUIROGA, 1477/8–1565

The political crisis in Mexico City brought New Spain to the verge of anarchy by 1530. The ambiguities of power and jurisdiction resulted in serious, often violent outbursts. The first Audiencia, which was charged with restoring public stability, had bungled its opportunity to bring about order. Instead of assuming a mediating position, it pursued its own selfish interests and joined in the contest for the spoils of conquest. Thus the crown and the Council of the Indies began to look for a solution to the atmosphere of corruption and greed in New Spain. Their answer was to appoint a second Audiencia whose members consisted of churchmen and proven jurists. One of the men selected was the *oidor* Don Vasco de Quiroga.

Vasco de Quiroga was born in Madrigal de las Altas Torres in Galicia. The town was not only famous for its beautiful church towers but also for being the site of Queen Isabella's birth in 1451. In addition, Isabella and Ferdinand had lived and held court in the town from 1475 to 1476.[53] The exact date of Don Vasco's birth is unknown. It has traditionally been placed at 1470, because of the opinion that he was ninety-five when he died in 1565.[54] Quiroga's most authoritative biographers, Aguayo Spencer and Fintan B. Warren, agree that "there is, however, considerable reason for fixing a later date for his birth. An Apostolic brief, *Exponi nobis*, of Paul III, dated May 12, 1549, indicates that after Quiroga received his appointment as Bishop he appealed for a dispensation from the triennial episcopal obligation of visiting Rome on the ground that he was in his sixtieth year."[55] If Quiroga was in his sixtieth year he would have been fifty-nine years old in 1537, fixing his year of birth at 1477 or 1478.

The Quirogas were aristocrats, and the family castle is still located in the province of Lugo, where there is "much rain, many somber clouds, and where ancient churches and monasteries rise gauntly among the green hills."[56] According to local tradition, in A.D. 715 a Christian knight heroically defended the valley against a Saracen invasion. The family's coat of arms commemorates the battle by superimposing five war pikes on a field of green. Felipe de la Gánara, a seventeenth-century Galician genealogist, stated that Vasco de Quiroga of Michoacán and the famous cardinal Gaspar de Quiroga of Toledo were the grandson and great-grandson of Gonzalo Rodríguez de Valcárcel and Emilia Vázquez de Quiroga. This would make Don Vasco's brother the father of Cardinal Quiroga.[57]

There is little information about Don Vasco's formative years. He apparently studied jurisprudence at the University of Valladolid (although Fintan B. Warren has noted the lack of matriculation records in existence at the university during Quiroga's enrollment, therefore making his schooling a mystery). In the papal bull that contains Quiroga's nomination to the bishopric of Michoacán, he is credited with a licentiate in sacred theology. Yet Quiroga later asked that this be corrected to state that his licentiate was in canon law.[58]

There is also a minimum of information about the influential people in Quiroga's life. In the most copious of his writings, *Información en derecho*, Don Vasco demonstrates familiarity with a range of Renaissance authors and draws on a formidable catalogue of authorities to support his position opposing the enslavement of the Amerindians. The latter includes Old and New Testament writers and the church fathers, Saints John Chrysostom, Cyril, Athanasius,

Basil, Augustine, and Ambrose. Quiroga also cites Saint Antonine, Pope Innocent III, the Spanish theologian Cardinal Cajetan, Johann Faber, and John Gerson. In addition, he borrows from the ideas of his humanist contemporaries like Guillaume Budé, Sebastian Brant, Antonio de Guevara, and Thomas More. Don Vasco's classical references include Aristotle, Lucian, and Horace. He also demonstrates his knowledge of the Aleric and Theodosian codes, and the jurists Angelo de Arecio, Christoforus, and Jason Maynus. This impressive list proves that Don Vasco was a capable intellectual. In fact, his thirst for knowledge led him to borrow Bishop Zumárraga's copies of Lucian's *Saturnalia* and Thomas More's *Utopia* when he arrived in Mexico City.[59]

We can only partially reconstruct Vasco de Quiroga's early career. Manuel Toussaint identifies a Vasco de Quiroga in the employ of the Archdiocese of Granada in 1492, but there is no verification of this information. It is certain that Quiroga became a *letrado*, that is, a member of the corps of royal jurists.[60] In the sixteenth century a career in law offered a young Spanish gentleman entry into well-paying and prestigious jobs in both church and state circles. Stafford Poole observes that

> *The growth of the Spanish empire and its government machinery created a demand for* letrados: *men from the middle ranks of society, skilled and trained in law, who formed a governing elite. Doctors and* licenciados *from Salamanca and other major universities could be found all over the New World, where they held positions as* oidores, alcaldes, *bishops, canons, university professors, and town councilmen. The* [letrados] *tended to be clannish and mutually supportive. They produced a long line of civil servants, lawyers, and churchmen, who maintained a kind of 'old boy' network that promoted their careers.*[61]

Quiroga was well connected to the "old boy" network in Spain through his friendship with Doctor Juan Bernal Díaz de Luco, a member of the Council of the Indies. The doctor served as a *letrado* for the powerful cardinal of Toledo, Juan de Tavera. According to Marcel Bataillon, *Información en derecho* was written as Quiroga's personal appeal to his close friend Bernal Díaz de Luco.[62]

The first solid information that we have of Quiroga concerns him as a middle-aged man in his fifties. Fintan B. Warren discovered certain legal records that place Don Vasco in the North African city of Oran in March 1520. Oran had been captured by Ferdinand's armies in 1509. The Spanish king had a difficult time, however, in establishing his sovereignty over the African city. Quiroga held the position of royal judge of *residencia* in Africa and was attached to the office of the *corregidor*, the *licenciado* Alonso Páez de Ribera.

Quiroga's primary task in Oran was to deal with the problems of corruption, greed, and division among the military that resulted from the subjugation of the Muslims.

Warren tracks Quiroga's activities through several legal complaints over which he presided. The first case was filed by Jewish, Muslim, and Christian merchants against one Páez de Ribera, whom they accused of extortion and other crimes.[63] Apparently the unscrupulous *corregidor* had irritated the Spanish military as well. Páez de Ribera had incarcerated a captain named Luis Álvarez for two months without recourse to Spanish law. The captain had committed the unpardonable act of selling a horse to a Muslim. This incident caused the Spanish officers to register a complaint before the Royal Council of Castilla, and the case was eventually ruled on by appeal to the Chancellery of Granada on March 21, 1522.

The precise starting date of Quiroga's work in Oran is absent from the historical record. Warren states that the earliest documents place Quiroga in the city of Oran on March 6, 1525.[64] He offers as evidence a civil suit filed by two Savoyan merchants, Glaudio Burdilion and Tomás Breton, against Páez de Ribera for confiscating their goods. In this incident Quiroga had Páez de Ribera imprisoned without bond. The trial spanned the summer of 1525. In the end Quiroga moderated his initial sentence but still ruled for the claimants. He ordered Páez de Ribera to return the items taken from the merchants or to compensate them. Páez de Ribera also had to pay the tax that the litigants had given the *corregidor*, along with all court costs.[65]

Another suit, between a Genoese merchant and a tailor, also contains information concerning Quiroga's activities in Oran. The case was fairly complicated, so the broadest of outlines follows. A merchant named Baptista Caxines and a tailor named Alexos de Pastrama had made a mutual agreement: they had exchanged a year of "services" from Pastrama's wife, María de Garay, and twenty-four *ducados*. In October 1524 the case went before Quiroga's predecessor, Licenciado Liminiana. Liminiana ruled that Caxines had to pay the agreed sum and the cost of repairs to several government buildings. In March of the following year Caxines appealed the decision to Don Vasco. Quiroga reversed Liminiana's decision, "not because he judged Caxines innocent but because he considered the *cámara real* and the city of Oran had no right to exact a fine in a case which neither of them had suffered damage."[66] Quiroga's strong sense of justice and literal reading of the law are traits that he manifested throughout his lifetime.

The last date Warren cites for Quiroga in Africa is August 1526. The date is taken from certain documents shrewdly drawn up by Quiroga to protect him from lawsuits stemming from his *residencia*. By securing a royal decree that limited appeals on lawsuits filed against him, Quiroga demonstrated his keen understanding of the law, especially when the legal system protected his personal interests.

In many ways North Africa was a training ground for Quiroga. The problems he dealt with there were similar to those he would confront in New Spain. In both Africa and New Spain, Quiroga wielded the power of a royal representative. As such he was required to mediate the conflicts that developed between a conquered people and their conquerors. In both situations Quiroga proved to be a legal literalist upholding royal law and order. In Mexico, Quiroga's legalist personality would be tempered by a pastoral compassion. And in both situations he was forced to immerse himself in the violence and corruption that threatened the crown's sovereignty.

In 1529, while Nuño de Guzmán was preparing for the conquest of Nueva Galicia, the crown began to solicit names for his replacement. As mentioned previously, Quiroga came by his appointment through his family connection with Juan Bernal Díaz de Luco.[67] The infamous Nuño de Guzmán charged, in an accusation dated 1540, that in removing him from his post Bernal Díaz de Luco had acted with prejudice. Guzmán argued that his rival, Archbishop Zumárraga, had actually sent a series of letters to Juan Bernal Díaz de Luco reporting unfavorably on his actions in Mexico. Bernal Díaz de Luco subsequently transmitted the letters to Cardinal Tavera, and both men used Zumárraga's accusations to remove Guzmán.

Guzmán also accused Bernal Díaz de Luco of using illegal tactics to destroy his credibility. He argued that in his zeal to remove him the doctor had sent Quiroga to Mexico with the aim of restoring the supremacy of the Cortés faction in New Spain. Guzmán further claimed that Bernal Díaz de Luco had written Quiroga many letters encouraging Quiroga to move against him. Guzmán appears to have had a point. Warren cites a letter dated April 23, 1553, which verifies the close friendship between the doctor and Quiroga. In the text Quiroga says that he is grateful for the careful attention that his good friend paid to his letters and requests.[68]

The young Cristóbal Cabrera, who lived in Quiroga's house in Michoacán, suggested a more spiritual reason for Don Vasco's acceptance of the post. He stated that after Quiroga completed his assignment in Africa, he was uncertain about what to do next. After all, he was a middle-aged man, and the court competition for a favorable position was fierce. Through the intervention of Cardinal Tavera, Carlos V offered Quiroga several positions. Cabrera informs us that Quiroga entered a monastery in order to make the proper decision.

One day, in the chapel of the monastery, Quiroga was listening to the monks sing the divine office: "While the monks were reciting their office, he was struck by the words of the psalm: 'Offer up the sacrifice of justice and trust in the Lord. Many say, who showeth us good things?'"[69] Quiroga interpreted the psalm as the voice of the Amerindians crying out to him, "Who will show us good things?" He believed that the message was a divine call for him to be the "sacrifice of justice," so that by accepting the position he could be God's instrument of "good things."

In January 1530, while the *cazonci* of Michoacán was being tried on the banks of the Lerma River, the empress Isabella informed Quiroga that he had been selected as a royal judge to the second Audiencia of New Spain. The appointment would have long-lasting implications for the people of Michoacán. Within three years Vasco de Quiroga would replace the *cazonci* as the spiritual and temporal guardian of the Purhépecha kingdom.

The Christianization
of the Purhépecha

The aim of the sixteenth-century evangelization project was to establish the millennial kingdom of God in the "New World." The missionaries hoped to accomplish this goal by isolating the Amerindians into towns called *repúblicas de indios*, or *congregaciones*. In the towns the natives would be governed by their own laws and guided by the spiritual direction of the friars. The mendicants' rationale for adopting this policy was to better protect the Amerindians from exploitation by lay Christians and to facilitate their conversion to Christianity.

In the sixteenth century a brand of apocalyptic mysticism resurfaced in Spanish religion. It was especially popular among the early mendicant missionaries who evangelized Mexico. The mendicants believed that after the last Amerindian gentiles had been converted, historical time would come to an end. At that point Christ would reappear to establish an eternal terrestrial paradise in the New World. The friars, however, could not agree amongst themselves on how to effect spiritual and social perfection in the Amerindians. This confusion led to a prolonged dispute over the various models of spiritual development to be imposed on the natives. Needless to say, the Christian project to perfect humanity had failed in the "Old World."

TATA VASCO, THE CATHOLIC *CAZONCI*

Vasco de Quiroga was the primary agent in the evangelization of the Purhépecha-Chichimec. Don Vasco's task in Michoacán was to rectify the disorder in which Nuño de Guzmán had left the province after the assassination of the *cazonci*. Fintan Warren expands Quiroga's mission to include caring for the needy, training the natives in a civilized way of life, and instructing the "pagans" in the Catholic faith.[1] The Purhépecha's current image of Quiroga as a *tata*, or benevolent father, is the best example of the success of Don Vasco's work. In acquiescing to the *tata* image, Quiroga assumed the pastoral role of protector, spiritual father, judge, and confessional physician. According to William Taylor, this traditional role of the parish priest, established by the mendicants and appropriated by bishop Quiroga, would survive intact until the Bourbon designs for a professional clergy in the eighteenth century.[2]

Quiroga arrived in México-Tenochtitlán at the end of 1530. On that occasion the *cabildo* (city council) ordered every *hidalgo* who owned a horse to welcome the new *oidores* at the outskirts of the city. Bishop Zumárraga commented later that the level of enthusiasm shown the second Audiencia was due to the anxiety caused by the pro-Amerindian mendicant lobby, which had been calling for a "redemption of the land," as well as by conquerors who hoped to win the favor of the royal representatives.[3]

In the sixteenth century the Roman Catholic tradition organized its members into areas known as dioceses. The diocese was constituted by the church members who lived in a given territory and who were under the sovereign protection of a spiritual leader called a bishop. The bishop resided in the principal seat of authority, which was the cathedral. In practice the bishop's powers and functions were similar to those of the *cazonci*; both posts had territorial and spiritual dimensions. In Michoacán the ecclesiastical constitution of the diocese was most responsible for the preservation of the preconquest province. Therefore, in successfully accomplishing his assignment, Quiroga's episcopacy retained the range of sovereignty that had belonged to the *cazonci*.[4]

In the summer of 1532 the second Audiencia began to work on a plan to divide New Spain into the four dioceses of Michoacán, Tlaxcala-Puebla, Antequera, and Nueva Galicia. The Audiencia also proposed that an archdiocese be located in Mexico City. By 1533 the plan had been completed, and the emperor Charles V approved it in early 1534.

The bishopric of Michoacán had been vacant for three years before Quiroga was formally installed in 1536.[5] Paul III canonically erected the episcopacy of Michoacán in the papal bull *Illus fulciti praesidio*, dated August 8, 1536.[6] The pope and the emperor hoped that the establishment of the dioceses would bring an end to the chaos and promote evangelical "pearls in the provinces."[7]

Quiroga was not the first to be nominated for bishop of Michoacán. Fray Luis de Fuensalida, one of the original twelve Franciscans, was first offered the position. But the mendicant declined out of humility, and because he hoped to pursue his ethnographic studies. On December 5, 1535, the Council of the Indies nominated Vasco de Quiroga. Juan de Zumárraga endorsed Quiroga's appointment with the following statement: "There is a good report of his life and his example and he is much inclined to the conversion and the good treatment of the Indians and to the instruction in the matters of the holy faith on which he has spent a large part of the salary that Your Majesty has commanded to be given to him."[8] The emperor's ambassador in Rome, the Conde de Cifuentes, informed the pope of Quiroga's nomination, and it was approved on December 9, 1536. Quiroga remained bishop-elect and *oidor* for about a year, until he was ordained by Archbishop Zumárraga in Mexico City in 1538.

During Quiroga's tenure as bishop he demonstrated that he had a complex personality. At times he was truly the gallant well-educated *letrado* and a benevolent man of peace. Yet he could be intensely stubborn and vengeful with his enemies, and he was unafraid of wielding great power. Quiroga also exhibited a mature political sophistication and an acute legal rigidity.

Upon arriving in Michoacán, Don Vasco began to consolidate his diocese through the establishment of three institutions that he believed would ensure a permanent evangelization: his cathedral, the Colegio de San Nicolás Obispo, and the *congregaciones*, the towns into which the Purhépecha were organized. It should be recalled that the Purhépecha believed themselves to be an autochthonous people generated from four huge stones called the *petázecua* that were located near Pátzcuaro. Quiroga shrewdly chose this site as the location of his new cathedral. In planting the cathedral atop the Purhépecha's sacred geography, Quiroga not only destroyed the idolatrous stones, replacing them with a symbol of Christian victory, but his action also sustained the Purhépecha's cosmos. Quiroga's foresight thus added to his credibility as a benevolent lord.

Don Vasco began the construction of the cathedral in the 1540s. It was to be built on a grand scale with five naves in the shape of a human hand, imitating the design of Saint Peter's Church in Rome. The main altar was to be built in the center of the building. At the time, Juan de Medina de Rincón stated that Quiroga's intention was to provide a space where each of the distinct native populations, along with the Spanish Christians, could concurrently listen to the "good news" preached in their own language. There is little information on the tremendous Purhépecha workforce that must have been required in order to construct the building. George Kubler states in *Mexican Architecture in the Sixteenth Century* that the grand design was aban-

FIGURE 7.   Bishop Vasco de Quiroga, 1477/8–1565

doned by midcentury, when Quiroga returned from Spain. Kubler contends that the size of the structure made its construction impractical.[9]

A second related undertaking in establishing Christianity in Michoacán was Quiroga's founding of the Colegio de San Nicolás Obispo. San Nicolás was a seminary in Pátzcuaro designed to provide the diocese with secular (diocesan) priests well trained in the languages of the province. Quiroga believed that the seculars were essential to the daily administration of the culturally diverse parishes and the *pueblo*-hospitals (the newly formed Amerindian towns). Don Vasco stated in his last will, the *Testamento*, that the *pueblo*-hospitals would work hand in hand with the Colegio de San Nicolás Obispo.[10] The towns would provide the seminary with financial support and students, while the seminary would provide the towns with clerics.

The Colegio de San Nicolás Obispo had a hierarchy of deans and a rector who served as administrator and spiritual head of the institution. Vasco de Quiroga had invited the Jesuits to run the college, but the Society of Jesus did not arrive in Pátzcuaro until 1573, well after Quiroga's death in 1565. Quiroga appointed his confessor, Juan Fernández de León, as the first rector of the seminary. The Jesuits took over the administration of the school after their arrival. In 1580 the college and the Holy See were moved to Valladolid.[11]

A third area of work in the establishment of the diocese was Quiroga's organization of the Purhépecha into *congregaciones*. The purpose of Quiroga's aggregation policy was to isolate the Amerindians in order to prevent their physical extermination and their religious corruption by Spanish Christians. Quiroga hoped that the towns would be centers of religious and social acculturation for the Purhépecha. This included education in Eurocentric social values, as well as moral instruction in how to live a "good" Christian life. Quiroga argued that congregating the Purhépecha into their own towns was necessary, so that they were not "scattered about like animals in the fields without good *policía* (order)." He asserted that warfare and abuses by conquistadors had created an unbearable situation in which the Amerindians "grow for these reasons evil, ferocious, bestial and cruel, prejudicial, inhuman and ignorant, and tyrants among themselves."[12]

The social polity of the *congregaciones* was translated into a daily regimen patterned after monastic communities in Spain. Quiroga's plans drew from theories of society that incorporated the educational and social principles of classical humanism. He took his model for the towns from Thomas More's *Utopia*. But Quiroga's reliance on More should not be overstated, because the myth of a communal paradise was already an ancient and recurrent theme in Christian history.

The ordinances of these communities called for a monastic lifestyle, hard work, plain dress, monogamous marriage, universal public education, a six-hour work day, and rigorous religious devotion. Among the Quiroga-sponsored towns were Santa Fe de México; Santa Fe de la Laguna, near the present town of Quiroga; and the Chichimec town of Santa Fe del Río.

During his episcopacy Quiroga sought to expand the boundaries of his diocese to conform to the maximum territorial extension reached under the *cazonci* Tangaxoan II. Quiroga extended his jurisdiction to the south, including Los Altos in Jalisco and Ciudad Guzmán. With the establishment of the Holy See of Nueva Galicia at Guadalajara in 1548, however, the expansion of the Diocese of Michoacán was curtailed. After this setback Quiroga turned his attention eastward, incorporating the *doctrinas* (evangelization towns) across the Lerma River into the town of Salamanca.[13]

Bishop Quiroga's territorial ambitions met with significant resistance from the *encomenderos*. The bishop and the *encomenderos* hoped to control the same resources and the same people. For example, Quiroga's protracted legal battle with Juan de Infante was a major characteristic of his tenure as bishop. At stake was the collection of tithes due to the bishop and tribute due to the *encomendero*, especially in the vicinity of Jilotepec, Querétaro, Maravatio, and the Gran Chichimec. Don Vasco also engaged his fellow bishop, Pedro Gómez Maraver of Nueva Galicia, in a sovereignty battle over the issue of tribute.[14] In each instance he acted to protect the absolute patrimony of his bishopric. Ultimately, his success was due to his obstinacy and to his comprehensive knowledge of the Spanish legal system.

THE MENDICANT EVANGELIZATION

It would be a mistake to think that Vasco de Quiroga was solely responsible for the Christianization of the people of Michoacán, for he shared parochial duties and power with the mendicant orders. At times this arrangement produced intense rivalry between the bishop and the regular orders. The ambiguous division of responsibilities remained the status quo until full-scale secularization occurred in the late eighteenth century.

In the classic work *The Spiritual Conquest of Mexico*, Robert Ricard puts forth the thesis that the mendicant parish system passed through three dynamic stages in the sixteenth century before a dominant pattern emerged— that of the colonial church. The first stage of this process, which bridged the period from the early conquest to approximately 1540, was characterized by a highly spontaneous, noninstitutional church. The second stage began with the creation of the diocese and included the introduction of various missionary orders from Spain. The third stage was initiated with the arrival of the Society of Jesus in 1572 and the decree of the new episcopal laws issued by the Council of Trent.[15]

The conversion of the natives in Michoacán was the shared venture of

Bishop Quiroga, the Franciscans, and the Augustinians. According to *The Chronicles of Michoacán*, the Franciscans were the first to arrive. Their work in Michoacán actually had begun in 1524, when Cortés ordered fifteen boys from elite Purhépecha families forcibly sent to Pedro de Gante's school, the Colegio de Santa Cruz de Tlaltelolco. Formally invited to Tzintzuntzan by Tzintzicha Tangaxoan II in 1525, the Franciscans established themselves in 1526. The Augustinians were appointed to the area by Viceroy Antonio de Mendoza in 1537. Quiroga also brought a number of secular priests with him when he established residency in the kingdom in 1538. Though he invited the Jesuits in 1547, they did not arrive until 1573.

The first Franciscans to set foot in Michoacán were Fray Martín de la Coruña, Fray Ángel de la Salceda, Fray Jerónimo, Fray Juan Badía, Fray Miguel de Bolonia, and Fray Juan Padilla. Martín de la Coruña organized the construction of the modest first chapel in Tzintzuntzan, which was dedicated to the Virgin Mary's mother Santa Ana. Coruña, who was also among the first evangelizers of Nueva Galicia, is identified early in *The Chronicles of Michoacán* as having vigorously objected to the torture of the *cazonci* by Nuño de Guzmán.

The Franciscan indoctrination efforts in Michoacán were modeled after their experience in the central valley. They focused on the densely populated fertile areas around Lake Pátzcuaro and the central *meseta*. After two failed attempts to convert the Purhépecha, a *doctrina* was finally established at San Francisco Tzintzuntzan in 1526 by Martín de la Coruña. This success was closely followed by the establishment of a conventual house at Santa Ana Zacapu in 1530. From Zacapu the mendicants of Saint Francis ventured to found a monastery at Uruapan (1533). Franciscan monasteries also were established at Pátzcuaro (1538) and San Buenaventura de Valladolid (1546). The province was named the Provincia de San Pedro y San Pablo, and the headquarters were later located in Valladolid. Toward the end of the century, Franciscan houses were founded at San Miguel Tarímbaro (1570), San Gerónimo Purenchécuaro (1583), and San Francisco y Santo Tomás Pichátaro (1585).[16]

The Chronicles of Michoacán informs us that the Franciscans began evangelizing by preaching against polygamous marriages and ritual drunkenness. Both these customs were quite acceptable to the Amerindians; polygamy and inebriation rites imitated the multiplicity and excesses of their cosmos. But excess of any kind fell into the category of lust and gluttony in Christianity. Thus polygamy and drunkenness were severely restricted by the Franciscans.

The friars also engaged in the unfortunate destruction of the public images of the old religion, such as the magnificent stone temples and the indigenous pictographic writings. The difficulty of the evangelization effort is verified by the Franciscans' two early failures. Nevertheless, by 1583 the Franciscan province contained forty-seven convents, twenty-one in Michoacán and twenty-six in Jalisco.[17]

The first Augustinians to enter Michoacán were Fray Juan de San Román and Fray Diego de Chaves, who arrived in 1537. Fray Alonso de la Veracruz, Fray Francisco Villafuerte, and Fray Juan Bautista Moya arrived shortly afterward. The Augustinians established *doctrinas* at San Juan Bautista Tiripitío (1537) and San Gerónimo Tacámbaro (1538). In 1550 they were given charge of the parish of San Nicolás Guango by Quiroga's seculars. Around the same time they began the construction of a massive monastery at Valladolid. Following 1575, the order established parishes at Chocándiro and Pátzcuaro. Santiago Tingambato was established in 1581, and San Juan Parangaricutiro, San Felipe de los Herreros, and Santiago Necotlán were founded in 1595. By 1602 the Augustinians had established more than twenty houses in Michoacán. Their missionary efforts had grown so large that they founded a new province, the Provincia de San Nicolás de Tolentino de Michoacán.[18]

The secular priests were also part of the early evangelization efforts in Michoacán. Bishop Zumárraga sent at least one secular priest to Michoacán before Quiroga's arrival, and in 1533 Quiroga named a secular curate to the *pueblo*-hospital at Santa Fe de la Laguna. In 1570 there were fifty-nine secular parishes in the episcopacy of Michoacán.[19] And over two hundred seculars had graduated from the Colegio de San Nicolás Obispo by 1576.

THE UNIVERSAL KINGDOM OF LOVE

One of the last flowerings of medieval Franciscan mysticism, represented variously in the images of the apocalyptic age, the messianic king, and the sanctity of poverty, is evident in the Franciscan missionary effort in Michoacán. The goal of the friars was to realize the kingdom of God in Mexico. It seems incredible that a scant number of barefoot friars, many of them wearing penitential hair shirts under their wool robes, helped the Hapsburg emperor to consolidate his great empire. Nevertheless, the regulars were crucial agents of Spanish dominance in Mexico. By incorporating the indigenous peoples into a new economic order and forcibly acculturating them into Europe's christocentric system of social and moral values, the mendicants assured the crown its sovereignty. According to Zumárraga's practical perspective, the mendicants' task was "to open the door to the apostolic conquest and to augment the royal domain."[20]

Sixteenth-century Franciscan mysticism is rooted in a complex combination of sources. The first is the order's founder, Saint Francis of Assisi (1181/2–1226). The son of a rich Italian merchant, Francis led a carefree and irresponsible life in his youth. In his early twenties, however, he underwent a profound religious conversion. Shortly afterward he gave away what money he had, cut off contact with his family, and set out in absolute poverty with a few followers to preach to the poor.

Francis practiced an austere form of asceticism and preached an extreme Christlike version of unrestricted love. Believing that poverty was a prerequisite condition for experiencing the transcendence of God, he idealized the poor, regarding them as innocents who are closest to God. Francis's view of poverty was in accordance with Christ's vision of the poor expressed in the Sermon on the Mount. Soon the tattered cloaks of mendicant friars became a familiar sight on every highway and in every slum of western Europe. The Franciscan order, along with other mendicant orders, represented a new model of monasticism in the history of Christianity in Europe. Strictly speaking, the friars were not monks because they did not live in monasteries. Rather, they were worldly renunciates who wandered among the people, earning their living by begging.

In Spain the Franciscan Spiritual branch of the order advanced the millennial ideas present in the prophetic writings of the Cistercian abbot Joachim of Fiore (1135–1202). Fiore was born near Cosenza in the Calabrian Mountains. Early in life he made a pilgrimage to the holy city of Jerusalem, where he saw a land ravaged by years of epidemics and war. This powerful experience transformed his life and so he joined the Cistercian order, attaining ordination in 1168. In 1191 Fiore left the monastery to found a more austere group, which he directed until his death. After he died legends sprang up concerning his writings and his esoteric understanding.

Joachim of Fiore's essential teachings are contained in three works: the *Liber concordie*, the *Expositio in apocalypsim*, and the *Psalterium decem chordarum*. The Joachimite theories relevant to this discussion may be summarized as follows. Fiore postulated that the pattern of human history parallels the structure of the Holy Trinity, and that the divine personages are dynamic active forces in history. Fiore organized the Trinity's progressive revelation into three ages or *status*. Each age was identified with one person in the godhead.

The first age spanned the time from Adam to Christ and corresponded to the Father. The second or middle age, which spanned the time from Christ to Saint Francis, pertained to the Son. The third age was to be a future time of the Holy Spirit. Scheduled to commence in 1260, it was supposed to culminate in the experience of the Parousia of the Christ and the universal perfection of humankind.[21]

Before his death Fiore stated that the third age would be initiated by two new religious orders of men, one dedicated to spreading the "good news," the other to contemplative piety. He predicted that signs of this last historical age would be the conversion of the Jews and the reconciliation of the Greco-Roman world. The third era would also bring about an end to violence and war; Fiore posited that at its end the theology of the Sermon on the Mount would be realized in universal love, which would reign to the end of time.

The Franciscan Spirituals were the preservers of Fiore's apocalyptic view of history. In 1254 a Franciscan mystic at the University of Paris, Gerard of Borgo San Donnino, proclaimed that the new age had arrived. In the years following Fiore's death various mendicant orders saw themselves as the "new men" of the "new age." The interpreters of Fiore's ideas frequently adopted the view that the transition to the "new age" would be led by either an angelic pope or a benevolent king.

The Franciscan Spirituals, or Friars Minor, as they also were known, believed that strict adherence to the ideal of poverty would provide an example through which lay people might gain salvation. Although the Spirituals lived and worked in the world rather than in the cloister, spiritual work could only be accomplished if they rejected the temptations of the material world. This ideal quite naturally challenged the institutional church, with its magnificent buildings and its elaborate ceremonialism. The ideal of corporate poverty was the engine behind the development of a Franciscan community in Spain that rivaled the institutional church at the beginning of the sixteenth century.

Not only did the Spirituals interpret the discovery of the New World according to Fiore's theory of history, but they also connected it with the apocalyptic vision expressed in the Book of Revelation, when the apostle John states:

Then I saw a new heaven and a new earth; for the first heaven and the first earth had passed away, and the sea was no more. And I saw the holy city, new Jerusalem coming down out of heaven from God, prepared as a bride adorned for her husband; and I heard a loud voice from the throne saying 'Behold the dwelling of God is with men. He will dwell with them, and they shall be his people and God himself will be with them; he will wipe away every tear from their eyes, and death shall be no more, neither shall there be mourning nor crying nor pain any more, for the former things have passed away.'[22]

John Leddy Phelan demonstrates in his remarkable study *The Millennial Kingdom of the Franciscans in the New World: A Study in the Life of Gerónimo de Mendieta, 1525–1604* that Christopher Columbus also was steeped in a brand of Joachimite mysticism. For Columbus three important events foreshadowed the end of the world: the discovery of the Indies, the conversion of the Gentiles, and the deliverance of the Holy Sepulcher. In the *Book of Prophecies* Columbus outlines the importance of both the transmission of Christianity to the Caribbean peoples and the restoration of Jerusalem to Christian control. He argues that the discovery of a new route to the Orient was a momentous event, because it "opened the door of the western sea." This "opening" was significant for Columbus in that it provided the Spaniards with the opportunity to spread the gospel to all inhabitants of the earth. In his text Columbus boldly recommends that the Catholic monarchs use the treasures taken from the New World to recapture the Holy Sepulcher and to rebuild the Temple of Zion.[23]

The first mendicants in Mexico imagined that they had been placed on a great historical field where the end of time would be realized, where they could finally be one with God and thus recover the paradisiacal state of Eden. The experience of the "discovery" of the "New World" was for them a sign of the climax of Christian history: the New World seemed to be what Fiore and the apostle John had predicted. The Amerindians, or the "last of the Gentiles," had to be converted according to Franciscan ideals in order for Christianity to be purged of its Old World corruption. Free of the pollution and decadence of Europe's failed attempt at Christianity, the segregated Amerindians and good friars would together usher in a golden age by living in unadorned poverty. The millennial community would thus constitute a new Christian commonwealth. Like Plato's Republic, the "New Jerusalem" would eventually become a terrestrial paradise. Only then would New Spain be a "City of God" as opposed to the European "City of Man." With the conversion of the Gentiles and the New Jerusalem complete, Christ would appear to announce the end of time. The belief that Spain would inaugurate the millennial kingdom of God on earth, by uniting under one universal Monarch all the races of humankind, was the dream that dazzled the adventurer and churchman alike.

During the early phases of the conquest, the crown needed the friars to serve as intermediaries with the native populations. But after midcentury—and the deaths of the early evangelizers, the collapse of the indigenous cultures, and the consolidation of the episcopacies—the apocalyptic fervor of the early mendicants turned into disillusionment. The dream of integrating the Amerindians into a purified form of Christianity was slowly transformed into a policy of strained coexistence.

THE ETHNOGRAPHIC AND TRANSLATION PROJECTS

The thought of a mendicant or begging monk does not usually bring to mind the picture of a university-educated man. Yet the early mendicant missionaries in Mexico were extremely well educated and very much influenced by the humanist writings then in vogue in Spain. When the mendicants entered Michoacán they immediately set out to collect and document an immense corpus of ethnographic information. In addition, they conducted meticulous investigations of the indigenous languages. Their goals were to understand the origins of the Purhépecha people and to translate the message of Christian salvation into the Purhépecha language.

The ethnographic and linguistic interests of the Mexican missionaries reflected a primary concern of Renaissance humanism. In the late fifteenth century there was a general consensus among humanist scholars that a reevaluation of European history should be undertaken. Erasmus in particular had called for an investigation of Europe's pre-Christian past. In his program he singled out the literature of the Romans and the philosophy of the Greeks as especially important pagan sources.

Erasmus also called for an intensive study of the Greek language. The reasoning behind his interest in Greek was fairly obvious: the New Testament manuscripts were written in Greek, and he believed the new methods of scholarship would be instrumental in discovering the original meaning of the Holy Scriptures. Erasmus stated that the goal of biblical scholarship should be to decipher a more accurate version of the New Testament through linguistic comparison. Once the original "truth" had been deciphered, Erasmus envisioned that scholars would then move to translate "God's words" into the vernacular languages. Erasmus angered quite a few of his fellow clerics with this idea, because the clerics knew that universal lay access to the Scriptures meant eliminating their traditional role as interpreters.

In Spain, Cardinal Jiménez de Cisneros provided an atmosphere for creative scholarly enterprises at the University of Alcalá. Cisneros was also responsible for filling the missions in Mexico with educated friars trained in linguistics and scriptural analysis. The mendicant ethnographers of Mexico hoped to renovate Christianity in the New World. But this reform could only be accomplished through each person's voluntary experience and acceptance of the "true" word of God. This was why the mendicants' ethnographic and evangelizing work was so important to them.

Various versions of this belief of Renaissance humanism—that individuals must freely accept God's word—came to Michoacán. They arrived with the educated people in the civil government and, more importantly, within the ranks of a network of early mendicants who were historians, ethnographers, and linguists.[24] The friars were humanists in a fuller sense as well, in that they believed that language was a key to the humanity of a culture. Christianizing the Purhépecha thus hinged on preserving the Purhépecha language. The early mendicants favored multicultural, multilingual access to Christianity. This position brought them into conflict with the crown, the conquistadors, and later missionaries, who held that Hispanicizing the Amerindians by forcibly teaching them Spanish was the key to their acculturation. From the outset the Franciscans decided that it was imperative for them to learn the Purhépecha language. The first example of their success was Fray Diego de Santa María, who served as interpreter for the group of Purhépecha ambassadors that visited Cortés in Tenochtitlán in 1531.

The friars' persuasiveness with the Amerindians of Michoacán depended on their knowledge of the Purhépecha worldview. Their success also hinged on their ability to translate abstract Amerindian concepts into comparable Christian symbols. Hence the mendicants' task was immense. The letters of the Roman alphabet composed single spoken words, in contrast to the multivocal pictographic writings of the Amerindians. Moving back and forth between linguistic systems required great skill and sensitivity. In actuality the friars were extremely limited in their capacity to render complex Spanish concepts in Purhépecha and vice versa. Gradually, as the primitive church became more institutionalized and more conservative, the mendicants lost their interest in native languages and thus became more restricted in their ability to alter the indigenous worldview.

The early missionaries' efforts to translate Purhépecha phonemes and hieroglyphics into the Roman alphabet seem crude by today's standards. Nevertheless, their desire to share the millennial fervor of God's "words" led to the preservation of the Mesoamerican languages. This pluralist approach to a "life in Christ" was mandated partly by the ecumenical tendency within Catholicism and was also due to the friars' daily recognition of the eloquence and dignity of the native cultures. Seen in a more negative light, however, the friars' knowledge of the Purhépecha language helped them to identify "the errors and superstitions of the older people," so that they could then monitor the native elders to see if they practiced the old religion in secret.[25]

Of the great ethnographers, Bernardino de Sahagún must be cited. He was born in the Tierra de Campos region of León in the village of Sahagún during the last part of the fifteenth century. He studied at the University of Salamanca, where he took the Franciscan habit. Sahagún went to Mexico as a young man of thirty in 1529, along with nineteen other Franciscans led by Fray Antonio de Ciudad Rodrigo (who was one of the original twelve, the first group of missionaries to arrive in Mexico). He remained in Mexico for more than sixty years until his death in 1590.

One work stands out among Sahagún's writings: the *Historia general de las cosas de Nueva España*, a monumental effort that was the work of a lifetime.[26] In the introduction to this work Sahagún likens the missionary's responsibility to gain knowledge of the native cultures to that of a medical doctor:

> *The physician would be unable to treat his patient properly unless he knew from the beginning the humor and cause of the disease. And just as it is necessary for the physician to have a perfect knowledge of remedies and maladies in order to apply to each of the latter that which tends to counteract it, in like manner it is necessary for preachers and confessors, who are the true physicians of the souls in spiritual sickness, to gain a knowledge of spiritual maladies and the medicines they require.*[27]

The *Historia* is intended to be an encyclopedia of the people of Mexico. It consists of twelve books that cover a range of topics: gods and goddesses, the native liturgical cycle, the Amerindian soul, funeral rites, astrology, auguries, intellectual life, rhetoric, history, merchants and artisans, the Náhuatl language, the animals and plants of Mexico, and the history of the conquest.

Two other Franciscans—Jerónimo de Alcalá and Maturino Gilberti—produced major works specifically about Michoacán. Fray Alcalá was responsible for compiling *The Chronicles of Michoacán*, the most important source for tracing the heritage of the pre-Columbian Purhépecha-Chichimec. In 1541 Viceroy Mendoza, who was leading an army to the Mixton wars in the north, stopped in Pátzcuaro. At that time Fray Alcalá and a Purhépecha delegation

presented *The Chronicles of Michoacán* to the viceroy.[28] Fray Alcalá's religious
aims and humanist training are evident in the following statement:

> *It is a common saying that says it is natural for everyone to learn. And towards
> acquiring this science, many years are consumed going back into books, burn-
> ing the midnight oil, and unlearning many languages, in order to inquire and
> learn how the many gentiles lived. Then a natural desire came to me as it came
> to the others, that desire to investigate among these new christians the way
> their life was in their infidelity, what their beliefs were, what their customs
> and government was like, and where they originated.*[29]

Fray Alcalá was concerned that the results of his investigation facilitate the
spiritual conversion of the Purhépecha. He was well aware of the tension between the goal of Christianization and the goals of humanism: "The religious
have another intent (besides linguistic interests), which is to plant the faith of
Christ, and to polish and adorn this people, and give them back new customs,
and fuse them into, if possible, men of reason after god."[30]

Although the mendicants employed many methods of translation, the most
popular was the painted picture. To suggest hell, for example, they pointed to
pictures of the earth, fire, or serpents and frogs. This process was often more
confusing than helpful, since the Purhépecha venerated serpents, frogs, fire,
and the earth. Other friars wrote sermons that were translated by bilingual
interpreters into the aboriginal tongue. The friars would then memorize the
texts. But there was no way to ensure that the translations were correct or that
the Amerindians understood the Eurocentric context of the message. The
sacrament of penance, particularly the rite of confession, put further pressure
on the mendicants to learn the native languages.[31]

The missionaries learned the languages of the peoples whom they missionized. (The Dominicans, who had no missions in Michoacán, never mastered
Purhépecha.) Between 1524 and 1572, mendicant orders printed 109 books
pertaining to the evangelization in various Amerindian languages, including
80 Franciscan texts, 16 Dominican texts, 8 Augustinian texts, and 5 anony-
mous texts.[32]

In 1542 a French Franciscan from Tolosa arrived in New Spain. His name
was Maturino Gilberti, and it is he who did the most to preserve the language
of Michoacán. The first solid evidence of Gilberti in Michoacán dates to
1556, when Gilberti was in Tzintzuntzan. In less than a year he had printed
two books in Purhépecha: a grammar entitled *Arte de la lengua de Mechuacan*

and a book of Christian contemplative prayers, *Tesoro espiritual en la lengua de Mechuacan.* In the last section of the grammar book Gilberti credits Erasmus of Rotterdam along with other teachers who inspired the work.[33]

THE RELIGIOUS RIVALRIES

In 1558 Gilberti wrote a monumental work that brought him into direct conflict with Bishop Quiroga. This work was the *Diálogo de doctrina cristiana en lengua de Mechuacan.* Five months after the text's publication Quiroga presented a letter of complaint before Archbishop Montúfar in Mexico City, demanding that it not be permitted to circulate. Apparently Gilberti had neglected to secure permission from Quiroga for the work. Yet Gilberti maintained that he had obtained permission from Archbishop Montúfar. The confusion apparently occurred because Gilberti had changed the title of the book.[34]

The harshness of Quiroga's actions against Gilberti clashed with his image of a benevolent patriarch. Quiroga ordered Gilberti's book translated into Spanish, so that the Purhépecha edition could then be compared to the Spanish text. He gave Gilberti's manuscripts to two clerical allies—Diego Pérez Gordillo Negrón and Francisco de la Cerda—for review. Apparently after reading only a few pages the bishop's clerics ruled against Gilberti. Shortly thereafter Pérez Gordillo Negrón presented himself before Montúfar's provisor, and the latter ruled against the book's distribution. Although the Mexican Inquisition later found no major wrong in the book, the Spanish Inquisition also ruled against it. In any case, Gilberti invoked the *obedezco pero no cumplo* (I obey but cannot comply) principle and ignored the ruling.[35] (Interestingly, it should be noted that Pérez Gordillo Negrón emerged, in the latter period of Quiroga's tenure, as the bishop's war captain in his numerous quarrels with the mendicants.)

The Quiroga-mendicant rivalry concerned money and spiritual authority. Quiroga and the mendicants both received their funds through the tithes and tribute imposed on the people of their *encomiendas.* Both factions claimed sovereignty over the souls of the Purhépecha. The early mendicants had acquired an extraordinary amount of power when they represented the only religious presence in the nascent Mexican church. As the only religious on the mainland, the friars grew accustomed to functioning on their own. The new situation of having to obey a bishop caused tensions at first and eventually open conflict. In these quarrels Bishop Quiroga, in his role as the ultimate authority in the province, proved that he could be an obstinate and ruthless player.

The struggle for power between the mendicants and Quiroga reached a climax in the summer of 1560. The battlefield was the Augustinian conventual house of Tlazazalca, which had been founded under the authority of the second viceroy of New Spain, Luis de Velasco. Quiroga believed that the Augustinian order had bypassed his authority in establishing their house in Michoacán. Moreover, Quiroga resented the Augustinian's seeming indifference to his authority and was determined to impose his will on them. While Don Vasco's lawsuit against Gilberti was being heard in Mexico City, Pérez Gordillo Negrón led a group of secular priests and Purhépecha warriors from Pátzcuaro to the Augustinian convent and burned the house to the ground.

Undaunted by this violence, the Augustinian friars rebuilt a large part of the building during the next year. But this only increased the Bishop Quiroga's resolve. Father Diego Pérez Gordillo Negrón returned the following year, this time with a written statement from Quiroga. On this occasion Quiroga's emissaries confiscated a large quantity of gold and silver ceremonial ornaments. They also tore down the altar in the main chapel. And to add insult to injury, Pérez Gordillo Negrón ordered that the corpses of the dead Augustinians be disinterred from the consecrated cemetery and transferred to the town's unconsecrated graveyard. Quiroga's armed force then destroyed the remaining conventual structures and carried the prior of Tlazazalca, Fray Sebastián de Trassierra, back to Pátzcuaro in shackles.

The attack on the Augustinian order was not an isolated incident. Shortly before Quiroga's move on the Augustinian house he ordered his strongman, Father Diego, to destroy a Franciscan baptismal font in Pátzcuaro. In establishing his authority in Michoacán, Quiroga demonstrated that he was not reluctant to use violence against his fellow religious. The severity of his actions, as well as the mendicants' resolve to maintain their power, attests to the strength of both factions' beliefs.

The aim of the sixteenth-century evangelization project had been to establish the millennial kingdom of God in the "New World." However, today it appears that a hybrid religious system was born in Michoacán. Perhaps because of the many disparate religious factions communicating the new religion, a variety of syncretisms appeared. To a great extent the new religion contained an amalgamation of distinct religious elements already familiar to the Purhépecha and thus easily incorporated into their worldview. James Lockhart addresses the two religions' ideological compatibility when he states that after the conquest the Amerindians "needed less to be converted than to be instructed. The mendicant ethnographers seem to have held a similar position, since the friars spoke mainly in terms of instruction or indoctrination rather than conversion, and never referred to themselves as missionaries, the word so many modern scholars have anachronistically preferred."[36]

SEVEN

Información en derecho
Quiroga's Report to the Royal
Council of the Indies

Vasco de Quiroga's longest written work carries the full title *Información en derecho del licenciado Quiroga sobre algunas provisiones del Real Consejo de las Indias* (Information on the law by the licentiate Quiroga concerning certain provisions of the Royal Council of the Indies).[1] The document demonstrates that a variety of religious, social, and legal concepts influenced the cultural synthesis that took place in Michoacán. Quiroga and the mendicants had come to the "New World" with a worldview patterned in part by their personal experiences and by the intellectual and religious currents prevalent in Spain. Both the bishop and the mendicant monks shared the Renaissance's optimism concerning the inherent potential of human beings. In the *Información en derecho*, Quiroga's observations and solutions for the crisis in Mexico reveal how the ideals of Christian universalism and Renaissance humanism hand in hand forged a bridge between the Purhépecha and Spanish Christian worldviews.

THE CONFLICTING PORTRAITS OF DON VASCO

Scholars have interpreted Vasco de Quiroga and his legacy in different ways. Quiroga's most authoritative Mexican biographer, Aguayo Spencer, describes him as a *taumaturgo* (miracle worker). Juan José Moreno, an earlier biographer, proclaims Quiroga the "best man who has lived in these blessed places of Michoacán." Enrique Cárdenas de La Peña focuses on Quiroga's *pueblo*-hospital efforts; he gives Quiroga the title of "Apostle of the New World" and argues that he laid the foundations of the Mexican social security system.

Silvio Zavala, Lewis Hanke, and Fintan B. Warren assume that because Quiroga was a humanist he was thus a humanitarian. Presenting Don Vasco in a positive light, they characterize him as a liberal defender of Amerindian rationality and culture.

If these descriptions contained the only information about Vasco de Quiroga available to the investigator, it would be impossible to understand the volatile and authoritative Quiroga. It would be equally difficult to comprehend Quiroga's complex character if he were primarily depicted as a gentleman-intellectual and compassionate human being. If he had been simply a political liberal and cultural pluralist, he would have allied himself with Bartolomé de Las Casas in the struggle between the church and state in New Spain. Instead, as Marcel Bataillon has noted, Quiroga opposed Las Casas' pro-Amerindian appeal and defended the *encomienda* system. Even the conservative theologian Ginés de Sepúlveda used Vasco de Quiroga as an example of an influential person who favored the conquest.

Quiroga himself contradicted his saintly image when he declared that the *Información en derecho* was dedicated to "God, the Crown, and the utility of conquerors and colonizers."[2] In actuality Quiroga was neither a saint nor a demon; rather, his actions demonstrate that he was a veteran politician capable of making difficult decisions. Throughout his career the *oidor-obispo* remained loyal to his king and country. Don Vasco was, at different times, both open-minded and resistant to change. Although he worked vigorously to realize his vision of an Amerindian utopia, he was sensitive enough to come to admire the indigenous people and to adapt his plans to their culture. Nevertheless, when his authority was challenged, he moved against his enemies with a forceful, even vengeful, persistence and always with a keen knowledge of the law.[3]

INFORMACIÓN EN DERECHO

The original text of *Información en derecho* resides in the National Library of Madrid. The longest of Don Vasco's writings, it contains 162 pages and is dated July 4, 1535. Although the manuscript was widely circulated among other colonial writings, it was not published during Quiroga's lifetime.[4]

The conversational style of the text is particularly characteristic of Quiroga's writing. Marcel Bataillon believes that Quiroga's treatise was addressed to his friend and ally on the Council of the Indies, Doctor Bernal. (Bataillon makes a strong case for this hypothesis since the bishop's last will, the *Testamento*, and his *Letter of 1531* also were addressed to Bernal.)[5] There is also a discourse written by one Licenciado Rojas following Quiroga's commentary. *Información en derecho* was written as a protest to the royal *cédula* of February 4, 1534, which permitted the taking of Amerindians as slaves. The *cédula* stated that enslaving the Amerindians was legal because the "slaves" had either been acquired in a "just" war or were already slaves when "ransomed" by the conquerors *(esclavos de rescate)*.

The Catholic sovereigns had forbidden the enslavement of the Amerindians during the Caribbean phase of the conquest and had quickly moved to make them free vassals of the crown. In theory the Amerindian population was subsumed under the royal patrimony of Ferdinand and Isabella. But in actuality they were required to pay a direct tribute to the Spanish monarchs. Even though the crown publicly forbade slavery, it too had its informal share of slaves. In this way the sovereigns reconciled their imperial and commercial goals with their religious obligation to Christianize the "infidels." Thus the rather liberal idea of free Amerindian vassalage soon gave way to widespread greed and corruption as the native peoples became the victims of *encomienda* assignment.[6] After Isabella's death in 1504 Ferdinand encouraged *encomendero* interests, and slavery became more widespread.

The lucrative profit gained from the royal fifth proved to be too strong an incentive for the king to stop the forces of enslavement. In 1512 and 1513, because of the devastation of the Caribbean people and the protests of an antislavery lobby led by the Dominicans, the crown produced the Laws of Burgos. These laws attempted to sanction the *encomienda* system, although with the proviso that the *encomenderos* were obligated to Christianize the Amerindians. Above all, the laws stated that the natives were not to be enslaved.

By the beginning of the 1530s the great population centers of the central valley of Mexico had been conquered. Endemic diseases had laid waste to large portions of the indigenous population, and infighting over the spoils of war brought the various Spanish factions in the colony to the brink of anarchy. The devastation of central Mexico threatened to duplicate the demographic collapse that had occurred in the Caribbean islands. *Información en derecho* is Quiroga's particular contribution to the great sixteenth-century religious and legal debate, by which he attempted to gain the freedom of the Amerindians and reestablish order in the colony. The antislavery effort eventually culminated in the New Laws of 1542–1543 that absolutely prohibited Amerindian enslavement.

The policy shift between 1512 and 1542 was partly due to Carlos V's more confident authority and to the influence exerted on the king by his more liberal advisers.[7] In the last analysis the New Laws of 1542–1543 were only partially successful. They did draw critical attention to *encomendero* abuses. Nevertheless, three years after their enactment they were repealed.

THE LEGALITY OF SPAIN'S CLAIM TO THE AMERICAS

Información en derecho indicates that Vasco de Quiroga was well aware of the intellectual and spiritual ideals popular in Renaissance Europe. In the text, the legalist bishop dares to dream of the possibility of creating a new kind of human being in Michoacán: one who at long last lives according to the radical love preached by Jesus of Nazareth. According to his plan, Purhépecha society would be reorganized into quasi-monastic village communities overseen by the church.

Of course Quiroga's ideal of spiritual and earthly perfection reflected his christocentric worldview and was informed by Spanish Christianity, especially the culture's idealization of the primitive apostolic church and its apocalyptic vision of a terrestrial paradise. Yet the pagan ideal of a golden age of classical antiquity was also attractive to the humanist in Quiroga. Actually the idealization of both the past and the future is a recurring theme in the broader history of European Christianity. In the sixteenth century this theme accompanied the ascendancy of Franciscan mysticism in Spain and the church's efforts to reform medieval Christianity. The result was a renewed interest in evaluating the human condition and in the possibility of achieving earthly perfection.

Erasmus best reflected this tendency when he called Christians to live their lives according to a *philosophia Christi*. The development of a "philosophy of Christ" represented the Christian social thinker's attempt to bridge the distance between the "City of Man" and the "City of God." Erasmus believed that the humanist project could facilitate the reform of Christianity, through its emphasis on the moral messages culled from the Greek classics as well as the spiritual lessons gained from contemplation. He asked Christians to cast off the impotent shadows of their former lives "and imitate him (Christ) whom you have drunk in."[8]

Early on in *Información en derecho* Quiroga introduces Doctor Bernal to the possibility of creating a Christian social utopia in Michoacán. He tells the doctor that only a complete rethinking and restructuring of native society will resolve the breakdown of law and order in New Spain. Unlike Thomas More's *Utopia*, however, where there existed the best of all possible political and religious worlds, Quiroga is faced with having to implement an imposed utopia on a defeated people in the grips of violence and social collapse.[9]

But before developing his ideas on a social utopia in Michoacán Quiroga must assess whether the claims and goals of the Spanish government are legitimate. In this regard the treatise actually represents part of a larger body of scholastic and legal writings concerning the legitimacy of the Spanish titles to the New World. The controversy had begun with the Dominican John Major in 1510. It intensified in the *Relectio de Indies,* presented by the Spanish Dominican Francisco de Vitoria at the University of Salamanca in 1539. The "Great Debate" at Valladolid in 1550 was the most famous public dialogue concerning the entitlement dispute. At the University of Valladolid the Dominican Juan Ginés de Sepúlveda presented the pro-imperial, pro-slavery position in his work *Democrates alter.* Bartolomé de Las Casas argued the pro-Amerindian, antislavery mendicant position. Although Las Casas was seventy-six years old, the strength of his conviction impelled him to undertake a five-day reading of his perspective. Las Casas' position in the debate is documented in his treatise *In Defense of the Indies.*[10]

The question of the conquest's legitimacy was extremely interesting to the humanists, who were concerned with legitimating history in general and with the question of justice. It was also an important topic for the *letrados* and the Scholastic theologians. In *Información en derecho* Don Vasco begins his evaluation of the conquest by quoting the jurist Cayetano and introducing the Roman concept of *dominium.* He asks the question of whether the Amerindians possessed legal *dominium* over their territories before the conquest. The idea of *dominium* originated with the Roman jurist Gaius and his categorization of the world into persons, actions, and things. The term was usually translated as "property," but Quiroga's concern is with *dominium jurisdictionis,* or those faculties and legal rights *(facultas et ius)* that give the individual and community jurisdictional control over their affairs.[11] Most Scholastic theologians taught that all forms of *dominium* were natural because they involved rights. The humanists, however, offered a different perspective:

> *But for the Roman jurist and their humanist commentators, most (rights) were part of the civil or positive law. A man, as an animal, might enjoy* "dominium corporis sui" *which was one of the reasons why the Indians could not be sold into slavery against their will. But only civil beings could be the subject of political rights. The canonist lawyers had argued that the paganism of the ancients—and hence of the Amerindians—deprived them* "ipso facto" *of any* dominium. *Both the civil jurist and the theologians rejected this claim, since for the jurist it threatened the universality of legal norms and for the theologians came perilously close to the Wycliffite, and more recently Lutheran, heresy of confusing God's laws with God's grace.*[12]

Quiroga argues that the natives had an undeveloped brand of *dominium* in Mexico: "even the lowliest know and guard the natural law, they do not honor many gods, possess a king, the law, or an ordered political life."[13] He says that the more rustic tribes existed in a pure state of nature but "in tyranny of themselves as a barbarous and cruel people, and ignorant of things and of how to live good politically."[14] For this reason, Quiroga concludes, the Amerindians must have lacked knowledge of the principles informing the operation of the natural world. The bishop contends that the Amerindians' ignorance of these principles rendered their societies inherently weak and defenseless against the Spaniards, who possessed a "true" knowledge of nature. The proof of this, states Quiroga, was the native people's "wildness and crudeness *[rusticidad]*, and their ignorance of things."[15]

Quiroga informs Doctor Bernal that the Amerindian communities did not constitute legitimate polities. To reinforce this position he cites the French nominalist Jean Gerson and states that legitimate forms of government must consist of a monarchy, an aristocracy, and a timocracy. In other words, in legitimate states political and civil honors must be distributed on the basis of property and economic status. Quiroga asserts that the absence of any of these factors leads to tyranny, oligarchy, and even democracy. He therefore draws the obvious but incorrect conclusion that the Amerindian states were illegitimate.

Quiroga describes the Aztecs as tyrants who were mistakenly venerated as gods and argues that they were illegitimate rulers because they were not fully human rational beings. He states that even the *cabecera* towns were not true commonwealths since they possessed no legal rights in the indigenous system. Quiroga concludes that no pre-Columbian state could legitimately claim *dominium jurisdictionis* over its own territory, for no one actually possessed political authority in the New World. All property was thus available to the first "civilized" men who took possession of it.[16]

Although the crown could legitimately possess the new territories, states Quiroga, it had the moral obligation to free everyone enslaved by tyranny. To leave the Amerindians "disorganized and barbarous in their savage and bestial life, uninstructed, insufficient without enough (food and shelter), and wild and miserable and uncultivated as they are" was tantamount to robbing them of their natural rights. The worst scenario would be to keep the natives "ignorant and wild," as some conquerors had done by enslaving them. Most importantly, "to deal them out and portion them as if they were livestock, or other irrational animals for the squandering" was criminal because it deprived them of the benefits of civility.[17]

Quiroga denounces the latter kind of enslavement as abominable. He tells Doctor Bernal that he recently witnessed a group of Amerindians at the slave market in Pátzcuaro. All in the group, which consisted of women and their small children, were branded in the face, leaving their faces remote behind thick scars. All captives had been branded without consideration of their age or sex.[18] In this situation, Quiroga laments, "[a] dog is more valuable than a human being, (because) the human being sells himself for only one or two or three *pesos* as a slave to the Spanish."[19]

Quiroga was deeply affected by the sight of this cruelty. Ironically, however, he does not totally negate the institution of slavery in his writings. Instead he remains a loyal subject and practical politician, knowing that the crown's justification for the conquest was based on the king's sovereign right to "pacify and socialize those barbarians" so they might be "humiliated of their power and bestiality" and come to "the true understanding of their Creator and of the thing created."[20]

Quiroga argues that slaves may be taken only in just, holy, and legal wars. But for a war to have been just it had to meet certain conditions. Warfare was legitimate only if the Amerindians attacked Spanish Christians, impeded the Spaniards' free passage, or obstructed the recovery of Spanish property. It was also justified if they violently rejected the evangelization, especially if the gospels had been peacefully preached to them.[21] Quiroga warns Bernal, however, that the conditions for a just war did not exist in New Spain. He states that the "Indians are not hostile nor are they enemies of the name of Christ; they are merely unbelievers who never received notice of Him, thus they do not deserve to be the victims of war through force of arms."[22]

Quiroga does affirm that slaves may be taken by the Spanish if they were already slaves in Amerindian society, because the latter were a kind of property exchanged through purchase or ransom *(rescate)*. But Quiroga hesitates in wholeheartedly endorsing slavery by ransom, for he believes that the Amerindian institution of slavery was different from European slavery. He says that indigenous slavery more closely resembled Europe's system of indentured servants. In the indigenous system slaves traded their services for long periods of time but did not sell their personhood.[23]

Don Vasco notes that the common laborers, the *macehuales, tamemes,* and *naborías,* were not slaves in Amerindian society. These people represented a caste of manual workers who "lived in their own tyranny as a cruel and barbarous people, some were barbarous nations (the Chichimec), who were victimized by their own tyrants who oppressed them."[24] Quiroga tells his friend that in Mexico the chaos of the conquest had reached inhumane levels: "For taking an ear of corn from a strange cornfield because of lack of funds, [the manual laborers] had to serve the owner by enslaving themselves for their entire life."[25] Quiroga's position on the enslavement of the Amerindians demonstrates that he was not uniformly opposed to the practice but was instead a moderate. His contention that certain kinds of slavery were natural and even beneficial adds fuel to the controversy surrounding his work and his historical image.

P. O. Kristeller defines humanism as a cultural and educational movement primarily concerned with the promotion of eloquence. Morality, philosophy, and politics were of secondary importance to the humanist. Kristeller asserts that humanism was preoccupied with "how ideas were obtained and expressed" rather than with "the actual substance of those ideas."[26] The humanist literary agenda was summed up in the slogan *ad fontes* (back to the sources). Humanist intellectuals overlooked the decadence of the medieval period and extolled the recovery of idealized glories. They abandoned commentaries written during the Middle Ages, whether on the Bible or legal treatises, instead advocating a return to the original texts. This particular definition of humanism more accurately characterizes men like Valla, Vives, More, Colet, Erasmus, and Luther, who believed that new lay practices of piety could be created that circumvented the clergy.

Quiroga cannot be easily located within the parameters of Kristeller's definition. His objection to slavery is based neither on the Christian ideal of fraternal love nor on the premise that the Gentiles were made in the image of God. Rather, "the crown had no obvious right to enslave the natives, because its *dominium* was restricted to *dominium juridisdictionis.*"[27] Don Vasco does demonstrate the humanist preoccupation with creating a Christian commonwealth. His hope is to construct an active community in which every citizen participates in communal political life. An active political life was a respected social ideal for the humanist writers. To qualify for this social responsibility the Amerindians had to be acculturated into Christianity and a classical curriculum. Don Vasco is closest to the European humanist tradition in his role as a social engineer.

NATURALES MADE OF SOFT WAX

The conquest of the great population centers in Mexico not only resulted in a great loss of life but also displaced tens of thousands of individuals. These people retreated into the distant jungles and, in the particular case of Michoacán, the remote mountain areas. In *Información en derecho* Quiroga often refers

to the natives of Michoacán as a "disorganized and barbarous" people living a
"savage and bestial life." However, when he wants to convince his reader of
their potential to fulfill the ideals of a renovated Christianity, Quiroga depicts the Amerindians in a more positive light. He describes them as *naturales*,
which in Spanish connotes both a native and a rough or unfinished person.

The bishop tells Doctor Bernal that the *naturales* can be remade into new
human beings who will form the vanguard of a purified Christianity. Quiroga
says the new territories provide a fertile terrain for conducting this experiment. He rhapsodizes about the paradise that could be realized in Michoacán
and describes the Amerindians as innocent creatures of nature embodying an
enviable simplicity and gentleness. Quiroga sees himself as an important actor
in the program to evangelize the Purhépecha with the "best" of Christianity.
In his *Letter of 1531* he writes: "I offer myself, to plant a primitive church and
to put it right."[28] He says that the success of his role in the evangelization can
be seen in the rapidity of the conversion and the sincerity shown by the natives for the sacraments.

In a passionate section of *Información en derecho* Quiroga tells Doctor Bernal that the Amerindians are not hopeless creatures even though they are "wild
and unordered," for they have been selected as candidates for God's divine
plan. And by giving the Amerindians "the good and perfect things of our
Christian religion, and not that which is imperfect, it would be possible to realize the reborn church in this golden age among the *naturales*, and the teachings of a Christian life, holy simplicity, gentleness, humility, piety, and charity."[29] Quiroga continues, "It seems to me certain that I see, if I do not deceive
myself of it, in the *[naturales]* an image of them [the Apostles], and a translation authorized by them." He builds upon the image of the apostolic ideal
when he says, "And in this primitive, new, and reborn church of the new world
there is a shadow and image of that primitive church of our known world, of
the time of the holy apostles, and of the early christians, the true imitators of
the apostles."[30]

To identify the Amerindians with the apostles of Christ is quite different
from describing them as *naturales*. Quiroga employs the latter term in speaking of them as the rustic victims of *encomendero* atrocities. In those situations
the *natural* is a "miserable beast" victimized by his own "ignorance." But when
Quiroga discusses the spiritual possibilities of the *naturales* he says they are
"humane and docile," with "the most gentle of natures." They are "a teachable
people of capacity and born so apt." Furthermore, they are eager to obey
"whatever is ordered by your Majesty. And for that which is the Royal Council of the Indies, they are without any resistance and very humble and obedi-

FIGURE 8. Tariácuri's daughter decapitates a *cacique*

ent."[31] Quiroga tells Bernal that the role of the Audiencia and the missionaries should be to introduce the best of Spanish civilization to the Amerindians and to impart to these "people of quality" a social order. This immense task, he contends, is part of a divine plan to reshape the bodies and souls of the *naturales*, which he describes as "soft wax."[32]

In his enthusiasm to engineer a new Amerindian, Don Vasco links the events in the New World to classical antiquity. But, he writes, the New World experience has been tarnished by the insatiable greed and the oppressive practices of some Spanish Christians. Quiroga places the blame for the chaos in the colony on misinformed officials in Spain who tried to impose laws upon the new territories that had no relevance within the native social system. In order to rectify this wrong he asks Bernal and the Council of the Indies for an imaginative legal approach to the situation in New Spain. He petitions that laws be written that are both sensitive to the native cultures and easily appropriated by them:

> *This [land] is named the New World with great cause and reason. It is the New World not because it was found new, but because its newness is its peoples, and almost everything that is encountered, is as it was in that first Golden Age. [However,] now because of the malice and great greed of our people, it has become an age of iron and worse. And because of all this, our ways cannot conform themselves with theirs [the Amerindians'], nor can they adapt themselves to our way of government ... if it is not ordered for them anew with laws that conform to the laws of this New World and of its* naturales.[33]

Quiroga states that the Spanish government must be sensitive to Amerindian laws and customs. This responsibility was outlined, says the bishop, in the Alexandrine Bulls of Donation in which the pope charged the Spanish crown with the care of the newly discovered cultures. Quiroga asserts that the new territories were granted to the crown as an obligation, not as possessions.[34] He argues that Spain's legal right to the Americas is intricately tied to the moral well-being of its people. In a letter he presented to the Council of the Indies in 1553 he restates his position by saying that the crown possessed New Spain not only through dynastic succession but also through papal concession.[35]

THE *REPÚBLICA AMERINDIA*

There is no clear evidence as to the source or inspiration for Quiroga's plan for congregating the Amerindians into *repúblicas de indios*. *Información en derecho* mentions three possible sources: the ideal of a golden age present in Lucian's *Saturnalia*, the primitive church or apostolic ideal popular among the mendicant friars, and Thomas More's concept of a utopian Christian commonwealth. Most probably Quiroga synthesized his ideas from various pagan and Christian communal models.

After a long descriptive passage concerning the living conditions in the *Saturnalia*, Quiroga states, "Examined carefully it will be discovered that these are the *naturales* from the new world. Almost without missing a point the *[nat-*

urales] have and enjoy the simplicity, gentleness and humility and liberty of mind as those people, without arrogance, without greed, and without any ambition." [36] Quiroga blends an idealization of the classical past with the primitive Apostolic ideal when he asserts that founding a new kind of Christianity is a necessary step in recapturing the simplicity and humility "of the Apostolic Golden Age." [37] Pedro Borges suggests that Quiroga's fascination with the apostolic ideal resulted from his contact with the millennial fervor of Franciscan Spirituals who predicted that the end of the world would occur in 1605.

Quiroga himself attributes the concept of an "Indian Republic" to Thomas More's book *Utopia*, stating that he was "inspired by the Holy Spirit" when he discovered the book. Quiroga argues that More's social ideals could be implemented among the Amerindians; doing so would help them "guard, conserve, and more easily manage" their own societies. More's plan would also introduce the Amerindians to "the faith and to an integrated social order *[policía mixta]*, which is the only thing they lack." [38] He calls More a "most prudent *señor*" for having translated from Greek to Latin some of the works of Lucian, from which More derived his model of a commonwealth. [39]

Quiroga believed that the *república indiana* was the only way for the Amerindians to achieve *polis*, the social order characteristic of European urban life. The term *polis* is used repetitively by Quiroga in a negative manner to describe what New Spain lacked. It also refers to a prerequisite lifestyle necessary for achieving a successful translation of Christianity. The term carries with it the idea of a cultivated person and in the Amerindians' case implies the abandonment of all inappropriate acts such as pantheism, polygamy, and nomadism. For Quiroga the idea of *polis* included his desire that the Amerindians live a regulated urban life similar to that found in the European cities. Only when the Amerindians were finally aggregated into urban settlements and instructed in the basics of "civility" could they begin to understand the word of God. [40]

An elaborate urban organization and a cultivated elite social caste were not foreign to the Purhépecha of Michoacán. However, Quiroga encountered many nomadic Chichimec tribal groups that had migrated from the Bajío region into the farming areas of Michoacán, as well as other people displaced by the Spanish invasion. The Chichimec in particular were still in the hunter-gatherer phase of social development and were noted for their fierceness. Bishop Quiroga's wish to Europeanize the Amerindians before they became Christians demonstrates cultural and racial prejudice. Yet if one recalls the social and ecological chaos prevalent in New Spain at the time of Quiroga's arrival, it is difficult to uniformly condemn the bishop's desire for peace and order.

The idea of "reducing" or congregating the Amerindian people into reorganized towns *(reducción y congregación)* in order to acculturate and evangelize them was not Quiroga's invention. When the mendicants arrived in New Spain they developed two social institutions that facilitated the work of evangelization. These social centers were designated the *doctrinas* and the *congregaciones*. The *doctrina* was a center or school of religious instruction usually located in a monastery or convent. There the friars preached to the natives outside, in the open atriums of the churches. The Amerindians were called to worship several times a day during the early evangelization. Grouped around large raised crosses, they were required to recite the catechism by rote, listen to sermons, and hear mass.[41]

The *congregaciones* were new Amerindian communities that were formed for two reasons: to facilitate the conversion by bringing the Purhépecha and the missionaries together, and to halt the disintegration of the aboriginal populations by isolating them from the conquistadors. The Franciscan Pedro de Gante, who initiated the missionary style of evangelization, had developed the institutions by requiring the sons of the native nobility to receive special training from the mendicant fathers. The boys were forcibly brought to the conventual house to live with the friars and to be schooled in the classical curriculum of Europe. In theory the boys were to serve as interpreters and catechists to their tribal groups.

Quiroga supported the *congregaciones* in his *Letter of 1531*.[42] In *Información en derecho* he calls upon Carlos V to "order such a living situation for the *naturales*, [both] for themselves and so that those who will be maintained are of sufficient numbers, and they conserve themselves and convert themselves as they should, and live and not die or perish, as they currently are dying and perishing . . . because of the lack of good polity."[43] He maintained that if the Amerindians were not congregated into their own towns "in good catholic polity," then "no conservation, no good treatment, no execution of ordinances, no justice, in this land and within the *naturales* can be hoped for."[44]

Organizing the Amerindians in centers of acculturation and indoctrination involved politicizing them. Thus the mendicants appointed governors from among the indigenous *caciques*. They also required the townsfolk *(vecinos)* to elect town officials called *alcaldes* and *regidores*. This primitive attempt at democracy was done in order to constitute the *cabildo*, or governmental body of the town. Congregation was also designed to provide the Amerindians with a method of subsistence and a means for paying the Spaniards their tribute. One mendicant described congregation as a way to teach "catechism and training in good habits."[45] The missionaries hoped to ameliorate physical suffering in the centers by providing medical care and lodging for those who were ravaged by epidemics and forced labor.

In his defense of the *repúblicas de indios* Quiroga states that isolating the Amerindians was the only way to resolve their "lack of *policía* and their dispersed wild and savage life, in which they resemble more irrational animals than human beings."[46] Reduction was a first step in creating a purified church in Michoacán. Without the Amerindian republics it would be impossible for the missionaries to weed out idolaters and nonconformists. According to Quiroga, a divine plan ordained that the Amerindians would be converted into good Christians. But first the church and the state had to conquer their "sinfulness."[47]

As the seasoned judge who had previously dealt with similar difficulties in Africa, Quiroga recognized that abolishing the indigenous social order was crucial to the Christianization process. As a "prince of the church" he recognized his responsibility to present the Amerindians with the best values and practices of Christianity. And as a royal judge he knew the harsh realities of conquest and the importance of establishing law and order in the new territories. Quiroga's answer to the crisis in New Spain demonstrates that he was well aware of the intellectual and social programs popular among European humanists at the time. Nevertheless, his brand of humanism could hardly be unequivocally lauded as humanitarian.

EIGHT

The Utopian Experiment
Santa Fe de la Laguna

Quiroga states in *Información en derecho* that the purpose of isolating the Purhépecha into *repúblicas de indios* was to reshape their behavior. Close supervision would allow the clergy to monitor the process of converting the Amerindians to Christianity. In employing the republican town model Don Vasco selected an ancient symbol of Europagan and Christian origin. The pagan sources of this symbol reach back to the Greek ideal of the *polis* and the idea of the enlightened rule of an elite group of males who strive for intellectual excellence. The root Christian meaning of the idea of the republic is found in the Book of the Apocalypse; it refers to the idea of spiritual and earthly perfection that is motivated by the fear of a cataclysmic end to the world and the salvific promise of the Parousia. This dual prophecy of terror and salvation, amazingly enough, continues to function to this day as a fundamental layer of modern Western civilization.

The Purhépecha had a similar prophecy of the end-time. According to their sages, the world would terminate with the appearance of strange "new men." The strangers would "spare no end of the earth . . . all the way to the edge of the sea and beyond."[1] The strangulation and immolation of the *cazonci* Tzintzicha Tangaxoan II on February 14, 1530, threw the people of Michoacán into a widespread panic and left the territory open to the ravages of military conquest. It seemed as if the two cultures' archetypes of the end-time were about to become real. After the *cazonci*'s assassination Guzmán marched northward to conquer Nueva Galicia. He took with him thousands of Purhépecha warriors, burden carriers, and women slaves. Stability in the region was painfully slow in coming. The *doctrinas*, where the church conducted its evangelical work with the dispossessed, provided the only safe havens in the province.

SANTA FE DE LA LAGUNA

Tzintzuntzan was proclaimed a *corregimiento* (royal town) by the first Audiencia. The institution of the *corregimiento* counterbalanced the *encomienda* in many ways. In the Amerindian towns that fell beneath the monarchs' auspices, the natives remained under the direct authority of the crown. In contrast, the *encomienda* system allocated the Amerindians to an *encomendero* as a private grant of vassals who provided service and tribute. The former towns soon became known as *corregimientos de indios*. They were administered by a royal representative who lived off the tribute he collected as well as the personal services of others whom he controlled.[2]

Pedro de Arellano was the first *corregidor* of Tzintzuntzan. Upon his arrival in the capital he presented a royal decree to the *cabildo* authorizing him to claim the richest towns in the province for Charles V. Arellano's governorship of Tzintzuntzan was short-lived, however. In 1532 a group of indigenous elders from Tzintzuntzan complained to the second Audiencia that Arellano had kidnapped and tortured three natives. Arellano's actions were apparently motivated by his greed; in torturing the three he hoped to force them into revealing the hiding place of the *cazonci*'s treasure.[3]

Cristóbal de Benavente conducted an investigation of the Arellano incident under the authority of the second Audiencia. Archbishop Zumárraga had entrusted Benavente with the title "Protector of the Indians" so that he was obliged to conduct an inquiry of the incident. Benavente's inquiry resulted in Arellano's arrest.[4] On February 15, 1532, Benavente was appointed as the new *corregidor* and *alcalde* of Tzintzuntzan, Colima, Zacatula, and the royal mines in Michoacán.

In April 1532 the Audiencia informed the crown of Benavente's appointment. The court also informed the Spanish king that it had recommended that one of its members visit Michoacán. The Audiencia had appointed Vasco de Quiroga to make the arduous trip by mule across the volcanic ranges. The decision to send Quiroga was prompted by an upsurge in violence in Michoacán due to the influx of gold speculators in the region.[5] Quiroga left for Michoacán sometime in June of 1532. Fintan B. Warren states that Quiroga delayed his journey a year in order to ensure that his first hospital town outside Mexico City got off the ground.[6]

On his first visit to Michoacán, Quiroga established a Spanish town near Tzintzuntzan called Granada. He appointed the local town officials and registered twenty-five citizens. The Audiencia later vetoed the town's application, however, on the grounds that the venture was poorly planned and would hamper colonization in the central valley.[7]

Vasco de Quiroga politically allied himself with the Amerindians during these early years. He believed that the basic problems between the conquered and their conquerors stemmed from cultural and religious differences. Quiroga's observation was subtle but keen. Amerindian religious iconography was particularly offensive to the Spaniards. Many actions and images, such as ritual bloodletting and serpents (which were symbols of fertility in the Mesoamerican worldview), had demonic values in Christianity. This led the Spaniards to believe that the natives' religious imagination was proof that Satan was working amongst them.

The humanist program to renovate Christianity aimed not only at purifying Christian theology but also cultivating Christian piety. For humanist reformers God was accessible through the intellect and the original scriptural message of Jesus of Nazareth. Erasmus used Platonic thought to argue the antimaterialist position that the phenomenal world was but a shadow of the world of ideas: "Wean your heart from the love of visible things, and attend rather to the things invisible."[8] Erasmus taught that the materialism of the late medieval world was "the ruin of Christendom."[9] The mendicants' horror with Amerindian religious imagery must be understood against the backdrop of this reformist tendency and the broader attack on the materialism of the European church.

Quiroga tried to convince the Purhépecha-Chichimec that their oppression resulted from their idolatry. While the bishop may have been correct, the indigenous religion proved more durable and adaptable to Christian syncretisms than the missionaries first thought. Pedro de Arellano had defended his brutal actions by arguing that if he had not taken the Amerindians' treasures, they would have persisted in offering them to their gods.[10] Yet it is difficult to believe that the Purhépecha were persuaded by Quiroga, since the conquistadors' insatiable greed was the more obvious source of the Amerindians' predicament.

Quiroga's reputation as a benevolent pastor was initially established by his first visit to Michoacán. Francisco Castillejo, the bishop's interpreter, informs us that Quiroga spent long hours "teaching [the Purhépecha] that there was one God in heaven and the Emperor on earth, and that God rewarded the

good and punished the evil."[11] Quiroga called upon the Purhépecha to abandon their deities, their bloodletting, and their drunkenness. He condemned
the Purhépecha religion as the "work of the devil" and talked with men and
women concerning the merits of monogamous marriage. Quiroga appears to
have been partially successful in convincing Purhépecha men to marry only
one wife. Aguayo Spencer reports that the Purhépecha elder Don Pedro Cuinierángari had many wives at the time Quiroga first began offering his sermons. But after a long conversation with Don Vasco the *cacique* gave up all
but one wife. The townsfolk followed Don Pedro's example because of the
Mesoamerican custom that says that a clan's religion must be the religion of
its leaders.[12]

Quiroga was profoundly affected by the reception given to him by the Purhépecha on this first visit, and he proposed that a hospital-hospice be built for
the dispossessed and the infirm.[13] A group of indigenous officials showed him
a favorable site for the hospital—near the village of Guayameo on the north
side of the lake—but the *encomendero* Juan de Infante had already located a pig
farm there. This inconvenience failed to discourage Quiroga, and he ordered
that the construction of the *pueblo*-hospital begin.[14]

CONFLICT AT SANTA FE

According to the eighteenth-century biographer Juan José Moreno, Quiroga
assumed his position in Michoacán by 1538. He quickly began the task of
consolidating his diocese and building up the *pueblo*-hospital community of
Santa Fe de la Laguna.[15] In the summer of 1538 Don Pedro Cuinierángari
and his wife, Doña Inez, presented themselves before the bishop to execute
the transaction of the ownership.[16] A bill of sale was drawn up and Quiroga
paid the Purhépecha governor 150 *pesos* for the land. Don Pedro retained some
tribute privileges over the community as part of the agreement.[17]

Quiroga's patronage of Santa Fe led directly to his difficulties with the
encomendero Juan Infante. The Quiroga-Infante power struggle would continue beyond the two men's lifetimes. The prize in the controversy was much
greater than the tribute derived from the small town: the reward was the control of the entire province.[18]

Juan de Infante was one of the *cazonci*'s formal accusers at his trial, along
with Francisco Villegas and Purándiro Villaseñor. The three *hidalgos* profited
enormously from the king's death.[19] Between 1540 and 1554 Infante amassed
more than sixty tribute towns in Michoacán. Exactly how Infante acquired

the *barrios de la laguna* grant (a group of twenty five-towns that included Santa
Fe) is unknown. Under the Purhépecha tribute system the towns fell under
the authority of Tzintzuntzan. Nevertheless, in 1531 Infante convinced the
Audiencia in Mexico City to give him the *encomienda* grant.

Fintan B. Warren states that the *corregidor* Arellano first rejected Infante's
request for ownership, arguing that the towns were part of the royal *corregimiento* of Tzintzuntzan. When the *licenciado* Benavente replaced Arellano,
Benavente testified that Infante had never been in actual possession of the
towns. Infante appealed the decision in 1532 and again in 1535, but the second Audiencia ruled against Infante. Infante then filed a countersuit accusing
Quiroga of biased judgment on the basis of his dual role as bishop of Michoacán and *oidor* of the Audiencia. Although the Audiencia ruled that the case was
closed, Infante presented an appeal before the Council of the Indies.[20]

In 1539 Infante returned triumphant from Spain, a *carta ejecutoria* in his
possession. The second Audiencia had no choice but to execute the royal order, and so it appointed a court official to accompany Infante to Tzintzuntzan
to enforce the decree. Don Pedro, the indigenous governor of Tzintzuntzan,
twice appealed the decision before the Audiencia, but on both occasions the
court ruled that the royal order should be obeyed. Quiroga entered the controversy with Don Pedro's second appeal. Quiroga's interest was motivated
by his concern that he was losing control of his new diocese to a powerful *encomendero*. Warren affirms this position: "in losing the *barrios de la laguna* the
City of Michoacán would not be able to support the Spanish and Indian population which was befitting his (Quiroga's) newly erected diocesan see."[21]

It was inevitable that two powerful men like Quiroga and Infante would
lock horns. On September 27, 1539, Juan Infante reached Lake Pátzcuaro.
Determined to take control of the towns, he was convinced that Quiroga
would not dare to resist the royal order he carried. Don Vasco was equally
confident that the towns would not fall into Infante's hands but would remain
under his own jurisdiction. Infante's bold actions in the conflict had moved
Quiroga to a state of "restrained fury," and although the bishop was sixty-five
years old, he was still a formidable adversary.[22]

In a later legal suit arising out this conflict Infante testified that Quiroga
told him that he "wanted nothing more than to be a hermit, and that he would
cause a serious disturbance in this affair so that he would lose his diocese and
could take up the eremitical life."[23] Quiroga's threat was fairly obvious. He was
willing to create a public scandal in order to uphold his convictions. Quiroga
also warned Antonio Godoy that if Infante took possession of the towns, he

would leave Michoacán with a pilgrim's staff and beg the crown to take away his bishopric.[24]

While Infante was making his way to Tzintzuntzan, Quiroga was lobbying the Purhépecha for their support. He informed the native elders of their legal rights and of the grave situation that would occur should Infante prevail. Thus by the time the *encomendero* and his party arrived from Mexico City, Quiroga had cultivated a solid block of indigenous resistance to turning over the towns.

Infante's party rested for three days before presenting their demands. Then on September 30 the court-appointed executor, Andrés Juárez, met with Quiroga's representative, Pedro Yepes. On this occasion Infante warned the executor that Quiroga was stalling the process to stir up anti-Infante sentiment among the Amerindians. Juárez cautioned Quiroga's representative that the bishop would have to assume responsibility for any riots that might break out.

Upon hearing of Infante's accusation Quiroga angrily presented himself before Juárez and challenged Infante to make the accusation to his face. Infante did exactly that. Then he presented the bishop with the decree that gave him ownership of the twenty-five towns. Infante later told the Audiencia that during the time Quiroga refused to comply with the order, he had advised the Purhépecha that if Infante was successful they should abandon their villages and move to Pátzcuaro, where he lived.[25]

On October 1, 1539, Juan Infante and two Audiencia officials headed north from Pátzcuaro on the lakeside road to Santa Fe. Infante was steadfast in his decision to take possession of the towns. The riders had not gone far when they were overtaken by the old bishop. Riding a large black mule, he was accompanied by eleven Spaniards carrying lances and by three armed clerics. Infante was nervous but unyielding. He again showed Quiroga the royal decree and asked him to withdraw before a serious disturbance occurred. But Quiroga responded that he was only there to prevent violence and that if violence did occur it would be due to Infante's stubbornness and greed. He asked Infante to refrain from taking any action until the viceroy and the Audiencia could find an answer to the crisis.

The royal executor then entered the fray. He warned the Spaniards accompanying the bishop that they would be punished if they continued to support Quiroga. He also informed the armed clerics that they would lose their temporal privileges if they persisted in blocking the decree's enforcement. Two Spaniards in the bishop's party obeyed the warning and turned back. But the others vowed to remain with their sovereign lord, the bishop of Michoacán.

In later testimony López de Agurto stated that in the interest of peace, he had tried to convince the bishop to back down. Agurto reported that Quiroga told him that the *encomendero*'s party would have to cut him into pieces before he would surrender the township to Infante. Don Vasco vehemently protested Infante's legal right to the land, arguing that the deed was not acquired according to the laws of the land.[26]

The two groups rode together for a short distance. Then one of the Spaniards accompanying Quiroga told Infante that six thousand Purhépecha and Chichimec warriors were waiting ahead to ambush him. The threat proved too much for Infante. He made one more protest to Quiroga and then turned back, saying he was returning to Mexico City to inform the viceroy of the bishop's outrageous actions.[27]

Whether Bishop Quiroga truly intended to kill Infante remains a mystery. He was certainly prepared to stop the powerful *encomendero* from taking the twenty-five towns. One of the court officials in the Infante party, who rode ahead on the road to Santa Fe, later claimed that he had seen many suspicious Amerindian men standing in the cornfields and on high ground. In any case the threat was sufficient to make the *encomendero* think twice about continuing on the road.

In the subsequent legal suit against Don Vasco, Infante accused the bishop of amassing ten thousand warriors to kill him. He also charged Quiroga with resisting a royal decree and committing treason by doing so. On October 23, 1539, the Audiencia recommended that Viceroy Mendoza should go to Michoacán to settle the controversy. When Mendoza arrived he informed the Purhépecha elders that the decree must be obeyed. But the Purhépecha protested, arguing that they were royal vassals and that they had not authorized that the towns be given to Infante. Mendoza countered by stating that the crown had ordered the Purhépecha to give the towns to Infante. The indigenous governor told the viceroy that if Infante prevailed, the native inhabitants would abandon the towns and move to Pátzcuaro.

Infante eventually took possession of the towns, and he forcibly ejected the Purhépecha who protested. Quiroga had encouraged the native resistance so that Infante could not claim they had peacefully capitulated. Yet the Quiroga-Infante feud did not end with this incident. Fintan B. Warren refers to a number of legal suits filed by both parties concerning the ownership of the twenty-five towns. Moreover, the rivalry continued well after both men were dead. Almost ten years after Quiroga's death Infante's son, Juan Infante Samaniego, sued the city of Tzintzuntzan for the towns. Eventually, the Council of the Indies ruled that the towns should remain subject to the city of Tzintzuntzan.[28]

THE ORDINANCES OF SANTA FE

Bishop Quiroga concluded that the only way to bring about the *optimus status reipublicae* was to train an active citizenry. He believed that the Amerindians first had to understand the concept of participative government before the republic could become a fact. Quiroga's ordinances for the town of Santa Fe de la Laguna provide the best example of how he hoped to realize the republican ideal.

The *Ordenanzas* were written as part of Quiroga's last will, the *Testamento*. As stated earlier, Quiroga found the prototype for the town's ordinances in Thomas More's musings about a pagan commonwealth.[29] More's *Utopia* was a city of aristocrats and intellectuals who adhered to the ideal of civic self-government. The premise behind More's model was that a republic could not function properly unless there were uniform intellectual and spiritual bonds and the citizenry was politically educated. The citizens of the perfect republic were truly noble (*vera nobilitas*), as opposed to those nobles whose status was based on lineage and inherited wealth. More scoffed at the lords of his day because "they believe themselves to be noble in the sense of being entitled to honour and respect, entitled to be met with bare heads and bent knees."[30] He stated, "what is alone noble and deserving of honor is the willingness to labour for the common good." Egalitarian labor promoted the virtue of selflessness, which More called *honestas*. *Honestas* was "the highest term of praise for those who had attained the full range of virtues and deployed them upon the betterment of the common good."[31]

Don Vasco encountered More's ideas when Juan de Zumárraga gave Quiroga his personal copy of *Utopia*. Quiroga first introduced the idea of a Christian republic in New Spain in his *Letter of 1531*. He subsequently developed the concept more fully in *Información en derecho*. By the time he wrote the *Ordenanzas*, sometime between 1555 and January 24, 1565, the idea had undergone many adaptations.[32]

One of the differences between Quiroga's social utopia and the one presented in More's work can be traced to Don Vasco's appropriation of Spanish Catholic folk elements such as the *cofradía* or *mayordomía* system. In the Spanish countryside these religious organizations were dedicated to the enactment of the liturgical and social calendar. The confraternities and sodalities provided widows and orphans with stipends, and they maintained and fostered communal piety. While in Michoacán, Quiroga recognized that the Spanish *cofradía* structure had remarkable similarities to existing indigenous institutions.[33]

It is not the intention of this essay to provide the reader with an evaluation of Quiroga's detailed ordinances for Santa Fe de la Laguna. Fintan B. Warren provides an excellent analysis of them in his work on the *pueblo*-hospitals, and Rafael Aguayo Spencer furnishes a good commentary with the fully published Spanish text. The specificity of the *Ordenanzas* does demonstrate that Quiroga sincerely hoped to preserve his ideas and life's work through civil regulations.[34]

Quiroga designed the *familia* (clan/kinship ward) as the basic social unit of the town. It consisted of a large extended family of between ten to sixteen married couples, all of whom were from the same tribal group. The *padre y madre de familia* were the ultimate authorities in the ward. Each town was composed of six thousand *familias*, or approximately sixty thousand adult males. A *jurado* was appointed to supervise every thirty families, while a *regidor* would regulate every four *jurados*. Above the *regidor* were two *alcaldes ordinarios* and a *tacatecle*. A Spaniard directly appointed by the crown or the Audiencia served as *corregidor* over the entire social structure.[35]

Quiroga imagined a patriarchally sanctioned agrarian community for Santa Fe, with tightly knit extended families as the scaffolding upon which life was built. When the clan townships, or *familias*, became overcrowded, new ones were formed. Parents were responsible for arranging the marriages of their offspring. Boys were to be married at fourteen and girls at twelve; the newlyweds were required to obtain permission to marry from both sets of parents and their respective tribal wards. Wives were obliged to live with their husband's parents. Ultimate authority resided with the eldest grandfather of the *familia:* children obeyed their parents, grandparents, great-grandparents, and so forth, creating a vertical network of kinship relationships based on a village gerontocracy. The elderly Quiroga believed that a gerontocracy was the best structure for eliminating the practice of privilege and the need for servants and slaves, since the latter "disturb the social tranquility."[36]

Transgressions within the *familia* were reported to the village priest and the town's indigenous *regidor*. The two functionaries were ultimately responsible for discipline and punishment, particularly if the *familia* did not carry out its duty in such matters. Quiroga stated that the workers in the fields and the fishermen on the lake should be supervised by the *padre de familia*. The workers labored six hours per day and spent a great amount of time in religious instruction and ceremony. In Quiroga's plan the *padre de familia* was a master craftsman who supervised the town's parks, farms, and ranches. The townsfolk rotated through this post every two years.

Quiroga wrote that the town should raise Spanish livestock such as sheep, goats, cows, pigs, and mules, along with native animals, primarily chickens,

FIGURE 9. A dialogue regarding the history of the ancestors

turkeys, and ducks. The townsfolk "had to plant twice as much as is necessary for the *pueblo* or at least one-third more than is necessary."[37] The agricultural surpluses were to be stored to prevent shortages in hard times. Acquired income from the sale of produce or livestock was to be placed in a large chest and locked with three keys. The rector of the hospital kept the coffer in his office, and the three keys were given to the rector, the *cacique* of the town, and the Spanish *regidor*.[38]

Quiroga's ordinances also provided for the material and spiritual well-being of the community. He stated that the people of Santa Fe should be clothed according to European styles and norms. But in actuality his idea of clothing reflected the mendicants' predisposition for simplicity. He ordered that the natives should refrain from wearing the bright colors and gaudy dress of the European nobility. Instead, their apparel should be made of cotton or wool "in their natural color, white, clean and modest, without decoration and other costly curious work."[39] All clothing was to be made by the *familia*. Quiroga further commanded that all married women were obliged to veil their heads and wear long garments *(tocas)*.

Each community member, regardless of sex or social status, had the right to a free public education. Quiroga required children to read and write in their own language. The youngsters were also taught Christian moral doctrine as outlined in Quiroga's catechism, the *Doctrina cristiana*.[40] Quiroga had this book printed while he was in Sevilla in 1553. The first part of the book defined virtuous social behavior, and the second section was a kind of initiation manual into the various sacramental stages of life. The book also included more specialized information for various segments of society. Unfortunately, the manuscript of the *Doctrina cristiana* has been lost. Fintan B. Warren contends that its aim was to inform the Purhépecha of the foundations of Catholicism and the principles of how to live a "civilized" life. The work is traditionally categorized as a lost appendix to the *Ordenanzas*, because its topic conforms to the subject matter of the town ordinances.

Don Vasco had a threefold goal in writing the ordinances: to give the Purhépecha clans a sound footing in Catholic doctrine, to establish a new social order, and to provide the town with an economic means of survival.[41] Quiroga stipulated that the entire community should attend daily mass. In addition, he designated which religious feast days the townsfolk should celebrate: the Exaltation of the Holy Cross, the Feast of San Salvador, and the Feast of the Assumption. Quiroga added that each holy day should be accompanied by an "abundant and cheerful" meal to be prepared by the *familias* on a rotating basis.[42]

The ordinances also stated that the townsfolk were to build a large hospital that conformed to the square design of their communal houses. People with contagious diseases would be housed on one side of the building and noncontagious clients on the other. The remaining building would include a dispensary and offices for the medical staff. Quiroga specified that the townsfolk were to practice Christian charity through daily visits to the sick.

Bishop Quiroga's ordinances also provided the town with a method of exorcising criminals. Community members could be expelled by general consensus, or by a majority vote of the *cacique, regidor,* and village priest. Citizens could be cast out for a variety of infractions including "doing a hideous thing or causing bad example, unruliness, living scandalously, being a bad Christian, drunkenness, excessive laziness, consistent violation of the ordinances, [and] acting against the common good of the hospital."[43] Transgressors were prohibited from taking any of their personal wealth accumulated during their residency.

In addition to the *pueblo*-hospital communities in Michoacán, Quiroga established many traditional hospitals, including the famous La Asunción and Santa Marta in Pátzcuaro.[44] Quiroga's success in Michoacán was due to his personal devotion, his persuasive power, and his willingness to experiment with traditional indigenous forms of social organization. Prior to the conquest the Purhépecha clans were organized into wards according to tribal affiliation. The tribal wards were subdivided into family plots, the smallest being the *ocámbeti.* The *ocámbeti* consisted of twenty-five houses that comprised the territorial dimensions of the ward. These indigenous wards closely resembled Quiroga's *familia* structure. It is therefore difficult to determine whether the social organization of the people of Santa Fe was due to Quiroga's utopian vision or to the preexisting native social pattern. More than likely Quiroga used those native institutions that worked well and conformed to his ideas.

Quiroga's use of Purhépecha social institutions was most evident at Santa Fe in the placement of the hospital in the *guatapera.* The *guatapera* was originally a women's community house where young girls were educated and trained in the crafts essential for marriage. They were also trained to provide certain services for female priests. In the Purhépecha language the word *guatapera* eventually came to designate the many hospitals that were established by Don Vasco.

Another example of this phenomenon concerns private and corporate ownership of the land. It has long been thought that Quiroga introduced this distinction to the people of Michoacán. However, in pre-Columbian Purhépecha towns, both the *principales* and the agricultural workers privately owned the land. Corporate ownership also existed prior to the conquest. Communal properties were cultivated for the lower chieftains and for the benefit of the temple complex. The Purhépecha probably held communal village territories, because these still exist today. The thesis that Quiroga introduced the Purhépecha to the concept of private and corporate ownership of the land is simply incorrect.[45]

THE RELIGIOUS CONFRATERNITIES

The pre-Columbian communal arrangement of Purhépecha society was similar in form to the social structure of the rural villages in Spain. It was logical, then, for Quiroga and the Franciscan friars to turn to the *cofradías* as the best vehicle for instilling a Eurocentric sense of civic and spiritual responsibility in the people of Michoacán.

Prior to the introduction of Christianity in Michoacán, religious responsibilities were carried out by the native priestly castes and the women of the *guatapera*, who were mainly responsible for organizing the ornate ceremonies at the temples. Ironically, the early mendicants, who sanctified the practice of poverty and criticized external forms of worship, were sensitive to the importance of providing ornate religious pageantries for their Amerindian converts. Robert Ricard argues that this was because the friars knew that they had to compete with the religious spectacles held at the pyramids. The monks feared that the Amerindians would find the mendicants' ceremonies and asceticism too austere and lacking in the kind of drama it took to move large populations. This led the friars "to construct vast and beautiful churches and to decorate them luxuriously, (and) to surround the mass with the most solemn pomp." The ceremonialism had a dual purpose: "It maintained the enthusiasm of the Indians, who were very sensitive to external spectacle, and it enhanced their devotion and their respect for the ceremony at the altar."[46]

The meticulous ethnographies compiled by the first mendicants are proof that the evangelizers took pains to inform themselves about the aboriginal cultures. In their studies they equated many features of Catholicism with the practices and concepts of the Mesoamerican religions. In turn, the Amerindians understood Catholicism according to their own religious concepts and rites.

As the Purhépecha began to actively participate in the Catholic rites, they flocked to the sacrament of baptism, which resembled their own initiation and purification rituals. The aged and infirm went to the local Catholic priest to confess their sins because they had always gone to the chief high priest *(petamiti)* to seek relief from suffering and illness. Both religious systems highlighted the concept of transformation through sacrifice, communion offerings, and funeral rites.

Gradually the Catholic saints were vested by the Purhépecha with the responsibilities of their older tribal, village, and household gods. In the Spanish countryside the cult of the saints was maintained by the confraternities and sodalities of each village. In Michoacán, as in other parts of New Spain, the implementation of the new religion through the veneration of patron saints was greatly facilitated by the evangelizers' translation of the institution of the *cofradía*.

In sixteenth-century Spanish Catholicism a confraternity was traditionally established under the protection of God the Father, the Virgin Mary in one of her many apparitions, the crucified Nazarene, or a spiritual. Postulates, who hoped to receive a spiritual good, were installed *(se asentaban)* in exchange for a vow *(promesa)* made to a supernatural being and to the confraternity members.

The temporal goal of the *cofradía* was to help its members live a purified Christian life through intense pious devotion. Ultimately the members of the *cofradía* hoped to attain the transcendent goal of eternal salvation. On a day-to-day basis salvation was practically achieved by way of the liturgical and cultic agenda—that is, through masses, rosaries, processions, catechetical instruction, retreats, meditations, sermons, and so forth. The most important public aspect of the *cofradía* was its emphasis on the spiritual merit gained from performing the "Spiritual and Corporal Works of Mercy." [47] Confraternity members believed that their transcendent rewards depended on their daily practice of charity and public service. The Amerindian confraternity was also characterized by this dual spiritual and worldly emphasis.

Sixteenth-century Spain had no organized philanthropic institutions dedicated to humanitarian relief such as those existing today. There were no public or private secular institutions that dispensed excess wealth to the dispossessed. Only the Christian obligation to love one's neighbor mandated the dissemination of social services. Since the catastrophic situation in New Spain called for humanitarian action, the mendicants found a means for providing others relief in the *cofradía* system. Within a short time after the conquest confraternities could be found throughout New Spain. They were also prominent in Santo Domingo, the Viceroyalty of Peru, the Captain Generalship of Guatemala, and the Philippines.

Three kinds of confraternities were introduced to New Spain: transplanted Spanish organizations, new confraternities established by recent émigrés, and

Amerindian *cofradías*.[48] The conquistadors established the first confraternity, which was dedicated to La Santa Cruz. The confraternities of the Santísimo Sacramento and La Caridad were installed shortly afterward by Spanish colonists. Cortés established the confraternity of Nuestra Señora de la Concepción for his troops. And Archbishop Zumárraga was responsible for beginning the hospital confraternity called Amor de Dios.

As the European population of Mexico City increased, the confraternities took on a more specialized character. For example, girls' colleges were organized under the protection of Nuestra Señora de la Caridad, and craft-guild brotherhoods were dedicated to particular saints who specialized in natural disasters. The tailors and shoemakers of the capital constructed a hospital in 1526 and consecrated it to Saints Cosme and Damián. And even the many orphaned children were grouped under the protection of Nuestra Señora de los Abandonados.

The *cofradía* system was also advanced in the provinces: the confraternity of Nuestra Señora de la Concepción was established for the hospital of San Juan de Letrán in Puebla, that of Nuestra Señora del Carmen was founded in Campeche, and the confraternity of La Vera Cruz was installed in Guadalajara. By the early seventeenth century Mexico City had more than twenty Spanish and eighty Amerindian confraternities.[49]

Membership in the *cofradía* was usually made by written application. The applicant paid an adjustable entry fee in return for an annual membership letter of privileges. The member was entitled to both spiritual and material aid. This included communal orations for the salvation of the member's soul and economic aid in times of extreme hardship. Confraternities often paid for the medical expenses of not only members but also their families. Furthermore, the organizations collected monthly dues to be used for the elderly and for members suffering from catastrophic illness. Orphaned children and widows also were given subsidies.[50]

The Amerindian confraternities in Michoacán, Jalisco, Colima, Guanajuato, Guerrero, Morelos, and the state of México had a similar pattern of development because of the uniform evangelization by the mendicant orders of those territories. They differed from their Spanish antecedents in their passion and style of devotion, and the economic restrictions of their participants. Thus Amerindian confraternity ceremonialism displayed a unique blend of unaffected piety and macabre passion.

Most of the Amerindian confraternities and sodalities were installed under the common name of La Purísima or La Inmaculada Concepción. This linked them to Cortés's hospital community, Nuestra Señora de la Concepción, which had been granted special spiritual benefits by Pope Julius II. Subsequent Amerindian confraternities incorporated themselves under this rubric to participate in the spiritual rewards granted by the pope.[51]

In Quiroga's *pueblo*-hospital town, each tribal ward belonged to a single confraternity. These people were the first participants in the process of religious syncretism in Michoacán. They were the first natives to appropriate European styles of dress and to practice monogamous marriage. The *pueblo*-hospital confraternity members were indoctrinated as a group, then baptized en masse.

Quiroga's *Ordenanzas* outlined the responsibilities of confraternity members. New members were to be initiated in solemn ceremonies. The precise times to sing hymns, pray, walk in processions, go on pilgrimages, and study the *doctrina* also were prescribed.[52] Quiroga warned the confraternity members against taking personal pride in their religious responsibilities.[53] He also cautioned them to "properly correct and castigate" their children so that they would learn discipline and humility.[54] In addition, he prohibited drunken and "immoral" individuals from joining in the *fiestas* of the *cofradía*. (By excluding such individuals from the *fiestas* the church gained influence over the townsfolk, because no one wanted to miss the festivals.)

Don Vasco's careful instructions aimed at eliminating any "deviant" behavior in order to create a unified religious and social consciousness. In making every public action religious, however, Quiroga encased village life in a rigid ritualism. The ideal of brotherly love became part of a coercive ideology of personal sacrifice for the common good. Caring for the images of the village saint resulted in extreme economic hardship for the families charged with the responsibility for the annual *fiesta*. Nonetheless, the *cofradía* or *mayordomía* system remains the predominant characteristic of religious life of the towns and villages in Michoacán today.

Quiroga's project to make Santa Fe de la Laguna a "true Christian" utopia by employing such detailed supervision of a conquered population was ultimately a form of coercion. This is clearly evident in the harsh measures taken to exorcise nonconformers from the community. Although Don Vasco found many things to admire about the Purhépecha people—notably their communal institutions and their gentleness—his experience of them represented an early form of the "noble savage" tendency.

Quiroga and the mendicant evangelizers found that the Spanish confraternity system was the best instrument for accomplishing the social and religious transformation of Amerindian society. In contrast, the Amerindians saw it as a means to create a native network that would preserve their religious and cultural autonomy. Ultimately Quiroga's utopian idealism proved useless in relieving the day-to-day suffering of the Purhépecha. What mattered to the Purhépecha was how to stabilize their precarious world. What mattered was the rain that swept down from the volcanoes to irrigate the cornfields, and what mattered was that their children were fed and that they had the proper tribute to pay their European overlords. Yet the Purhépecha-Chichimec were accomplished survivors. Their appropriation of the *cofradía* system enabled them to maintain their religious worldview under the guise of honoring the Catholic saints. Michoacán indeed became a New World under its Spanish conquerors —but it was hardly the millennial kingdom hoped for by the clergy.

EPILOGUE

Don Vasco de Quiroga spent his last years in Michoacán making pastoral visits to the many institutions he helped establish. In 1563 he became ill and entered the hospital of Santa Fe de la Laguna to convalesce. The frail patriarch prepared his last will and testament in Pátzcuaro on January 24, 1565. The *Testamento* is a precise document in which Quiroga meticulously outlines the transfer of his pastoral responsibilities and the legacy of his favorite projects. Almost all of the *Testamento* deals with the administration of the *pueblo*-hospitals, the Colegio de San Nicolás Obispo, and the Cathedral of Santa Ana.

According to Fintan Warren, there is some confusion concerning the date and place of the bishop's death. One account states that he died on March 14 during a visit to Uruapan. But in 1573 the executor of Quiroga's will, Juan Velasco, testified that Quiroga had passed away in Pátzcuaro. A subsequent letter written by the secular Lázaro Díaz to the bishop of Verapaz states that Quiroga expired on March 20, 1565, in Pátzcuaro.

The death of Don Vasco marked the end of a generation of passionate and well-educated missionaries who hoped to impart a form of apocalyptic Christianity to the Amerindians. After Quiroga's death the community of Santa Fe de la Laguna, no longer in the limelight, slowly grew accustomed to a more modest existence. The historical record mentions it only in passing. In 1582 Quiroga's successor, Bishop Juan Medina Rincón, testified that the economy of the town was unstable,

> since it (the town's income) resulted mainly from the work and industry of the
> residents. They harvest wheat and maize and have some looms. They have one

diocesan priest who was in charge of the pueblo *and who taught* doctrina. *The town paid their 150* ducados *annually to the college as stipulated in Quiroga's will. If they had anything left, they bought ornaments for their church, something to which all the Indians were very much attached.*[1]

At some point the overall success of Don Vasco's republican dream for the township of Santa Fe must be called into question. But unfortunately we know next to nothing of the community's daily operations. Also absent from the record is how the Purhépecha responded to Quiroga's precise plans to resocialize them. History teaches us the hard lesson that even the best blueprints for social change are often ignored. Fintan Warren verifies this perspective when he cites a "disturbing piece of evidence" discovered in the mid-eighteenth century. He states that when José Moreno was compiling the first biography of Quiroga in 1766, only a partial transcript of the *Ordenanzas* could be located in the cathedral archives. Warren concludes that this probably meant that the ordinances were no longer significant two hundred years after Quiroga's death. On the other hand, some aspects of Quiroga's plans may have survived in the folk traditions of the community, especially in the *cofradía.* Yet the Rincón report states that by 1582 Santa Fe had lost about half of its two hundred households. Therefore, it is impossible to ascertain either how long the *familias* scheme was in place or how successful Quiroga's plan was.[2]

It is safe to say that Quiroga himself believed his efforts in Michoacán were successful. The tedious legal stipulations he made in his will, in order to ensure the perpetuity of his work, attest to his faith in the town's survival. In the *Testamento* the cathedral, the Colegio de San Nicolás Obispo, and the hospital-villages are woven together into a network of financial supports. To ensure their continuance Quiroga designated Felipe II and the archbishop of Mexico as the three institutions' special patrons. Furthermore, he ordered that his ordinances should be followed precisely and not altered in any way.[3]

In a limited way Don Vasco's dream persists to this day in the continued existence of the township of Santa Fe de la Laguna, in the splendid hilltop church of Santa Ana, and in the integrity of the very boundaries of the state of Michoacán. The Colegio de San Nicolás Obispo, however, was taken over by the Jesuits and moved to Valladolid in Morelia in 1580. It continued to be an important educational force in New Spain until the expulsion of the Society of Jesus in 1767. Yet the college's goal of developing a native clergy for the colonies was never realized.[4]

FIGURE 10. A couple prepares for their wedding feast

ON EVALUATING THE EVANGELIZATION OF MICHOACÁN

The issue of the successes and failures of the Catholic friars remains controversial in the religious history of Mexico. Today there exists a plethora of diverse positions that usually vary according to the degree of accommodation and resistance effected by the evangelization. According to most historians, the highly disciplined friars found a captive audience in the war-weary Amerindians. The desperate natives either were forced to convert or became Christians in great numbers, conforming to the example of their chieftains. Historians also agree that there existed, and continues to exist, a love-hate relationship between indigenous peoples and their cultural overlords.

Most observers of the religious history of Mexico detect obvious changes in the public rites of the native cultures since the conquest. It is difficult to explain the meaning of these changes, however. The historical record demonstrates that the friars themselves became more skeptical about the success of the evangelization as the first generation of mendicants died off. Scholars today argue that the acceptance of Christian ritual and theology was superficial. Most likely the bipolar absolutism of the Mesoamerican godhead, and its multilayered pantheism, absorbed and transformed Christianity's monotheistic ideals. This is clearly evident in the syncretistic process wherein the cult of the Catholic saints replaced the worship of the old anthropomorphic deities. The central question is whether the Spanish conquest and occupation left behind any vestige of the pre-Columbian religions.

In the study of religion this question is located within the complex category of analysis called syncretism. Religious syncretism usually describes a historical process where a new cultural entity is superimposed on an existing system. In the subsequent blending of the two cultures, the older system either survives through a process of acculturation or a kind of symbiosis. However, we must take care in labeling a religious tradition syncretistic, because a clear definition of change is impossible without taking into account each group's particular historical and cultural experience. In other words, the concept of syncretism is merely an interpretive tool and cannot be applied in a universal way.[5]

In this study I have focused on the religious and political changes that occurred in Iberia and Michoacán in the watershed age of the sixteenth century. Most particularly, I examined the process of "spiritual conquest" in Michoacán and the mutual adjustments of the natives and missionaries to that process, which culminated in the natives' appropriation and transformation of the Catholic saints. Special attention was devoted to historical horizons, with the assumption that a people's historical origins inform how they know them-

selves and their world. A significant part of my analysis was dedicated to il-
lustrating that each culture's religious worldview contributed to the misunderstandings that it had of the other. Spaniards and Amerindians interacted
with one another according to cultural and mythic presuppositions concerning the nature of the world in which they lived. I have attempted to clarify the
uniqueness of these two worlds and to outline the transformations experienced
by each culture after their catastrophic encounter. One simple but important
observation surfaces: that human beings and their ideals of civilization are
shaped by the dynamics of change. People respond to historical uncertainty
with some sense of peril and a small hope of survival. With this idea in mind
it is easier to understand how the Amerindians and Spaniards accommodated
themselves to one another's sociopolitical and religious contexts. Each civilization was shaped by the processes of an invisible historical trajectory. On the
field of their collision near Lake Pátzcuaro, they met and judged one another
according to the ancient forces that they believed controlled and ordered
human life.

In a fine work on the Yucatec Maya, Nancy Farriss suggests an approach
for evaluating the changes that occurred in the sixteenth century. She states
that if we view different cultures as containing sets of core ideas concerning
"the way things ought to be," it is possible to measure how one culture influences the other. Farriss asserts that scholars should use these core ideas
as interpretive tools for understanding a culture's worldview. She writes that
core concepts "provide not only the principles according to which change will
take place but also the measure of its extent; they indicate whether we are
dealing merely with a variation on a theme or an altogether new theme."[6]

Farriss maintains that it is possible to speak of a unique kind of cultural
survival in the case of the Yucatec Maya. She interprets their cultural response
to the Spanish invasion and evangelization as a conscious counteraction designed to keep the Maya cosmos in operation. The Maya's collective survival
was shaped by their reaction, which in turn determined the kind of people
they were to become. The colonization experience did not simply result in
Amerindian society existing unmodified under a veneer of Spanish customs,
as most scholars contend. In the case of the Maya, they tended to selectively
preserve central aspects of their worldview. Their deliberate responses to the
Spanish invasion not only ensured their survival but became the ideological
foundation of subsequent cultural modifications and adjustments.[7]

Farriss's ideas are also useful in examining other Amerindian cultures. Her
analysis suggests that although many indigenous cultures were transformed
under the influence of their European overlords, the transformations occurred

according to each culture's understanding of the world. This means that the indigenous people remained identifiably Amerindian in spite of the colonization efforts and their own cultural appropriations. Through their selective adoption of European ideas, customs, and values, the Amerindians were able to preserve the old cosmos and society, only in new public forms more acceptable to their colonial masters.[8] In the long run the disintegration of the Amerindian cultures depended on the level of their integration into the Western-controlled system of economic exchanges.[9]

Louise Burkhart demonstrates a similar idea of cultural accommodation in her thoughtful work *The Slippery Earth: Nahua-Christian Moral Dialogue in Sixteenth-Century Mexico.* Burkhart argues that when the first mendicants encountered the native Mexican populations, they attempted to evangelize them through moral dialogue. The earliest missionaries believed that the Amerindians would willingly convert to Christianity if they could hear the "good news" in their own language. As a consequence the friars methodically translated the Bible and catechistic texts into the native languages. Analysis of these marvelous books and of the rhetorical devices employed by the mendicants demonstrates how Spanish Catholicism was accommodated to the Aztec worldview and also how Catholicism itself was altered by the marriage of the Amerindian and European worldviews. Burkhart thus challenges the spiritual conquest thesis:

> *The friars were confronted with an impossible challenge—the remaking of an entire culture in their own image. They responded to some extent, remaking themselves: the encounter could not help but expand their own sensitivity to human diversity; the molding of their Christianity to fit the Nahua context demanded a doctrinal flexibility which, though they rarely admitted it to non-Indian audiences, is clearly evident in their Nahua writings. . . . The Nahuas, on the whole, were able to get by in the colonial social and political setting without compromising their basic ideological and moral orientation.[10]*

When the conquest of Michoacán is evaluated in light of Farriss's and Burkhart's work (and the colonization of the Yucatán), an interesting picture emerges. Subjugation and evangelization occurred much later in the Yucatán than in Michoacán. Although the conqueror of the peninsula, Francisco Montejo, arrived in 1526, the Yucatán remained a colonial backwater well into the late 1500s. Maya towns and villages located in the isolated depths of the rain forests were distant targets for the conquerors. The absence of large wealthy

urban populations in the peninsula contributed to the Spaniards' relative dis-
interest in exploring it.

On the other hand, the Purhépecha of Lake Pátzcuaro represented a dense
population located in the amiable climate of the western highlands. By the
time the Spanish arrived the Purhépecha-Chichimec were largely an urban
people. They had a well-trained, powerful army that could be used by the conquerors in further exploratory ventures, as well as a highly organized labor
force. This, together with the large silver strikes and the abundance of virgin
grasslands suitable for livestock ranches and cereal-producing *haciendas*, accelerated the Spaniards' exploration of Michoacán and intensified their need
to control the Purhépecha.

Interestingly, in Michoacán the pressure of incessant Spanish land claims
to native property also tended to confuse the issue of who "really" owned the
land. The Michoacán historian Delfina López Sarrelangue asserts that the
Vanacaze elites of the core area of Lake Pátzcuaro resisted Spanish dominance
throughout the colonial period, up to 1810. Except for the serious threat to
Spanish hegemony posed by the Chichimec Wars, however, the Purhépecha's
resistance was minimal. This was due to several factors, but foremost was the
peaceful capitulation of the *cazonci* Tangaxoan II. The *cazonci*'s actions saved
the province from the ravages of war experienced in the Valley of Anáhuac.

This is not to suggest that the people of Michoacán did not suffer from the
invasion. Many people were lost to various forms of violence, pillaging, forced
labor, and virulent epidemics. The collapse of the native social order due to
the death of so many nobles and priests, as well as the large number of *mestizo* orphans abandoned by both races, also quickened the assimilation of the
people of Michoacán. By the end of the sixteenth century, while the Maya
nobles could still claim their status as lords, the native nobility of Pátzcuaro
had lost their pre-Cortés ceremonial and economic base. After this period the
traditional distinction between elites and commoners became more and more
blurred. The subjugation of the Purhépecha thus represents a more accelerated historical process of assimilation than that of the Maya.

As far as the evangelization is concerned, however, the Maya were evangelized solely by the Franciscan order. Although the Franciscans played a
significant role in the Christianization of Michoacán, the work of the Augustinians and of Vasco de Quiroga and his seculars cannot be neglected. Furthermore, in the jungles of the Yucatán the Maya religious worldview more
clearly eclipsed Spanish Catholicism than it did in Michoacán. For more than
two centuries after the arrival of the mendicants, the people of the rain forests

successfully pursued their old rituals in the privacy of their homes. They also preserved religious ceremonial objects and sacred writings in remote caves.

The situation in Michoacán was quite different. Although the rugged terrain and the population displacement following the initial invasion seemed to promote a similar kind of underground religion, the *cazonci*'s peaceful capitulation, along with the sheer speed of the conquest, evoked a different cultural response. In the quickened atmosphere of crisis and cultural collapse, Don Vasco de Quiroga's ideals of humanitarianism and Christian charity had a critical influence on the conversion process. The catechisms and ethnological works by Maturino Gilberti and Jerónimo de Alcalá, written in the Purhépecha language, were also instrumental in more rapidly facilitating the Christianization of the people of Michoacán.

In the Yucatán, under the Franciscan provincial and bishop Diego de Landa, idolatry was dealt with severely. Beginning in 1562, Diego de Landa conducted a series of Inquisition trials at which more than forty-five hundred Maya were tortured, beaten, and forced to renounce their religion. Although this repression helped to promote the appearance of public Christian rites in the towns, it also created enmity and mistrust. The Catholic Church's aggression resulted in the retreat of the Maya religion into the jungles, and in its survival today in the form of the old agrarian rites such as forest rituals and the *milpa* ceremonies performed for rain and good harvests.[11]

In Michoacán, although Quiroga proved to be a stern *tata* to the *indios*, there was never a massive repression of the Purhépecha by church authorities. On the contrary, the Purhépecha recognized the advantages in converting to Christianity and allying themselves with Quiroga and the mendicants against their more formidable enemies, the *encomenderos* and the diseases they had brought. Compared with forced labor in the mines, public floggings in the *doctrina* towns might have seemed like a blessing. In any case, the Purhépecha took advantage of the benefits of Quiroga's *pueblo*-hospital communities. Although they were forced to renounce their old religion and to conform to the aesthetics of their mendicant masters, the Purhépecha were housed, fed, and protected from the demands of the *encomenderos*. While Don Vasco remained alive, his dream of a *república de indios* shielded the Purhépecha-Chichimec living in his diocese.

The practice of baptisms en masse also contributed to different theological understandings and different forms of religious syncretism for the Maya and the Purhépecha. In late-sixteenth-century Maya society this difference was dramatically illustrated in a series of crucifixions of young girls. Imitating the example of Jesus, Maya Christians hung the girls on crosses and then threw them into deep wells called *cenotes*. These crucifixions demonstrate that the Christian idea of sacrifice had not been appropriated correctly and that the core Maya concept of "feeding the gods" was still in place. Mass baptisms of the native populations thus promoted the syncretistic process and the survival of indigenous religious concepts.

Among today's Purhépecha, although the old gods and forces of nature are mere shadows of their pre-Columbian selves, they are still remembered in times of crisis, when dangerous events remind the people of their existence. During these critical times the original patrons of the Amerindian cosmos are appeased. For example, according to Van Zantwijk, "Villagers sometimes try to protect the crop in the fields from damage by hailstorms by frightening (or propitiating) the Rain and Thunder Gods by letting off fireworks. The fishermen sometimes bring small offerings to the lake, when there is a heavy storm and the high waves are dangerous to the dugout canoes."[12]

Concerning social and liturgical activity, it should be noted that both Maya and Purhépecha religious praxis was originally designed to keep the cosmos in operation in order to ensure the survival of the community. Farriss contends that Christianity produced little conflict between behavior and belief in the Maya private sphere. This was most obvious in the realm of food production. After the initial period of evangelization, while the Maya would invoke the Holy Trinity, they still called upon the divine forces of nature as the primary sources of fertility and production activities. The friars interpreted this behavior as mere superstition and ignorance. Their leniency in permitting agrarian rites seems to have been due to the fact that rural religion was not as threatening as the state cult. The Maya elites were considered a significant idolatrous group because their social structure linked public ritual performances to the private sphere through a network of family lineage, totems, and rites. In Michoacán, the public performance of the state religion at the *yácatas* was also considered more threatening to the establishment of Christianity than the villagers' popular practices.

The cosmic tensions between private and public worship created a dilemma for the Amerindians: worshipping the old gods invited not only military repression but also floggings by the mendicants. And yet if the gods were not cared for as the ancestors had taught, the cosmic order would surely come apart. Failing to venerate the old gods was an invitation that courted terrifying consequences. Overcoming this dilemma attests to the Amerindians' ingenuity in adapting to the rapid changes occurring in their world. The Spanish intrusion thus produced a split between the public corporate observance of Christianity and the private clandestine adherence to the old religion. The

Yucatec Maya consciously made a public adaptation to the Spaniards' practice of religion, and as a consequence Christianity became more prominent in the urban areas, especially as the friars replaced the native priests. Maya religious practices remained in the dense jungle villages as "a parallel system driven underground."[13]

The enthusiasm with which Cortés and the mendicants pursued the conversion and destroyed the focal values of the indigenous religions also influenced the many syncretisms occurring in Mexico. When the Spaniards destroyed the state cult in Tenochtitlán they caused a severe disruption in the Aztec value system. Restrictions on the public performance of sacrificial rites resulted in the eventual abandonment of the premise that the successful functioning of the universe depended on sacrificial offerings to the gods.[14] In Michoacán, the speedy decimation of the state cult and the priestly castes left only a handful of disorganized resisters and people able to offer instruction in the old religion.

In the early stages of the evangelization the Amerindians were attracted to the mendicants' spartan discipline, particularly as it contrasted with the violent and opulent behavior of the conquistadors. The Amerindians' identification with and empathy for mendicant asceticism partly accounts for the early missionaries' phenomenal success. The Franciscan evangelization was supplemented by a policy of forced acculturation of the native children in mendicant schools at Texcoco, Tlaxcala, and Huejotzingo. Each school had from six hundred to one thousand pupils, all of whom were required to learn the doctrines and rituals of Christianity. Since many Purhépecha children attended these assimilation centers, they may have become more informed about Catholicism and European culture than their Maya counterparts. The Franciscan attempt to gather Maya children into monastery schools was thwarted by the *encomenderos*, who engaged in bitter feuds with the friars because they believed that this form of relocation reduced the number of people available for forced labor and tribute.

Moreover, by the time the evangelization of the Maya occurred, the millennial ideals of the first missionaries were being called into question. The later missionaries and the post-Trent bishops mistrusted the early friars' alleged successes. This attitude was voiced most strongly at the end of the century in the writings of the later chroniclers. Gerónimo de Mendieta used the phrase "Fall of the Indian Jerusalem" to describe his disillusionment with the missionary project. Even the old Franciscan ethnographer Bernardino de Sahagún mistrusted the apparition of the Virgin of Guadalupe, characterizing her appearance as the "invention of the devil."[15] By the end of the century it had become clear to the clergy that the Amerindians had not correctly appropriated Christian moral values and metaphysical concepts. The violent action taken by Bishop Diego de Landa to curtail the Maya's underground rites was most likely fueled by this embittering awareness. In contrast, in the 1530s evangelization of Michoacán, the hope of creating a purified form of Christianity among the Purhépecha was still quite ardent.

In the last analysis the New World enterprise fell far short of its ideological goals. This was partly due to the fact that the monotheistic god of Christianity had become diluted by an incorporation of rich Mediterranean paganism. Catholicism, for all its orthodox denial, had itself become heterodoxical and pantheistic. The Catholic cosmos was inhabited by a variety of sacred beings: a triune god, a mother goddess, angels, saints, dead souls, demons, and powerful spirits in nature, among others. Catholicism was almost as densely populated as the Mesoamerican cosmos. The two religious systems encountered each other as multilayered symbol systems, and so they interacted with one another on many levels. A clean, direct translation of Christianity was thus impossible from the outset. Any observation concerning theories of cultural survival or changes in the Amerindians' worldview should take this into account, or it quickly becomes impossible to make sense of the superabundance of cultural responses to the conquest.

The mendicants did not provide uniform ideological translations for the various tribal groups they missionized, and the Amerindian cultures had no common ideological experience upon which to base judgments of Christianity. The Mesoamerican cosmos actually consisted of many cosmos, each defining and being defined by specific peoples. The Amerindians were introduced to Christian ideas and symbols through rituals that were often comparable to their own indigenous rites. However, they had different meanings for each religious concept introduced to them. Christianity had to change in the New World because it was shaped by the historical circumstances and cultural landscapes it encountered there. Moreover, the Amerindians quickly learned that they could not overcome the spiritual and material obstacles posed by the Spanish invasion until they took active control of the Christian rites. And this fact led them to look to the institution of the *cofradía* as the best mechanism for preserving their cultural traditions and maintaining control of their religious practices.

In Michoacán, Christianity did not replace the autochthonous religion at the state level, nor did it fuse with the native religion. Both religions lost out to a "syncretic parochialism": that is, private indigenous forms of venerating nature and the household gods were transformed into the Catholic cult of the saints. Furthermore, with the gradual blurring of caste distinctions and the relegation of the common folk to an agrarian socioeconomic base, only those divinities most efficacious in meeting the people's needs remained. The divine principle, the Lord and Lady of Duality, became a remote power far from ordinary human life on earth, remembered only in times of crisis.

As the indigenous nobility disappeared it became increasingly clear that the question of survival was not limited to any one group but pertained to the Amerindians as an autonomous unit. In this critical situation each culture's boundaries had to be rethought within compatible Christian categories. The appropriation and transformation of the cult of the Catholic saints had undergone a similar process in the Spanish countryside when Christianity encountered the old pagan religions of Iberia.

The new canopy of religious imagery and practice erected in Mexico in the colonial period is a monumental testament to the ongoing tensions between a doctrinal form of Roman Catholicism and the Amerindians' accommodation to it. The Amerindians venerate the Catholic saints as divine beings. The saints represent various sacred powers of the natural world that can influence human existence from beyond the phenomenal plane. It is through the veneration of the saints, and through the confraternities and sodalities dedicated to their care, that the Amerindians of Mexico have preserved their identity and dignity.

NOTES

INTRODUCTION

1. An *encomendero* was a tribute-receiving nobleman who was given an *encomienda* (grant) in the form of land, municipalities, or Amerindian laborers. For a more comprehensive discussion of Vasco de Quiroga's conflicting image in Mexico see Chapter 7 of this study.

2. Enrique Florescano, *Memory, Myth, and Time in Mexico: From the Aztecs to Independence*. O'Gorman has written a fine introductory essay that details the intellectual process in Mexican historiography. See his introduction to *Evolución política del pueblo mexicano*, by Justo Sierra. Benjamin Keen also has written an excellent study that explores the shifting attitudes and foci of scores of historians who deal with the theme of the Aztecs in the five centuries since the conquest. See Benjamin Keen, *Aztec Image in Western Thought*.

3. Keen, *Aztec Image*, 563–567.

4. Francisco López de Gómara was Cortés's first biographer. His biography, which depicts the conqueror as a hero, was written as a polemic against Las Casas' interpretation of the conquistadors as gold-hungry mercenaries who sought to forcibly convert the Amerindians. Gonzalo Fernández de Oviedo portrayed the Amerindians as "dirty, lying cowards who commit suicide out of sheer boredom, just to ruin the Spaniards by dying." See Francisco López de Gómara, *Cortés: The Life of the Conqueror by His Secretary*, trans. and ed. Lesley Byrd Simpson; and Gonzalo Fernández de Oviedo, *Historia general y natural de las Indias*, 4 vols., ed. Juan Pérez de Tudela Bueso.

5. Keen, *Aztec Image*, 293.

6. On Voltaire, Montesquieu, and Raynal see Keen, *Aztec Image*, especially the chapter entitled "The Eyes of Reason I." On Rousseau's treatment of the Amerindians see Arthur O. Lovejoy, *Essays in the History of Ideas*. In this work Lovejoy analyzes Rousseau's concept of primitivism presented in the *Discourse on Inequality*.

7. Keen, *Aztec Image*, 381. For a good perspective on the effects of the theories of Morgan and Tylor on Mexican archaeology see Ignacio Bernal, *A History of Mexican Archaeology: The Vanished Civilizations of Middle America*, especially pages 142–159.

8. I am relying here on the definition of "worldview" provided by Kees W. Bolle in Mircea Eliade, ed., *The Encyclopedia of Religion* 4:100–107. In addition, I have found two works particularly useful in formulating my understanding of communities: Anthony P. Cohen, *The Symbolic Construction of Community*; and Benedict Anderson, *Imagined Communities: Reflections on the Spread of Nationalism*.

CHAPTER ONE. THE PURHÉPECHA-CHICHIMEC OF MICHOACÁN

1. Sherburne F. Cook and Woodrow Borah, *The Indian Population of Central Mexico, 1531–1610*.

2. This section is taken from two important sources: *Atlas geográfico del estado de Michoacán;* and Robert C. West, *Cultural Geography of the Modern Tarascan Area*.

3. *Chronicles of Michoacán: The Description of the Ceremonies, Rites, Population, and Government of the Indians of the Province of Michoacán, 1540–1541*, trans. and ed. Eugene R. Craine and Reginald C. Reindorp, 11.

4. Richard Adams has written an informative work on the development of the Mesoamerican cultures from the earliest agricultural settlements to the rise of the city-states. See Richard E. W. Adams, *Prehistoric Mesoamerica*. For a comparative approach to this question see C. C. Lamberg-Karlovsky and Jeremy A. Sabloff, *Ancient Civilizations: The Near East and Mesoamerica*, 213–320. Also useful is the anthropological text by Eric Wolf that interprets the development of Mexico in terms of class struggle; see Eric Wolf, *Sons of the Shaking Earth*, 48–69. A unifying historical concept that is important to consider in the continuing development of Amerindian cultures is whether they ever existed in pristine isolation, or rather, if the Amerindians should be viewed as peoples continuously accommodating and rejecting larger international and national networks. A suggestive contemporary study which examines the complex relations between nation-states and Amerindian peoples in Latin America is Greg Urban and Joel Sherzer, eds., *Nation-States and Indians in Latin America*.

5. Lamberg-Karlovsky and Sabloff, *Ancient Civilizations*, 218–219, quoting Kent V. Flannery, "The Origins of Agriculture" in *Annual Review of Anthropology*.

6. Lamberg-Karlovsky and Sabloff, *Ancient Civilizations*, 224–225, quoting Richard S. MacNeish, "Speculation about How and Why Food Production and Village Life Developed in the Tehuacán Valley, Mexico," in *Archaeology*.

7. George Kubler, *The Art and Architecture of Ancient America: The Mexican, Mayan, and Andean Peoples*, 106–114.

8. Jacques Soustelle, *The Olmecs: The Oldest Civilization in Mexico*, 160–195.

9. Adams, *Prehistoric Mesoamerica*, 134.

10. Soustelle, *Olmecs*, 193.

11. Adams, *Prehistoric Mesoamerica*, 130.

12. Dogs were important to the pre-Columbian people for a number of reasons. Canines were bred hairless and fattened to be consumed. They were placed in tombs

to help the deceased advance through the various obstacles they encountered in their journey in the subterranean paradise. The famous canine ceramic effigies of western Mexico date from this period; see Adams, *Prehistoric Mesoamerica*, 66, 130.

13. Soustelle, *Olmecs*, 33.

14. On Teotihuacán see Wolf, *Shaking Earth*, 69–129. For an account of the Toltecs' mystical ideology from an archaeological perspective see Laurette Sejourné's controversial but thought-provoking work, *Burning Water: Thought and Religion in Ancient Mexico*.

15. Wolf, *Shaking Earth*, 94.

16. Paul Gendrop, "Mesoamerican Temples," in Eliade, *Encyclopedia of Religion*, 14:388–390.

17. Sejourné, *Burning Water*, 121.

18. Robert Ricard, *The Spiritual Conquest of Mexico: An Essay on the Apostolate and the Evangelizing Methods of the Mendicant Orders in New Spain, 1523–1572*, 176. See also John McAndrew, *The Open-Air Churches of Sixteenth-Century Mexico*.

19. Nigel Davies, *The Ancient Kingdoms of Mexico*, 141–163.

20. Davies, *Ancient Kingdoms*, 111.

21. Wolf, *Shaking Earth*, 102–129; see also Davies, *Ancient Kingdoms*, 114–130.

22. *Chronicles of Michoacán*. The manuscript, better known as *La Relación de Michoacán*, is located in the Real Biblioteca of the Escorial in Madrid. There it is known as Codex C-IV-5, though it is sometimes called the Codex of the Escorial. It contains 140 sheets, plus 3 additional pages about the Purhépecha calendar and 44 illustrations. The historian Nicolás León believes that the Escorial manuscript is a copy. Three other copies of the text also exist: one in the Peter Force Collection of the Library of Congress, a second copy in the Obadiah Rich Collection of the New York Public Library, and a third copy in the Aubin Collection of the Bibiliothéque Nationale in Paris. *The Chronicles of Michoacán* is the most important single source for recovering the culture of the Purhépecha. It was compiled around 1540, most likely by the Franciscan mendicant Fray Martín de la Coruña, with the help of Amerindian informants. It should be noted that this edition is not without its critics. Charles Gibson, in his review in the *Hispanic American Historical Review*, criticizes Craine and Reindorp for their use of the 1903 edition of the *Relación* and for the authors' failure to cite José Tudela's 1956 facsimile edition. I have examined both editions and have not found significant problems with the specific passages that I have selected from the Craine and Reindorp study. For a history of the text and good discussion of the problems of authorship see Georges Baudot, *Utopía e historia en México: Los primeros cronistas de la civilización mexicana (1520–1569)*.

23. Antonio de Mendoza belonged to one of the most powerful and prestigious families of Castile. An aristocratic cosmopolitan, he was raised in the Alhambra and was familiar with the diverse cultural influences of southern Spain. Mendoza attended the university in the early sixteenth century, when Erasmian humanism was popular at Spanish institutions of higher learning. Only a man of his stature could have dealt with the problems in New Spain. See Erika Spivakovsky, *Son of the Alhambra: Don Diego Hurtado de Mendoza, 1504–1575*.

24. J. Benedict Warren, *The Conquest of Michoacán: The Spanish Domination of the*

Tarascan Kingdom in Western Mexico, 1521–1530, 328. See also Warren's article, "Fray Jerónimo de Alcalá: Author of the *Relación de Michoacán?*" in *Americas.*

25. *Chronicles of Michoacán,* vii.

26. J. B. Warren, *Conquest of Michoacán,* 328–329.

27. For a detailed interpretation of the *Lienzo of Jucutacato* see Nicolás León, *Studies on the Archaeology of Michoacán.*

28. On the Chichimec migrations into the central valley of Mexico from Aztlán see Nigel Davies, *The Toltec Heritage: From the Fall of Tula to the Rise of Tenochtitlán,* 72–134.

29. *Chronicles of Michoacán,* xiv.

30. *Chronicles of Michoacán,* 69.

31. Fray Bernardino de Sahagún, *Historia general de las cosas de Nueva España,* ed. Ángel María Garibay K., 609–610. For a discussion of the god Tharés Upeme see José Corona Núñez, *Mitología tarasca,* 11–12.

32. J. B. Warren, *Conquest of Michoacán,* 7

33. Maturino Gilberti, *Diccionario de la lengua tarasca de Michoacán.* This is a facsimile of the Mexican edition of 1902.

34. *Chronicles of Michoacán,* xi–xii.

35. R. A. M. Van Zantwijk, *Servants of the Saints: The Social and Cultural Identity of a Tarascan Community in Mexico,* 24–27.

36. *Chronicles of Michoacán,* 103–107.

37. For a discussion of the Purhépecha nobility and of dynastic succession in pre-Hispanic Michoacán see Delfina Esmeralda López Sarrelangue, *La nobleza indígena de Pátzcuaro en la época virreinal,* 26–45.

38. Tariácuri was both a great *cazonci* and a cultural hero in Purhépecha-Chichimec history. *The Chronicles of Michoacán* devotes almost one hundred pages to his exploits. These two incidents are examples of his darker side. He is also extolled as a quasi-divine figure. See *Chronicles of Michoacán,* 129–196.

39. *Chronicles of Michoacán,* 140.

40. *Chronicles of Michoacán,* 142.

41. For two excellent discussions of family life and the institution of marriage in Purhépecha society see Van Zantwijk, *Servants of the Saints,* 36–42, 51–56; and Augustín Jacinto Zavala, "La visión del mundo y de la vida entre los Purhépecha," in Francisco Miranda, ed., *La cultura purhé: Segundo coloquio de antropología e historia regionales,* 143–158.

42. Van Zantwijk, *Servants of the Saints,* 51–56.

43. Van Zantwijk, *Servants of the Saints,* 51–56.

44. *Chronicles of Michoacán,* 40.

45. Zavala, "La visión del mundo," 151.

46. Carrasco is cited in Zavala, "La visión del mundo," 151.

47. López Sarrelangue, *La nobleza indígena,* 38–45, 109–148.

48. López Sarrelangue, *La nobleza indígena,* 38–45.

49. Van Zantwijk, *Servants of the Saints,* 46. The Aztecs had a similar system of public education for boys and girls from seven to twenty years of age that was known as *calmecac.* Interestingly, the Purhépecha did not have an educational institution for boys. Their training was conducted by their fathers or elder brothers.

50. *Chronicles of Michoacán,* 44–47.
51. *Chronicles of Michoacán,* 11.
52. *Chronicles of Michoacán,* 17.

CHAPTER TWO. THE PURHÉPECHA RELIGIOUS WORLDVIEW

1. It is difficult to speak of Mesoamerican religion using Western categories of analysis. My approach draws from phenomenological categories developed in the History of Religions school. See Mircea Eliade, *The Quest: History and Meaning in Religion;* Mircea Eliade and Joseph M. Kitagawa, eds., *The History of Religions: Essays in Methodology.* To see the fusion of Christian and Amerindian ideas in the early colonial period through the eyes of native authors see Louise M. Burkhart, *Holy Wednesday: A Nahua Drama from Early Colonial Mexico,* 98.

2. León-Portilla has explored the various theories of Ometeotl in the historiography of Náhuatl thought. See Appendix 2 in Miguel León-Portilla, *Aztec Thought and Culture: A Study of the Ancient Nahuatl Mind,* 179. He discusses the entry of the concept of the sacred dualism into Chichimec culture in *Native Mesoamerican Spirituality: Ancient Myths, Discourses, Stories, Doctrines, Hymns, Poems from the Aztec, Yucatec, Quiche-Maya and Other Sacred Writings,* 1–55.

3. Van Zantwijk, *Servants of the Saints,* 172.
4. Van Zantwijk, *Servants of the Saints,* 172.
5. Van Zantwijk, *Servants of the Saints,* 172.
6. León-Portilla, *Aztec Thought,* 221.
7. León-Portilla, *Aztec Thought,* 214–217.
8. León-Portilla, *Aztec Thought,* 206–207.
9. León-Portilla, *Aztec Thought,* 207.
10. León-Portilla, *Aztec Thought,* 217.
11. Sejourné, *Burning Water.* See the chapter entitled "The Heart of Penitence," 119–129.
12. Corona Núñez, *Mitología tarasca,* 16. Stars were symbolically represented by the sacred three-pronged staff, the *parátacuqua,* which was used to light the temple fires. The heavenly bodies were worshipped by the Náhuatl-speaking Amerindians under the name of *mamalhuaztli.*
13. Corona Núñez, *Mitología tarasca,* 39–56.
14. The Purhépecha-Chichimec were the spiritual heirs of the Toltecs and thus inherited Toltec cultural and metaphysical concepts. For a discussion of Toltec ideas of harmony and transcendence see Sejourné, *Burning Water,* 80–129; and León-Portilla, *Aztec Thought,* 62–103. For a thought-provoking analysis of the human body and the human condition in pre-Columbian thought see Alfredo López Austin, *Cuerpo humano e ideología: Concepciones de los antiguos nahuas,* 395–442. For a recent study of the idea of the soul in ancient Mexico see Furst McKeever and Jill Leslie, *The Natural History of the Soul in Ancient Mexico.* Yolotl González Torres has written a useful study that examines transcendence in terms of human sacrifice. González Torres writes that in ritual death, "the essential thing was precisely the act of killing, because with this action the energy necessary to conserve the harmony of the cosmos was liberated." See Yolotl

González Torres, *El sacrificio humano entre los mexicas*, 95–129. For a comparative perspective of Náhuatl thought from an idiomatic perspective see Louise Burkhart's *The Slippery Earth: Nahua-Christian Moral Dialogue in Sixteenth-Century Mexico*.

15. In general, human sacrifices occurred in times of crisis when the fabric of the Mesoamerican cosmos was in danger of coming undone. In these critical moments only by giving back the energy contained in human blood could the gods be sustained. One such moment for the Purhépecha came as the first Spaniards led by Cristóbal de Olid entered Tzintzuntzan. *The Chronicles of Michoacán* states, "Before the Spaniards arrived, the people of Mechuacán sacrificed eight hundred slaves held in prison." See *Chronicles of Michoacán*, 77.

16. Mircea Eliade and Lawrence Sullivan, "Center of the World," in Eliade, *Encyclopedia of Religion*, 3:166–171.

17. Eliade and Sullivan, "Center of the World," 171.

18. Corona Núñez, *Mitología tarasca*, 121–122.

19. As the anthropomorphic feline deity of rain, Tlaloc can be traced to the Olmecs. The deity appears in his heaven (Tlalocan) in the famous murals of Teotihuacán, and his temple is located next to that of the Aztec patron god Huitzilipochtli on the great pyramid of Tenochtitlán. See Fray Diego de Durán, *Book of the Gods and Rites of the Ancient Calendar*, 154–171.

20. Wheatley is quoted in David Carrasco, *Quetzalcóatl and the Irony of Empire: Myths and Prophesies in the Aztec Tradition*, 67–68.

21. J. B. Warren, *Conquest of Michoacán*, 5.

22. For a detailed analysis of the various transformations of the hummingbird in Mesoamerican cultures, see Eva Hunt, *The Transformation of the Hummingbird: Cultural Roots of a Zinacantecan Mythical Poem*.

23. Quiroga planned to build a cathedral with five naves in the shape of a human hand on the spot that the Purhépecha believed was an entryway to the subterranean paradise, but the plan proved too costly. The massive project is outlined in George Kubler, *Arquitectura mexicana del Siglo XVI*, 182, 353–354.

24. *Chronicles of Michoacán*, 121.

25. On the Purhépecha calendar see *Chronicles of Michoacán*, 241.

26. Julien Ries, "Cross," in Eliade, *Encyclopedia of Religion*, 4:158–160.

27. Sejourné, *Burning Water*, 89–94.

28. This section is based on the work of Burr Cartwright Brundage, especially his interpretation of Mesoamerican concepts of the numinous. See Burr Cartwright Brundage, "The Quality of the Numinous," in *The Fifth Sun: Aztec Gods, Aztec World*, 50–79.

29. José Corona Núñez, *Mitología tarasca*, 57–62.

30. See Pablo Velásquez Gallardo, *Diccionario de la lengua phorhépecha*. Apparently the Purhépecha had no term comparable to the Náhuatl term *teotl*, which refers to sacred power manifest in natural forms.

31. *Chronicles of Michoacán*, 103.

32. *Chronicles of Michoacán*, 20–21.

33. On Curita-caheri see Corona Núñez, *Mitología tarasca*, 85–86. For pictographs see *Chronicles of Michoacán*, Plate 19.

34. Corona Núñez, *Mitología tarasca*, 94–97.

35. Corona Núñez, *Mitología tarasca*, 97–100.

36. Corona Núñez, *Mitología tarasca,* 101–103.
37. Cristiano Grotanelli, "Agriculture," in Eliade, *Encyclopedia of Religion,* 1:139–149.
38. Grotanelli, "Agriculture," 143.
39. Soustelle, *Olmecs,* 185.
40. *Chronicles of Michoacán,* 15–16.
41. Corona Núñez, *Mitología tarasca,* 27–29.
42. Corona Núñez, *Mitología tarasca,* 63–64.
43. Seler quoted in Corona Núñez, *Mitología tarasca,* 28.
44. Corona Núñez, *Mitología tarasca,* 28.

CHAPTER THREE. THE HISTORICAL LANDSCAPE OF SPAIN

1. This section is developed from the following texts: William Bayne Fischer and Howard Bowen-Jones, *Spain: A Geographical Background; Spain and Portugal,* vol. 3, *The Peninsula;* and John A. Crow, *Spain: The Root and the Flower.*
2. Américo Castro, *The Spaniards: An Introduction to Their History,* trans. Willard F. King and Selma Margaretten, 31.
3. Crow, *Spain,* 23–24.
4. W. B. Fischer and Bowen-Jones, *Geographical Background,* 54–55.
5. The Basques have largely had no voice in the historical life of the peninsula. Castro believes that their marginalized role in Spanish history has caused the Spaniards to act, in an exaggerated way, as Castilian *hidalgos.* In the Indies, Basques were trusted to be *apartadores de oro y plata* (collectors of the king's gold and silver). See Castro, *Spaniards,* 29–31.
6. Castro, *Spaniards,* 174–208.
7. For an excellent discussion of Islamic life in the peninsula, see Miguel Asín Palacios, *Huellas de Islam.* See also Castro, *Spaniards,* 209–324. For a broader historical study see J. J. Saunders, *A History of Medieval Islam.*
8. For a discussion of Aryan Christianity in Spain see Marcelino Menéndez y Pelayo, *Historia de los heterodoxos españoles,* vol. 1, especially the chapter entitled "Herejías de la época visigoda."
9. Stanley Payne, *Spanish Catholicism: An Historical Overview,* 25. This is the best overview of Spanish Catholicism that exists in English.
10. Payne, *Spanish Catholicism,* 6.
11. Castro writes: "Peninsular life was reconstituted after the Muslim occupation in accordance with a system of castes based on one's being Christian, Moorish, or Jewish. After the disappearance of Moors and Jews from the social scene, respect for the pure lineage *(lo castizo)* of people—in other words, for their 'Old Christian' ancestry—continued to be very intense." He contends that what is known as Spanish today is a weaving of the three threads of Christianity, Islam, and Judaism. See Castro, *Spaniards,* 48–95.
12. Alister E. McGrath, *Reformation Thought: An Introduction,* 29–34. See also Marcel Bataillon, *Erasmo y España: Estudios sobre la historia espiritual del Siglo XVI,* especially Chapter 1, "Cisneros y la prereforma española."
13. On the social structure of the *cristiano* cultures in the peninsula see Lyle N.

McAlister, *Spain and Portugal in the New World, 1492–1700*, especially "Reconquest Hispania," 13–40. Also helpful is Jaime Vicens Vives, *Approaches to the History of Spain;* and Leslie Bethell, ed., *The Cambridge History of Latin America.* On Muslim society see Asín Palacios, *Huellas de Islam.* For a thorough discussion of Jewish culture see Yitzhak F. Baer, *A History of the Jews in Christian Spain.* Also indispensable for examining Reconquista society is volume 1 of Menéndez y Pelayo, *Historia de los heterodoxos.*

14. Payne, *Spanish Catholicism*, 24.

15. Payne, *Spanish Catholicism*, 24.

16. Payne, *Spanish Catholicism*, 24.

17. Payne, *Spanish Catholicism*, 24–25.

18. McAlister, *Spain and Portugal*, 39–40.

19. See Chapter 1 of Roland Monsier, *Social Hierarchies, 1450 to the Present*, trans. Peter Evans.

20. Payne, *Spanish Catholicism*, 27.

21. Payne, *Spanish Catholicism*, 32.

22. Payne, *Spanish Catholicism*, 9.

23. Castro, *Spaniards*, 380.

24. Castro, *Spaniards*, 381.

25. Castro, *Spaniards*, 422–426.

26. Castro, *Spaniards*, 382–419.

27. Castro, *Spaniards*, 471–472.

28. Cited in Castro, *Spaniards*, 411.

29. Cited in Castro, *Spaniards*, 411.

30. Castro, *Spaniards*, 414.

31. Payne, *Spanish Catholicism*, 25.

CHAPTER FOUR. RELIGION IN SPAIN ON THE EVE OF THE CONQUEST

1. John Lynch, *Spain under the Hapsburgs*, 1:1.

2. Lynch, *Spain under the Hapsburgs*, 1:15.

3. Lynch, *Spain under the Hapsburgs*, 1:7.

4. "Degenerate" Christianity must be understood as an imperial or high-church characterization of the popular beliefs and religious customs that had developed in the peninsula during the Muslim occupation. It refers to the heterodoxical thinking of the diverse cultures that make up Spain and represents a critique of the materialism of medieval Catholicism. For a discussion of popular beliefs in the sixteenth century see William Christian, *Local Religion in Sixteenth-Century Spain.*

5. Payne, *Spanish Catholicism*, 39.

6. For a historical analysis of the *converso* phenomenon see Baer, *Jews in Christian Spain*, 2:244–299. An account of medieval anti-Semitism among the mendicant friars can be found in Jeremy Cohen, *The Friars and the Jews.* The *conversos* were barred entry into New Spain during the sixteenth century. However, many wealthy families bribed or bought their way into the Americas. See also Alicia Gojman Golberg, *Los conversos en la Nueva España.*

7. Payne, *Spanish Catholicism*, 44–52. The Catholic Reformation had as its goal

the standardization of the Roman liturgy and the establishment of the ecclesiastical Church. In Spain, this was accomplished through the institutionalization of the Inquisition, which sought to establish a uniform religion in the peninsula. In practice, the Inquisition often reflected Spanish Christian racism against various populations living amongst them, especially people of Moorish and Jewish descent. See Henry Kamen, *Inquisition and Society in Spain;* and Edwards Peters, *Inquisition.*

8. W. Eugene Shields, *King and Church: The Rise and Fall of the Patronato Real,* 61–71.

9. Payne, *Spanish Catholicism,* 49–50.

10. Christian, *Local Religion,* 20–21.

11. Christian, *Local Religion,* 3–22.

12. Christian, *Local Religion,* 36–37, 143–146.

13. Christian, *Local Religion,* 23–69.

14. Victor Turner and Edith Turner, *Image and Pilgrimage in Christian Culture,* 140–171.

15. Turner and Turner, *Image and Pilgrimage,* 155.

16. Turner and Turner, *Image and Pilgrimage,* 21.

17. On the image of the Nazarene in the art of Renaissance Europe see Leo Steinberg, *The Sexuality of Christ in Renaissance Art and in Modern Oblivion.*

18. Payne, *Spanish Catholicism,* 44.

19. On Catholicism in Mexico today see William Madsen, *The Virgin's Children;* Anita Brenner, *Idols behind the Altars;* and John Ingham, *Mary, Michael, and Lucifer: Folk Catholicism in Central Mexico.*

20. Menéndez y Pelayo, *Historia de los heterodoxos,* 2:209–350.

21. For a fine discussion in English of mysticism among the mendicant orders see E. Allison Peers, *Studies of the Spanish Mystics.*

22. Castro asserts that although a great number of the Illuminists were Jewish, the influence of Muslim mystics (especially the Sufis) in the movement cannot be overestimated. See Castro, *Spaniards,* 331. Bataillon has demonstrated that Muslim and Jewish *conversos* were particularly interested in the mode of spirituality proposed by Erasmus. See Bataillon, *Erasmo y España,* 166–225. On the Spanish mystics see Peers, *Spanish Mystics.*

23. Concerning the doctrine of *limpieza de sangre,* Castro writes, "In the sixteenth century . . . purity of the blood would become a basic thought pattern of noble and ecclesiastical society as a result of the preoccupation with which the converts had . . . injected it." He states caustically that as the most just cause gives rise to the most injustice, "the frantic opposition to the Jews was impregnated, through dramatic mimicry, with the habits of its adversary." See Castro, *Spaniards,* 76.

24. Bataillon calls the experience of the Alumbrado devotees *un sentimiento vivo de la gracia.* See Bataillon, *Erasmo y España,* 166–167.

25. Peers, *Spanish Mystics,* 1:65–106.

26. Osuna is quoted in Peers, *Spanish Mystics,* 1:68–69.

27. Peers, *Spanish Mystics,* 1:109–181.

28. Quoted in Peers, *Spanish Mystics,* 1:125.

29. Quoted in Peers, *Spanish Mystics,* 1:124. Teresa does not differentiate between

ideas of the mind, soul, or spirit: "They all seem the same to me, though the soul sometimes issues from itself like a fire that is burning and has become wholly flame, and
sometimes this fire increases with great force" (Peers, *Spanish Mystics,* 1:128).

30. Bataillon, *Erasmo y España,* 69–71.

31. Bataillon, *Erasmo y España,* 176–178. See also Julio Caro Baroja, *The World of
the Witches.*

32. Paul Oskar Kristeller, *Renaissance Thought: The Classic, Scholastic, and Humanist
Strains,* 8–9.

33. Kristeller, *Renaissance Thought,* 9–10.

34. Kristeller, *Renaissance Thought,* 10.

35. Bataillon, *Erasmo y España,* 1–2.

36. Lynch, *Spain under the Hapsburgs,* 1:65.

37. Lynch, *Spain under the Hapsburgs,* 1:66–67. On the effect of Luther's movement
in Spain see Bataillon, *Erasmo y España,* 22–36.

38. Peter Gay, *The Enlightenment: An Interpretation,* 274.

39. Richard L. DeMolen, *The Spirituality of Erasmus of Rotterdam,* 1–15.

40. Erasmus is quoted in Lynch, *Spain under the Hapsburgs,* 1:71. For a thorough
treatment of the events surrounding Cisneros's invitation to Erasmus see Bataillon,
Erasmo y España, 77–78.

41. Bataillon argues that Erasmus's popularity in Spain among intellectuals and
Alumbrados was due to his advocation of a brand of Pauline mysticism that employed
militant metaphors. Erasmus imitates the "soldier of God" metaphor of Saint Paul's
Letter to the Ephesians when he states, "Put on the Armor of God." Bataillon makes
this point in his prologue to the Spanish edition of *The Enchiridion;* see Marcel Bataillon, prologue to Erasmus, *El enquiridion o manual del caballero cristiano,* ed. Dámaso
Alonso, 8–84. See also *The Enchiridion of Erasmus,* trans. and ed. Raymond Himelick.

42. *Enchiridion of Erasmus,* 15.

43. *Enchiridion of Erasmus,* 37.

44. John C. Olin, ed., *Christian Humanism and the Reformation: Selected Writings of
Erasmus,* 8.

45. Olin, *Christian Humanism,* 10.

46. From *In Praise of Folly,* cited in Olin, *Christian Humanism,* 13.

47. Lynch, *Spain under the Hapsburgs,* 1:71.

48. Peggy Liss, *Mexico under Spain, 1521–1556: Society and the Origins of Nationality,* 80.

CHAPTER FIVE. THE CONQUEST OF MICHOACÁN
AND THE APPOINTMENT OF VASCO DE QUIROGA

1. *Chronicles of Michoacán,* 55–60.

2. *Chronicles of Michoacán,* 55–60.

3. Gerónimo de Mendieta, *Historia eclesiástica indiana,* 375–379.

4. Pablo Beaumont, *Crónica de Michoacán,* cited in J. B. Warren, *Conquest of Michoacán,* 25–26.

5. J. B. Warren, *Conquest of Michoacán,* 28.

6. J. B. Warren, *Conquest of Michoacán,* 28. For a discussion of the demographic de-

cline in America that integrates ecology and politics see William H. McNeill, *Plagues and People*, especially the chapter "Transoceanic Exchanges, 1500–1700."

7. *Chronicles of Michoacán*, 68.

8. J. B. Warren, *Conquest of Michoacán*, 29–31.

9. Hernán Cortés, *Letters from Mexico*, ed. Anthony R. Pagden.

10. Bernal Díaz del Castillo, *Historia verdadera de la conquista de la Nueva España*, ed. Miguel León-Portilla, 2:74–75.

11. Cristóbal de Olid had joined the mainland expedition in Cuba. According to Bernal Díaz del Castillo, he was a close confidant of Cortés. Olid was captain general of three divisions. Cortés had appointed him quartermaster of the army and charged him with the responsibility of guarding Moctecuhzoma. He participated in the conquest of Michoacán and Pánuco. He was eventually beheaded by Cortés's cousin, Francisco de Las Casas, for leading a rebellion in the Honduras. See J. B. Warren, *Conquest of Michoacán*, 42. Also, for a pro-Cortés account see López de Gómara, *Cortés*, 365–369.

12. *Chronicles of Michoacán*, 70–71.

13. *Chronicles of Michoacán*, 72.

14. For a discussion of why the Amerindians viewed the Spaniards as gods see David Carrasco, *Quetzalcóatl*, 148–205. Carrasco argues that the fall of the Aztecs can be attributed in great part to the impact of the Quetzalcóatl prophecy.

15. *Chronicles of Michoacán*, 72–73.

16. J. B. Warren, *Conquest of Michoacán*. See Appendix B, 260–285.

17. J. B. Warren, *Conquest of Michoacán*, 53–54, 67–69.

18. J. B. Warren, *Conquest of Michoacán*, 71.

19. J. B. Warren, *Conquest of Michoacán*, 73.

20. J. B. Warren, *Conquest of Michoacán*, 78–79. For a complete list of Cortés's tributary towns along with a list of the early *encomenderos* of Michoacán see Appendix B in J. B. Warren, *Conquest of Michoacán*, 260–285.

21. J. B. Warren, *Conquest of Michoacán*, 70.

22. Cortés, *Letters from Mexico*, particularly the letter dated September 11, 1526, that is addressed to Carlos V.

23. For a thorough discussion of royal administration in the colonies see L. E. Fischer, *Viceregal Administration in the Spanish American Colonies*, 99–101.

24. J. B. Warren, *Conquest of Michoacán*, 123.

25. J. B. Warren, *Conquest of Michoacán*, 135–136.

26. Lesley Byrd Simpson, *The Encomienda in New Spain: The Beginning of Spanish Mexico*, 74–75.

27. J. B. Warren, *Conquest of Michoacán*, 143. For a contemporary account of Guzmán see Donald E. Chipman, *Nuño de Guzmán and the Province of Pánuco in New Spain, 1518–1533*.

28. Joaquín García Icazbalceta, *Don Fray Juan de Zumárraga: Primer obispo y arzobispo de México*, ed. Rafael Aguayo Spencer and Antonio Castro Leal, 1:27–125. Volume 1 contains valuable information on the relationship between Zumárraga and the first Audiencia.

29. Icazbalceta, *Juan de Zumárraga*, 2:190.

30. Icazbalceta, *Juan de Zumárraga*, vol. 2, especially Chapter 5, 49–67.

31. Ricard, *Spiritual Conquest,* 258.
32. For the details of this event see Icazbalceta, *Juan de Zumárraga,* 2:57–62.
33. Fray Toribio de Benavente Motolinía, *Motolinía's History of the Indians of New Spain,* trans. Francis Borgia Steck, 13–14.
34. Ricard, *Spiritual Conquest,* 239.
35. J. B. Warren, *Conquest of Michoacán,* 144.
36. J. B. Warren, *Conquest of Michoacán,* 146.
37. J. B. Warren, *Conquest of Michoacán,* 148.
38. J. B. Warren, *Conquest of Michoacán,* 214.
39. J. B. Warren, *Conquest of Michoacán,* 221.
40. J. B. Warren, *Conquest of Michoacán,* 233.
41. *The Chronicles of Michoacán* states that an embassy of Purhépecha brought back from Tenochtitlán an endemic disease called *cocolitztli,* probably measles or smallpox. For a discussion of the population of Michoacán in this period, see Cook and Borah, *Indian Population.*
42. Nicolás Sánchez-Albornoz, "The Population of Colonial Spanish America," in Bethell, *Cambridge History,* 2:7. See pages 805–811 of the same volume for a detailed bibliographical essay on the indigenous populations in the Americas.
43. Bartolomé de Las Casas, *In Defense of the Indies,* trans. Herma Briffault. Las Casas' portrait of the violent and brutal Spaniard and of the Amerindian as his innocent victim has led in part to the "Black Legend." See Charles Gibson, ed., *The Black Legend: Anti-Spanish Attitudes in the Old World and the New.*
44. McNeill, *Plagues and People,* 175–207; and Sánchez-Albornoz, "Colonial Spanish America," 3–35. See also Charles Gibson, *The Aztecs under Spanish Rule: A History of the Indians in the Valley of Mexico, 1519–1810,* especially Appendix 4, 448–451.
45. François Chevalier, *Land and Society in Colonial Mexico: The Great Hacienda,* trans. Alvin Eustis and ed. Lesley Byrd Simpson, 84–116. The chapter entitled "The Preponderance of Cattle Raising" gives the reader an idea of the immense dimensions of the livestock problem for the Amerindians.
46. Charles Gibson, *Spain in America,* 49.
47. On the rich silver strikes in Zacatecas see Philip Wayne Powell, *Soldiers, Indians, and Silver.*
48. Gibson, *Spain in America,* 65.
49. Simpson, *Encomienda in New Spain,* viii.
50. George Foster, *Tzintzuntzan: Mexican Peasants in a Changing World,* 3–16.
51. J. B. Warren, *Conquest of Michoacán,* 158.
52. See Florescano, *Memory, Myth, and Time,* 110. There are only a few ethnographies on contemporary Purhépecha culture. See Van Zantwijk, *Servants of the Saints;* also Robert West, *Cultural Geography of the Modern Tarascan Area.* For an ethnography by a Mexican author see Miranda, *La cultura purhé.* See also Foster, *Tzintzuntzan.*
53. Don Vasco's birthplace is verified in his will. See Don Vasco de Quiroga's *Testamento,* reproduced in Rafael Aguayo Spencer, *Don Vasco de Quiroga: Taumaturgo de la organización social.*
54. Aguayo Spencer, *Don Vasco de Quiroga: Taumaturgo,* 193, n. 3.
55. Felipe de Gándara, *Nobilario, armas y triunfos de Galicia hechos heróicos de sus hijos y elogios de su nobleza y de la mayor de España,* 284. The Quiroga family's genealogy is

mapped out in Fintan B. Warren, *Vasco de Quiroga and His Pueblo-Hospitals of Santa Fe,* 9–11.

56. John A. Crow, *Spain: The Root and the Flower,* 17.

57. Manuel Toussaint, *Pátzcuaro,* 24.

58. Quiroga's correction was made in the apostolic brief *Exponi nobis,* dated July 8, 1550. See F. B. Warren, *Vasco de Quiroga,* 11.

59. F. B. Warren, *Vasco de Quiroga,* 12.

60. F. B. Warren, *Vasco de Quiroga,* 13.

61. Stafford Poole, *Pedro Moya de Contreras: Catholic Reform and Royal Power in New Spain, 1571–1591,* 10–12.

62. Marcel Bataillon, "Vasco de Quiroga et Bartolomé de Las Casas," *Revista de Historia de América.*

63. F. B. Warren, *Vasco de Quiroga,* 14.

64. F. B. Warren, *Vasco de Quiroga,* 12.

65. F. B. Warren, *Vasco de Quiroga,* 14–15.

66. F. B. Warren, *Vasco de Quiroga,* 15.

67. F. B. Warren, *Vasco de Quiroga,* 18–20.

68. F. B. Warren, *Vasco de Quiroga,* 19.

69. F. B. Warren, *Vasco de Quiroga,* 21; Psalms 4, 6.

CHAPTER SIX. THE CHRISTIANIZATION OF THE PURHÉPECHA

1. F. B. Warren, *Vasco de Quiroga,* 28.

2. The Purhépecha still refer to Quiroga as Tata Vasco. *Tata* is a term of endearment akin to the English word "Daddy." The thesis that Quiroga assumed the political and religious functions vacated by the *cazonci* is presented by Wigberto Jiménez Moreno in Carlos Herrejón Perredo, ed., *Humanismo y ciencia en la formación de México: Quinto coloquio de antropología e historia regionales,* 151. See also William Taylor, *Magistrates of the Sacred: Priests and Parishioners in Eighteenth-Century Mexico,* 450.

3. Icazbalceta, *Juan de Zumárraga,* 1:107–108.

4. Herrejón Perredo, *Humanismo y ciencia,* 137. The essay by Francisco Miranda entitled "Vasco de Quiroga, artífice humanista de la provincia de Michoacán" is particularly relevant.

5. José Bravo Ugarte, *Historia sucinta de Michoacán,* 64.

6. Bravo Ugarte, *Historia sucinta,* 62.

7. F. B. Warren, *Vasco de Quiroga,* 85.

8. F. B. Warren, *Vasco de Quiroga,* 85.

9. Kubler, *Arquitectura mexicana,* 353–360.

10. Herrejón Perredo, *Humanismo y ciencia,* 137.

11. The last will and testament of Vasco de Quiroga is published in Aguayo Spencer, *Don Vasco de Quiroga: Taumaturgo,* 273–292.

12. Vasco de Quiroga, *Información en derecho del licenciado Quiroga sobre algunas provisiones del Real Consejo de las Indias,* ed. Paulino Castañeda Delgado, 142.

13. Aguayo Spencer, *Don Vasco de Quiroga: Taumaturgo,* 122.

14. Quiroga, *Información en derecho,* 142.

15. Ricard, *Spiritual Conquest,* 1–12.

16. Peter Gerhard, *A Guide to the Historical Geography of New Spain*, 38. For a complete list of the Franciscan houses and their history in Michoacán see Fray Isidro Félix de Espinosa, *Crónica de la Provincia Franciscana de los Apóstoles San Pedro y San Pablo de Michoacán*.

17. Bravo Ugarte, *Historia sucinta*, 50.

18. Nicolás P. Navarrete, *Historia de la Provincia Agustiniana de San Nicolás de Tolentino de Michoacán*.

19. Bravo Ugarte, *Historia sucinta*, 54–55.

20. Juan de Zumárraga, "Carta de don Fray Juan de Zumárraga al Príncipe don Felipe. México, 2 de junio 1544," in Mariano Cuevas, *Documentos inéditos del Siglo XVI para la historia de México*, 120.

21. Joachim of Fiore's interpretation of history appears throughout the course of European history "from Müntzer in the sixteenth century through Campanella in the seventeenth and Lessing in the eighteenth centuries. When translated into secular terminology the 'three states' of Joachimism became, in the nineteenth century, the dominant philosophy of history ending in a utopia." See Frank E. Manuel and Fritzie P. Manuel, *Utopian Thought in the Western World*, 33–34; Delno C. West and Sandra Zimdars-Swartz, *Joachim of Fiore: A Study in Spiritual Perception and History*; and Marjorie Reeves and Warwick Gould, *Joachim of Fiore and the Myth of the Eternal Evangel in the Nineteenth Century*. See also Bernard McGinn, *The Calabrian Abbot: Joachim of Fiore in the History of Western Thought*.

22. Revelation 21.1–22.5.

23. John Leddy Phelan, *The Millennial Kingdom of the Franciscans in the New World: A Study in the Writings of Gerónimo de Mendieta, 1525–1604*, 103. See the chapter entitled "The Apocalypse in the Age of Discovery," 17–27.

24. Bethell, *Cambridge History*, 1:511.

25. Herrejón Perredo, *Humanismo y ciencia*, 114.

26. Sahagún, *Historia general*, 17.

27. Sahagún, *Historia general*, 17.

28. Herrejón Perredo, *Humanismo y ciencia*, 114.

29. Herrejón Perredo, *Humanismo y ciencia*, 119.

30. *Chronicles of Michoacán*, vii.

31. Ricard, *Spiritual Conquest*, 48–49.

32. For a complete list of the native-language works published in sixteenth-century New Spain see Ricard, *Spiritual Conquest*, 406–414.

33. Herrejón Perredo, *Humanismo y ciencia*, 120–121.

34. Herrejón Perredo, *Humanismo y ciencia*, 120.

35. Herrejón Perredo, *Humanismo y ciencia*, 121.

36. James Lockhart, *The Nahuas after the Conquest: A Social and Cultural History of the Indians of Central Mexico, Sixteenth through Eighteenth Centuries*, 203.

CHAPTER SEVEN. *INFORMACIÓN EN DERECHO* QUIROGA'S REPORT TO THE ROYAL COUNCIL OF THE INDIES

1. Quiroga, *Información en derecho*.

2. Quiroga, *Información en derecho*, 227.

3. My interpretation of Quirogan humanism is grounded in the work of Anthony Pagden. Pagden argues that the ambiguity of meaning surrounding Quiroga's political and religious philosophy results from historians' confusion about the meaning of humanism. He states that a number of humanists like Erasmus, More, and Lefevre d'Etaples were concerned with the primacy of the world and with the role of the human being as a person in it. These humanists were theologically liberal, because they were concerned with the development of personhood. However, many schoolmen were neo-Thomist Scholastics, like Sepúlveda and Melchor Cano. Undoubtedly theological conservatives, they were shaped to a great extent by the Counter Reformation. In Quiroga, Pagden contends, "we are dealing with legal humanism, the humanism of Alciato and Connan, rather than the humanism of Valla and Bruni." Legal humanism emphasized the Roman legal tradition and the civic values of Ciceronian moral philosophy. This amounted to placing the human or positive law above the natural law. See Anthony Pagden, "The Humanism of Vasco de Quiroga's *Información en derecho*," in *Humanismus und Neue Welt*.

4. Pagden, "Humanism," 133, n. 2.

5. Both the *Ordenanzas* and the *Letter of 1531* are published in Aguayo Spencer, *Don Vasco de Quiroga: Taumaturgo*.

6. Gibson, *Spain in America*, 52–53.

7. Gibson, *Spain in America*, 59. For a work that analyzes Spanish just-war theories and colonization see Lewis Hanke, *The Spanish Struggle for Justice*.

8. DeMolen, *Spirituality of Erasmus*, 182.

9. Thomas More, *The Best State of the Commonwealth, the Discourse of the Extraordinary Character, Raphael Hythlodaeus, as Reported by the Renowned Figure, Thomas More, Citizen and Sheriff of the Famous City of Great Britain London*, ed. Edward Surtz.

10. Leslie Bethell, ed., *Colonial Spanish America*, 77–82.

11. Pagden, "Humanism," 137.

12. Pagden, "Humanism," 137.

13. Quiroga, *Información en derecho*, 141.

14. Quiroga, *Información en derecho*, 142.

15. Quiroga, *Información en derecho*, 200.

16. Pagden, "Humanism," 138.

17. Quiroga, *Información en derecho*, 160–161.

18. Quiroga, *Información en derecho*, 256.

19. Quiroga, *Información en derecho*, 260.

20. Quiroga, *Información en derecho*, 148.

21. Quiroga, *Información en derecho*, 70–71.

22. Quiroga, *Información en derecho*, 139–140.

23. Quiroga, *Información en derecho*, 74–75.

24. Quiroga, *Información en derecho*, 81.

25. Quiroga, *Información en derecho*, 199–200.

26. McGrath, *Reformation Thought*, 32. See also Kristeller, *Renaissance Thought*.

27. Pagden, "Humanism," 140.

28. Quiroga, *Información en derecho*, 98.

29. Quiroga, *Información en derecho*, 268.

30. Quiroga, *Información en derecho*, 271.

31. Quiroga, *Información en derecho*, 160.
32. Quiroga, *Información en derecho*, 269.
33. Quiroga, *Información en derecho*, 147.
34. Quiroga, *Información en derecho*, 90.
35. Quiroga, *Información en derecho*, 91.
36. Quiroga, *Información en derecho*, 269.
37. Quiroga, *Información en derecho*, 269–270.
38. Quiroga, *Información en derecho*, 273.
39. Quiroga, *Información en derecho*, 273.
40. Quiroga, *Información en derecho*, 107–108.
41. Lyle N. McAlister, *Spain and Portugal in the New World, 1492–1700*, 170.
42. Quiroga, *Información en derecho*, 107.
43. Quiroga, *Información en derecho*, 151–152.
44. Quiroga, *Información en derecho*, 151–152.
45. Ricard, *Spiritual Conquest*, 143.
46. Quiroga, *Información en derecho*, 168.
47. Quiroga, *Información en derecho*, 168.

CHAPTER EIGHT. THE UTOPIAN EXPERIMENT SANTA FE DE LA LAGUNA

1. *Chronicles of Michoacán*, 57.
2. McAlister, *Spain and Portugal*, 161–163.
3. F. B. Warren, *Vasco de Quiroga*, 79.
4. *A.G.I., Justicia, leg. 187. ramo 1*, cited in F. B. Warren, *Vasco de Quiroga*, 79.
5. *A.G.I., Justicia, leg. 187. ramo 1*, cited in F. B. Warren, *Vasco de Quiroga*, 80.
6. F. B. Warren, *Vasco de Quiroga*, 80.
7. *A.G.I., Justicia, leg. 187. ramo 1*, cited in F. B. Warren, *Vasco de Quiroga*, 81.
8. Erasmus of Rotterdam, quoted in Carlos M. N. Eire, *War against the Idols: The Reformation of Worship from Erasmus to Calvin*, 33.
9. Eire, *War against the Idols*, 37.
10. Cited in F. B. Warren, *Vasco de Quiroga*, 82.
11. Aguayo Spencer, *Don Vasco de Quiroga: Taumaturgo*, 422.
12. The clearest example of this practice is the mass baptisms of the Amerindians. Ricard writes that baptism was administered to the Indians without delay, the custom being to baptize them in great numbers. When a local indigenous ruler was converted and baptized, the people of his village also asked to be baptized. The Franciscans had baptized more than one million Amerindians by 1524. Fray Pedro de Gante writes in a letter dated June 27, 1529, of having baptized fourteen thousand people daily. See Ricard, *Spiritual Conquest*, 83–95.
13. Don Vasco had started a hospital-community outside Mexico City before he established Santa Fe de la Laguna. See F. B. Warren, *Vasco de Quiroga*, 43–54.
14. Aguayo Spencer, *Don Vasco de Quiroga: Taumaturgo*, 43.
15. Juan José Moreno, *Fragmentos de la vida y virtudes del V. Illmo. y Rmo. Sr. Dr. Don Vasco de Quiroga primer obispo de la Santa Iglesia Catedral de Michoacán, y fundador del Real,*

y Primitivo Colegio de S. Nicolás Obispo de Valladolid, 1766, ed. Jorge Diez González Cosio, cited in F. B. Warren, *Vasco de Quiroga,* 85.

16. F. B. Warren, *Vasco de Quiroga,* 87.

17. For a description of the deeded land see F. B. Warren, *Vasco de Quiroga,* 88.

18. For a list of the properties of the *encomendero* Juan Infante see Carlos S. Paredes Martinez, "El tributo indígena en la región del lago de Pátzcuaro," in *Michoacán en el siglo XVI,* particularly the subsection entitled "El sistema tributario bajo la encomienda de Juan Infante."

19. Paredes, *Michoacán en el siglo XVI,* 47.

20. F. B. Warren, *Vasco de Quiroga,* 90. While in Spain Infante married Catalina Samaniego, who was a close relative of the royal secretary Juan de Sámano. Through this influential connection he was able to reverse the Audiencia's decision.

21. F. B. Warren, *Vasco de Quiroga,* 91.

22. F. B. Warren, *Vasco de Quiroga,* 93.

23. F. B. Warren, *Vasco de Quiroga,* 93.

24. F. B. Warren, *Vasco de Quiroga,* 94.

25. F. B. Warren, *Vasco de Quiroga,* 95.

26. F. B. Warren, *Vasco de Quiroga,* 97.

27. F. B. Warren, *Vasco de Quiroga,* 98.

28. F. B. Warren, *Vasco de Quiroga,* 103.

29. The relationship between the structure of Thomas More's *Utopia* and Vasco de Quiroga's *Ordenanzas* has been well established by Silvio Zavala. See Silvio Zavala, *Recuerdo de Vasco de Quiroga.*

30. Quentin Skinner, "Sir Thomas More's *Utopia* and the Language of Renaissance Humanism," in Anthony Pagden, ed., *The Languages of Political Theory in Early-Modern Europe,* 128–129.

31. Skinner, "Thomas More's *Utopia,*" 142–143.

32. F. B. Warren, *Vasco de Quiroga,* 35.

33. There has been considerable investigation in recent years of the confraternity and ritual kinship *(compadrazgo)* in the Amerindian *pueblos.* Two works stand out for their scholarly attempts to explain the *cofradía* as an instrument of change in the syncretic process: see Hugo G. Nutini and Betty Bell, *Ritual Kinship: The Structure and Historical Development of the Compadrazgo System in Rural Tlazcala;* and Hugo G. Nutini, *Todos Santos in Rural Tlazcala: A Syncretic, Expressive, and Symbolic Analysis of the Cult of the Dead.* For a discussion of the *cofradía* among the Purhépecha in the village of Ihuatsio, Michoacán, see Van Zantwijk, *Servants of the Saints.* For a Mexican perspective see Josefina Muriel, "Las cofradías hospitalarias en la formación de la conciencia communitaria," in Miranda, *La cultura purhé,* 225–236.

34. F. B. Warren, *Vasco de Quiroga,* 36–42; Aguayo Spencer, *Don Vasco de Quiroga: Taumaturgo,* 243–269.

35. F. B. Warren, *Vasco de Quiroga,* 38. By selecting the *pueblo*-hospital town model, Quiroga demonstrates that he recognized the value of the Amerindian social order, since the model of township he selected parallels the pre-Columbian town, the *altepetl.* Quiroga reshapes the indigenous social pattern to conform to the sixteenth-century Spanish-style *municipio.* To this basic structure he adds the ideal of a terrestrial utopia

popular within the humanist literature of the 1530s. For a copious analysis of Meso-american territorial patterns see Lockhart, *Nahuas after the Conquest,* 28. For a very fine appraisal of contemporary indigenous townships in central Mexico see John Monaghan, *The Covenants with Earth and Rain: Exchange, Sacrifice, and Revelation in Mixtec Sociality,* 244.

36. F. B. Warren, *Vasco de Quiroga,* 41.
37. Aguayo Spencer, *Don Vasco de Quiroga: Taumaturgo,* 257–258.
38. F. B. Warren, *Vasco de Quiroga,* 39.
39. F. B. Warren, *Vasco de Quiroga,* 39.
40. F. B. Warren, *Vasco de Quiroga,* 39.
41. F. B. Warren, *Vasco de Quiroga,* 40.
42. F. B. Warren, *Vasco de Quiroga,* 42.
43. Aguayo Spencer, *Don Vasco de Quiroga: Taumaturgo,* 257–258.
44. Muriel, "Las cofradías hospitalarias," 230.
45. Van Zantwijk, *Servants of the Saints,* 41.
46. Ricard, *Spiritual Conquest,* 176.
47. Muriel, "Las cofradías hospitalarias," 227–228.
48. Muriel, "Las cofradías hospitalarias," 227–228.
49. Muriel, "Las cofradías hospitalarias," 226–235.
50. Muriel, "Las cofradías hospitalarias," 229.
51. Muriel, "Las cofradías hospitalarias," 229.
52. Muriel, "Las cofradías hospitalarias," 230–231.
53. Quiroga, *Información en derecho,* 258.
54. Aguayo Spencer, *Don Vasco de Quiroga: Taumaturgo,* 253.

EPILOGUE

1. F. B. Warren, *Vasco de Quiroga,* 115.
2. F. B. Warren, *Vasco de Quiroga,* 118–119.
3. For the *Testamento* see Aguayo Spencer, *Don Vasco de Quiroga: Taumaturgo,* 273–292.
4. For a discussion of the Colegio of San Nicolás Obispo see Bravo Ugarte, *Historia sucinta,* 122–124. The training of a lay and clerical elite was essential for the perpetuation of the missionaries' efforts. However, the mendicants were only partially successful in training a group of lay catechists, and they completely failed in their attempt to create a native clergy. The Colegio de Santiago Tlatelolco, which was designed to be the first native seminary in the New World, was unable to provide the indigenous population with a single priest of their own race. While the early mendicants knew that a colonial church could not survive on a purely European base, they were vigorously opposed by the anti-Amerindian colonials. The latter faction felt that hispanicizing the natives was preferable to creating an indigenous form of Christianity. This rendered the Catholic Church a foreign institution throughout the sixteenth century and beyond. When indigenous priests did appear in the colonial period they were relegated to inferior positions. See Ricard, "Training an Elite: The Problem of a Native Clergy," in *Spiritual Conquest,* 217–238.

5. For an evaluation of religious syncretism see Carsten Colpe, "Syncretism," in Eliade, *Encyclopedia of Religion*, 14:218–227.

6. Nancy M. Farriss, *Maya Society under Colonial Rule: The Collective Enterprise of Survival*, 8. For a classic work on the spiritual conquest of the Yucatec Maya see Inga Clendinnen, *Ambivalent Conquests: Maya and Spaniard in Yucatan, 1517-1570*. Also, a very fine study that explores how today's Maya of Santiago Chimaltenango define their community and their distinctiveness is John M. Watanabe, *Maya Saints and Souls in a Changing World*.

7. Farriss, *Maya Society*, 9. Many fine studies have recently appeared which examine the natives' responses to the early years of the conquest. Most of these studies develop the thesis that the Amerindians consciously manipulated their "reality" to survive. They argue that the extent of change was the product of the human imagination, historical events, and environmental factors. For an excellent book that discusses the cultural adjustments of northern Peru to the Spanish conquest see Susan Elizabeth Ramírez, *The World Upside Down: Cross-Cultural Contact in Sixteenth Century Peru*.

8. Farriss, *Maya Society*, 9, 10.

9. López Sarrelangue, *La nobleza indígena*, 291–304.

10. Burkhart, *Slippery Earth*, 184.

11. For a recent work that highlights the 1562 crisis between the Maya and Bishop Diego de Landa see Clendinnen, *Ambivalent Conquests*, 72–92.

12. Van Zantwijk, *Servants of the Saints*, 175.

13. Farriss, *Maya Society*, 290.

14. William Madsen, "Religious Syncretism," in *Handbook of Middle American Indians*, 6:369–492.

15. Madsen, "Religious Syncretism," 377–378. The Virgin of Guadalupe is said to have appeared to Juan Diego, an Amerindian convert, at the hill of Tepeyac in 1531. Guadalupe is a major symbol of the Mexican national identity. She bridges the world of the Amerindian past with the Spanish domination. In the early colonial period she is employed as a means of evangelizing the natives; later on, Guadalupe acts as an *axis mundi* of liberation in various independence movements. Stafford Poole has written a monumental work that focuses on the historical sources of the Virgin of Guadalupe's apparition. See Stafford Poole, *Our Lady of Guadalupe: The Origins and Sources of a Mexican National Symbol, 1531–1797*.

BIBLIOGRAPHY

Acevedo Barba, Cruz Refugio, et al. *Mitos de la meseta tarasca: Un análisis estructural.* With a prologue by Genaro Zalpa Ramírez. Mexico City: Universidad Nacional Autónoma de México, 1982.

Actas de Cabildo de la Ciudad de México. 50 vols. Mexico City, 1889–1916.

Adams, Richard E. W. *Prehistoric Mesoamerica.* Boston: Little, Brown, 1977.

Aguayo Spencer, Rafael. *Don Vasco de Quiroga: Documentos.* Mexico City, 1939.

———. *Don Vasco de Quiroga: Taumaturgo de la organización social.* Mexico City: Ediciones Oasis, 1970.

Aldridge, John W. *The Hermeneutic of Erasmus.* Richmond, Va.: John Know Press, 1966.

Anderson, Benedict. *Imagined Communities: Reflections on the Spread of Nationalism.* London: Verso, 1983.

Aristotle. *Politics.* Translated by H. Rackham. Cambridge: Harvard University Press, 1944.

Arriaga Ochoa, Antonio. *Don Vasco de Quiroga y la ciudad de Pátzcuaro.* Mexico City: Editorial Libros de México, 1978.

———. *Organización social de los tarascos.* Morelia, Mexico: Departamento de extensión universitaria, 1938.

Asín Palacios, Miguel. *Huellas de Islam.* Madrid: Espasa-Calpe, 1941.

Atlas geográfico del estado de Michoacán. Mexico City: Universidad Nacional Autónoma de México, 1979.

Augustinus, Aurelius. *Concerning the City of God against the Pagans.* New York: Penguin Books, 1980.

Ávila, Santa Teresa de. *Las moradas.* Madrid: Editorial de Espiritualidad, 1982.

Baer, Yitzhak F. *A History of the Jews in Christian Spain.* 2 vols. Philadelphia: Jewish Publication Society of America, 1978.

Bainton, Roland H. *Erasmus of Christendom.* New York: Crossroads, 1969.

———. *The Reformation of the Sixteenth Century.* Boston: Beacon Press, 1952.

Basalenque, P. Diego. *Historia de la Provincia de San Nicolás de Tolentino de Michoacán del Orden de N.P.S. Agustín.* Mexico City: Editorial Jus, 1963.

Bataillon, Marcel. *Erasmo y España: Estudios sobre la historia espiritual del Siglo XVI.* Mexico City: Fondo de Cultura Económica, 1950.

———. Vasco de Quiroga et Bartolomé de Las Casas. *Revista de Historia de América* no. 33 (June 1952): 83–95.

Baudot, Georges. *Utopía e historia en México: Los primeros cronistas de la civilización mexicana (1520–1569).* Madrid: Espasa-Calpe, 1983.

Beaumont, Pablo. *Crónica de Michoacán.* 3 vols. Mexico City: Editorial Porrúa, 1932.

Bernal, Ignacio. *A History of Mexican Archaeology: The Vanished Civilizations of Middle America.* London: Thames and Hudson, 1980.

Bethell, Leslie, ed. *The Cambridge History of Latin America.* 5 vols. Cambridge: Cambridge University Press, 1984.

———, ed. *Colonial Spanish America.* Cambridge: Cambridge University Press, 1987.

Boff, Leonardo. *Saint Francis: A Model for Liberation.* New York: Crossroads, 1982.

Bolle, Kees W. Cosmology. In *The Encyclopedia of Religion,* edited by Mircea Eliade. Vol. 4. New York: Macmillan, 1987.

Boorstin, Daniel. *The Discoverers.* New York: Vintage Books, 1983.

Borah, Woodrow. *The Aboriginal Population of Central Mexico on the Eve of the Spanish Conquest.* Berkeley: University of California Press, 1963.

Boxer, C. R. *The Church Militant and Iberian Expansion, 1440–1770.* Baltimore: Johns Hopkins University Press, 1978.

Boyer, Louis. *Erasmus and the Humanist Experiment.* London: Newman Press, 1959.

Bravo Ugarte, José. *Historia sucinta de Michoacán.* Mexico City: Editorial Jus, 1963.

Brenner, Anita. *Idols behind the Altars.* Boston: Beacon Press, 1970.

Brundage, Burr Cartwright. *The Fifth Sun: Aztec Gods, Aztec World.* Austin: University of Texas Press, 1979.

Brunschvig, Robert. Abd. In *The Encyclopaedia of Islam.* Vol 1. London: Luzac and Company, 1960.

Burkhart, Louise M. *Holy Wednesday: A Nahua Drama from Early Colonial Mexico.* Philadelphia: University of Pennsylvania Press, 1996.

———. *The Slippery Earth: Nahua-Christian Moral Dialogue in Sixteenth-Century Mexico.* Tucson: University of Arizona Press, 1989.

Cabrera, Cristóbal de. Cristóbal Cabrera on the Missionary Methods of Vasco de Quiroga. Translated by Ernest Burrus. In *Manuscripta V.* 1961.

Callens, Paul L. *Tata Vasco: A Great Reformer of the Sixteenth Century.* Mexico City: Editorial Jus, 1959.

Cárdenas de la Peña, Enrique. *Precursor de seguridad social.* Mexico City: Instituto Mexicano del Seguro Social, 1968.

Caro Baroja, Julio. *The World of the Witches.* Chicago: University of Chicago Press, 1965.

Carrasco, David. *Quetzalcóatl and the Irony of Empire: Myths and Prophesies in the Aztec Tradition.* Chicago: University of Chicago Press, 1982.

Carrasco, Pedro. *Tarascan Folk Religion.* New Orleans: Tulane University Press, 1952.

Caso, Alfonso. *La religión de los aztecas.* Mexico City: Secretaría de Educación Pública, 1945.

Castro, Américo. *De la edad conflictiva*. Madrid: Taurus, 1961.

———. *The Spaniards: An Introduction to Their History*. Translated by Willard F. King and Selma Margaretten. Berkeley: University of California Press, 1971.

Chavero, Alfredo. *México a través de los siglos: Historia general y completa del desenvolvimiento social, político, religioso, militar, artístico, científico, y literario de México desde la antigüedad más remota hasta la época actual*. Mexico City: G. S. López, 1940.

Chevalier, François. *Land and Society in Colonial Mexico: The Great Hacienda*. Translated by Alvin Eustis and edited by Lesley Byrd Simpson. Berkeley: University of California Press, 1963.

Chipman, Donald E. *Nuño de Guzmán and the Province of Pánuco in New Spain, 1518–1533*. Glendale: A. H. Clark, 1967.

Christian, William. *Local Religion in Sixteenth-Century Spain*. Princeton, N.J.: Princeton University Press, 1981.

Chronicles of Michoacán: The Description of the Ceremonies, Rites, Population, and Government of the Indians of the Province of Michoacán, 1540–1541. Translated and edited by Eugene R. Craine and Reginald C. Reindorp. Norman: University of Oklahoma Press, 1970.

Clendinnen, Inga. *Ambivalent Conquests: Maya and Spaniard in Yucatan, 1517–1570*. Cambridge: Cambridge University Press, 1987.

Cohen, Anthony P. *The Symbolic Construction of Community*. Chichester, England: Ellis Horwood, 1985.

Cohen, Jeremy. *The Friars and the Jews*. Ithaca, N.Y.: Cornell University Press, 1982.

Colpe, Carsten. Syncretism. In *The Encyclopedia of Religion*, edited by Mircea Eliade. Vol. 14. New York: Macmillan, 1987.

Cook, Sherburne F., and Woodrow Borah. *The Indian Population of Central Mexico, 1531–1610*. Berkeley: University of California Press, 1960.

Corona Núñez, José. *Mitología tarasca*. Morelia, Mexico: Balsal Editores, 1973.

Cortés, Hernán. *Cartas de relación*. Mexico City: Editorial Porrúa, 1983.

———. *Letters from Mexico*. Edited by Anthony R. Pagden. New York: Grossman Press, 1971.

Couliano, Ioan P. *Eros and Magic in the Renaissance*. Chicago: University of Chicago Press, 1987.

Cronon, William. *Changes in the Land*. New York: Hill and Wang, 1983.

Crow, John A. *Spain: The Root and Flower*. Berkeley: University of California Press, 1985.

Cruces Caravajal, Ramón. *La obra educativa de Pedro de Gante en Tezcoco*. Texcoco, Mexico: Editorial Futura, n.d.

Cruz, Juan de la. *Dark Night of the Soul*. Garden City, N.Y.: Doubleday, 1959.

Cuevas, Mariano. *Documentos inéditos del Siglo XVI para la historia de México*. Mexico City: Editorial Porrúa, 1975.

———. *Historia de la Iglesia en México*. 5 vols. Mexico City: Editorial Porrúa, 1921–1928.

Davies, Nigel. *The Ancient Kingdoms of Mexico*. London: Allen Lane, 1982.

———. *The Toltec Heritage: From the Fall of Tula to the Rise of Tenochtitlán*. Norman: University of Oklahoma Press, 1980.

DeMolen, Richard L. *The Spirituality of Erasmus of Rotterdam*. Nieuwkoop: De Gaaf, 1987.

Díaz del Castillo, Bernal. *Historia verdadera de la conquista de la Nueva España.* 2 vols. Edited by Miguel León-Portilla. Madrid: Historia 16, 1984.

Douglas, Mary. *Natural Symbols: Explorations in Cosmology.* New York: Pantheon Books, 1982.

Durán, Fray Diego de. *Book of the Gods and Rites of the Ancient Calendar.* Norman: University of Oklahoma Press, 1971.

Eire, Carlos M. N. *War against the Idols: The Reformation of Worship from Erasmus to Calvin.* Cambridge: Cambridge University Press, 1986.

Eliade, Mircea. *The Myth of the Eternal Return, or Cosmos and History.* Princeton, N.J.: Princeton University Press, 1959.

———. *The Quest: History and Meaning in Religion.* Chicago: University of Chicago Press, 1969.

———. *The Sacred and the Profane: The Nature of Religion.* New York: Harcourt Brace Jovanovich, 1959.

———, ed. *The Encyclopedia of Religion.* 16 vols. New York: Macmillan, 1987.

Eliade, Mircea, and Lawrence Sullivan. Center of the World. In *The Encyclopedia of Religion,* edited by Mircea Eliade. Vol. 3. New York: Macmillan, 1987.

Eliade, Mircea, and Joseph M. Kitagawa, eds. *The History of Religions: Essays in Methodology.* Chicago: University of Chicago Press, 1959.

Elliott, John H. *Imperial Spain, 1469–1716.* 2 vols. New York: Mentor Books, 1966.

Erasmus, Desiderius. *The Education of a Christian Prince.* Translated by Lester Born. New York: Columbia University Press, 1936.

———. *El enquiridion o manual del caballero cristiano.* Edited by Dámaso Alonso with a prologue by Marcel Bataillon. Madrid: S. Aguirre, 1932.

———. *The Enchiridion of Erasmus.* Translated and edited by Raymond Himelick. Bloomington: Indiana University Press, 1963.

———. *In Praise of Folly.* London: G. Allen and Unwin Ltd., 1937.

Espinosa, Isidro Félix de. *Crónica de la Provincia Franciscana de los Apóstoles San Pedro y San Pablo de Michoacán.* Mexico City: Editorial Santiago, 1945.

Evans-Pritchard, E. E. *The Theories of Primitive Religion.* Oxford: Clarendon Press, 1982.

Farriss, Nancy M. *Maya Society under Colonial Rule: The Collective Enterprise of Survival.* Princeton, N.J.: Princeton University Press, 1984.

Fernández, Justino, and Edmundo O Gorman. *Santo Tomás More y la utopía de Tomás Moro en la Nueva España.* Mexico City: Alcancía, 1937.

Fiedel, Stuart J. *Prehistory of the Americas.* Cambridge: Cambridge University Press, 1987.

Fischer, L. E. *Viceregal Administration in the Spanish Colonies.* Berkeley: University of California Press, 1926.

Fischer, William Bayne, and Howard Bowen-Jones. *Spain: A Geographical Background.* London: Chato and Windus Educational Books, 1958.

Flannery, Kent V. The Origin of Agriculture. *Annual Review of Anthropology* 2 (1973): 271–310. Quoted in C. C. Lamberg-Karlovsky and Jeremy A. Sabloff, *Ancient Civilization: The Near East and Mesoamerica* (Menlo Park, Calif.: Benjamin/Cummings, 1979), 218–219.

Florescano, Enrique. *Memory, Myth, and Time in Mexico: From the Aztecs to Independence.* Austin: University of Texas Press, 1994.

Foster, George M. *Tzintzuntzan: Mexican Peasants in a Changing World.* Boston: Little, Brown, 1967.

Gándara, Felipe de. *Nobilario, armas y triunfos de Galicia hechos heróicos de sus hijos y elogios de su nobleza y de la mayor de España.* Madrid, 1677.

Gante, Pedro de. *Cartas.* Edited by F. de J. Chauvanet. Mexico City, 1951.

García Carrafa, Arturo, and Alberto García Carrafa. *Diccionario heráldico y genealógico de apellidos españoles y americanos.* Vol. 1. Madrid, n.d.

Gay, Peter. *The Enlightenment: An Interpretation.* New York: Knopf, 1967.

Geertz, Clifford. *The Interpretation of Cultures.* New York: Basic Books, 1973.

Gendrop, Paul. Mesoamerican Temples. In *The Encyclopedia of Religion*, edited by Mircea Eliade. Vol. 14. New York: Macmillan, 1987.

Gerhard, Peter. *A Guide to the Historical Geography of New Spain.* Cambridge: Cambridge University Press, 1972.

Gibson, Charles. *The Aztecs under Spanish Rule: A History of the Indians of the Valley of Mexico, 1519–1810.* Stanford, Calif.: Stanford University Press, 1964.

———. Review of *The Chronicles of Michoacán*, by Eugene R. Craine and Reginald C. Reindorp. *Hispanic American Historical Review* 51, no. 3 (August 1971): 512–513.

———. *Spain in America.* New York: Harper and Row, 1966.

———. *The Spanish Tradition in America.* Columbia: University of South Carolina Press, 1968.

———, ed. *The Black Legend: Anti-Spanish Attitudes in the Old World and New.* New York: Knopf, 1971.

Gilberti, Maturino. *Diccionario de la lengua tarasca de Michoacán.* Guadalajara, 1962.

Ginsberg, Carlos. *The Cheese and the Worms: The Cosmos of a Sixteenth Century Miller.* New York: Penguin Books, 1982.

Gojman Golberg, Alicia. *Los conversos en la Nueva España.* Mexico City: Universidad Nacional Autónoma de México, 1975.

González, Luis. *San José de Gracia: Mexican Village in Transition.* Translated by John Upton. Austin: University of Texas Press, 1972.

González Sánchez, Isabel. *El obispado de Michoacán en 1765.* Mexico City: Comité Editorial del Gobierno de Michoacán, 1985.

González Torres, Yolotl. *El sacrificio humano entre los mexicas.* Mexico City: Fondo de Cultura Económica, 1985.

Great Britain. Naval Intelligence Division. *Spain and Portugal.* Vol. 3, *The Peninsula.* Geographical Handbook Series. 1941.

Greenleaf, Richard. *The Mexican Inquisition.* Albuquerque: University of New Mexico Press, 1969.

———. *Zumárraga and the Mexican Inquisition, 1536–1543.* Washington, D.C.: Academy of American Franciscan History, 1961.

Grijalba, Juan de. *Crónica de la Orden de N.P.S. Augustín en las Provincias de la Nueva España.* Mexico City, 1927.

Grotanelli, Cristiano. Agriculture. In *The Encyclopedia of Religion*, edited by Mircea Eliade. Vol. 1. New York: Macmillan, 1987.

Gutiérrez Casillas S. J., José. *Historia de la Iglesia en México.* Mexico City: Editorial Porrúa, 1984.

Hanke, Lewis. *The Spanish Struggle for Justice.* Philadelphia: Little, Brown, 1949.

Herrejón Perredo, Carlos. *Humanismo y ciencia en la formación de México: Quinto coloquio de antropología e historia regionales.* Zamora, Mexico: Colegio de Michoacán, 1984.

Hunt, Eva. *The Transformation of the Hummingbird: Cultural Roots of a Zinacantecan Mythical Poem.* Ithaca, N.Y.: Cornell University Press, 1977.

Hutton, Lewis J. *The Christian Essence of Spanish Literature.* Lewiston, N.Y.: Edwin Mellen Press, 1988.

Icazbalceta, Joaquín García. *Don Fray Juan de Zumárraga: Primer obispo y arzobispo de México.* 4 vols. Edited by Rafael Aguayo Spencer and Antonio Castro Leal. Mexico City: Editorial Porrúa, 1947.

Ingham, John. *Mary, Michael, and Lucifer: Folk Catholicism in Central Mexico.* Austin: University of Texas Press, 1986.

Isaac, Claudia B. Witchcraft, Cooperatives, and Gendered Competition in a Purhépecha Community. *Frontiers: A Journal of Women Studies* 16, no. 2–3 (1996): 161-189.

Jarnés, Benjamin. *Don Vasco de Quiroga, obispo de utopia.* Mexico City, 1942.

Kamen, Henry. *Inquisition and Society in Spain.* Bloomington: University of Indiana Press, 1985.

———. *The Spanish Inquisition.* London: Weidenfeld and Nicolson, 1965.

Katz, Steven, ed. *Mysticism and Religious Traditions.* Oxford: Oxford University Press, 1983.

Keen, Benjamin. *Aztec Image in Western Thought.* New Brunswick, N.J.: Rutgers University Press, 1971.

Klein, Herbert S. *African Slavery in Latin America and the Caribbean.* New York: Oxford University Press, 1986.

Kristeller, Paul Oskar. *Renaissance Thought: The Classic, Scholastic, and Humanist Strains.* New York: Harper and Row, 1961.

Kubler, George. *The Art and Architecture of Ancient America: The Mexican, Mayan, and Andean Peoples.* New York: Penguin Books, 1962.

———. *Mexican Architecture in the Sixteenth Century.* 2 vols. New Haven, Conn.: Yale University Press, 1948. Published in Spanish as *Arquitectura mexicana del Siglo XVI* (Mexico City: Fondo de Cultura Económica, 1948).

Lacas, M. M. A Social Welfare Organizer in the Sixteenth-Century New Spain: Don Vasco de Quiroga, First Bishop of Michoacán. *Americas* 14 (1957–58): 57–86.

Lafaye, Jacques. *Quetzalcóatl and Guadalupe: The Formation of the Mexican Consciousness.* Chicago: University of Chicago Press, 1974.

Lamberg-Karlovsky, C. C., and Jeremy A. Sabloff. *Ancient Civilizations: The Near East and Mesoamerica.* Menlo Park, Calif.: Benjamin/Cummings, 1979.

Landa, Rubén. *Don Vasco de Quiroga.* Mexico City: Biografías Gandesa, 1965.

Las Casas, Bartolomé de. *Breve relación de la destrucción de las Indias Occidentales.* Mexico City: Libros Luciér Naga, 1957.

———. *Del único modo de atraer los pueblos a la verdadera religión.* Edited by Augustín

Millares Carlo and Lewis Hanke. Mexico City: Fondo de Cultura Económica, 1942.

———. *In Defense of the Indies.* Translated by Herma Briffault. New York: Seabury Press, Continuum Books, 1974.

Leclercq, Jean, et al. *A History of Christian Spirituality.* Vol. 2, *The Spirituality of the Middle Ages.* New York: Seabury Press, 1982.

León, Nicolás. *El libro de doctrina cristiana.* Mexico City, 1928.

———. *El Ylmo. Señor Don Vasco de Quiroga, primer obispo de Michoacán.* Mexico City, 1904.

———. *Studies on the Archaeology of Michoacán.* N.p., n.d.

León, Nicolás, and José Quintana. *Documentos inéditos referentes al ilustrísimo señor Don Vasco de Quiroga.* Mexico City, 1940.

León-Portilla, Miguel. *Aztec Thought and Culture: A Study of the Ancient Nahuatl Mind.* Norman: University of Oklahoma Press, 1963.

———. *The Broken Spears: The Aztec Account of the Conquest of Mexico.* Boston: Beacon Press, 1962.

———. *Los Franciscanos vistos por el hombre náhuatl.* Mexico City: Universidad Nacional Autónoma de México, 1985.

———. *Native American Spirituality: Ancient Myths, Discourses, Stories, Doctrines, Hymns, Poems from the Aztec, Yucatec, Quiche-Maya and Other Sacred Writings.* The Classics of Western Spirituality. New York: Paulist Press, 1980.

———. *Pre-Columbian Literatures of Mexico.* Norman: University of Oklahoma Press, 1969.

Levi-Strauss, Claude. *The Savage Mind.* Chicago: University of Chicago Press, 1966.

Lietz, Paul S. Vasco de Quiroga: Oidor Made Bishop. *Mid-America* 32 (1936): 13–32.

———. Vasco de Quiroga, Sociologist of New Spain. *Mid-America* 32 (1936): 247–259.

Liss, Peggy K. *Mexico under Spain, 1521–1556: Society and the Origins of Nationality.* Chicago: University of Chicago Press, 1975.

Lockhart, James, and Stuart Schwartz. *Early Latin America: A History of Colonial Spanish America and Brazil.* Cambridge: Cambridge University Press, 1983.

———. *The Nahuas after the Conquest: A Social and Cultural History of the Indians of Central Mexico, Sixteenth through Eighteenth Centuries.* Stanford, Calif.: Stanford University Press, 1992.

López Austin, Alfredo. *Cuerpo humano e ideología: Concepciones de los antiguos nahuas.* 2 vols. Mexico City: Universidad Nacional Autónoma de México, 1984.

López de Gómara, Francisco. *Cortés: The Life of the Conqueror by His Secretary.* Translated and edited by Lesley Byrd Simpson. Berkeley: University of California Press, 1964.

López Sarrelangue, Delfina Esmeralda. *La nobleza indígena de Pátzcuaro en la época virreinal.* Mexico City: Universidad Nacional Autónoma de México, 1965.

Lovejoy, Arthur O. *Essays in the History of Ideas.* Baltimore: Johns Hopkins University Press, 1948.

Lynch, John. *Spain under the Hapsburgs.* 2 vols. New York: New York University Press, 1974.

MacNeish, Richard S. Speculation about How and Why Food Production and Village Life Developed in the Tehuacán Valley, Mexico. *Archaeology* 24(4): 307–315. Quoted in C. C. Lamberg-Karlovsky and Jeremy A. Sabloff, *Ancient Civilizations: The Near East and Mesoamerica* (Menlo Park, Calif.: Benjamin/Cummings, 1979).

Madsen, William. Religious Syncretism. In *Handbook of Middle American Indians*, edited by Robert Wauchop. Vol. 6. Austin: University of Texas Press, 1967.

———. *The Virgin's Children*. Austin: University of Texas Press, 1960.

Manuel, Frank E., and Fritzie P. Manuel. *Utopian Thought in the Western World*. Cambridge: Harvard University Press, 1982.

Mariátegui, José Carlos. *Seven Interpretive Essays on Peruvian Reality*. Austin: University of Texas Press, 1971.

Mariéjol, Jean Hippolyte. *The Spain of Ferdinand and Isabella*. New Brunswick, N.J.: Rutgers University Press, 1961.

Marín, Tomás. La biblioteca del obispo Juan Bernal Díaz del Luco, 1495–1556. *Hispania Sacra* 5 (1952): 263–326.

McAlister, Lyle N. *Spain and Portugal in the New World, 1492–1700*. Minneapolis: University of Minnesota Press, 1984.

McAndrew, John. *The Open-Air Churches of Sixteenth Century Mexico*. Cambridge: Harvard University Press, 1965.

McGinn, Bernard. *The Calabrian Abbot: Joachim of Fiore in the History of Western Thought*. New York: Macmillan, 1985.

McGrath, Alister E. *Reformation Thought: An Introduction*. Oxford: Basil Blackwell, 1988.

McKeever, Furst, and Jill Leslie. *The Natural History of the Soul in Ancient Mexico*. New Haven and London: Yale University Press, 1995.

McNeill, William H. *Plagues and People*. Garden City, N.Y.: Anchor Press, 1976.

Méndez Arceo, Sergio. Contribución a la historia de Don Vasco de Quiroga. *Abside* 5 (1941): 59–68, 196–208.

———. Dos libros sobre Don Vasco de Quiroga. *Abside* 4 (1940): 62–64.

Mendieta, Gerónimo de. *Historia eclesiástica indiana*. 3 vols. Mexico City: Editorial Porrúa, 1980.

Menéndez y Pelayo, Marcelino. *Historia de los heterodoxos españoles*. 3 vols. Mexico City: Editorial Porrúa, 1982.

Merino, J. Antonio. *Humanismo franciscano*. Madrid: Ediciones Cristiandad, 1982.

Miller, Robert Ryal. *Mexico: A History*. Norman: University of Oklahoma Press, 1985.

Miranda, Francisco. Vasco de Quiroga, artífice humanista de la provincia de Michoacán. In *Humanismo y ciencia en la formación de México: Quinto coloquio de antropología e historia regionales*, by Carlos Herrejón Peredo, 131–156. Zamora, Mexico: Colegio de Michoacán, 1984.

———, ed. *La cultura purhé: Segundo coloquio de antropología e historia regionales*. Zamora, Mexico: Colegio de Michoacán, 1980.

Monaghan, John. *The Covenants with Earth and Rain: Exchange, Sacrifice, and Revelation in Mixtec Society*. Norman and London: University of Oklahoma Press, 1995.

Monsier, Roland. *Social Hierarchies, 1450 to the Present*. Translated by Peter Evans. New York: Schochen Books, 1973.

More, Thomas. *The Best State of the Commonwealth, the Discourse of the Extraordinary*

Character, Raphael Hythlodaeus, as Reported by the Renowned Figure, Thomas More, Citizen and Sheriff of the Famous City of Great Britain London. Edited by Edward Surtz. New Haven, Conn.: Yale University Press, 1964.

Moreno, Juan José. *Fragmentos de la vida y virtudes del V. Illmo. y Rmo. Sr. Dr. Don Vasco de Quiroga primer obispo de la Santa Iglesia Catedral de Michoacán, y fundador del Real, y Primitivo Colegio de S. Nicolás Obispo de Valladolid, 1766*. Edited by Jorge Diez González Cosio. Morelia, Mexico: Impreso de los Talleres Gráficos del Gobierno del Estado, 1965.

Morin, Claude. *Michoacán en la Nueva España del Siglo XVIII*. Mexico City: Fondo de Cultura Económica, 1979.

Mörner, Magnus. *Race Mixture in the History of Latin America*. Boston: Little, Brown, 1967.

Motolinía, Fray Toribio de Benavente. *Motolinía's History of the Indians of New Spain*. Translated and edited by Francis Borgia Steck. Washington, D.C.: Academy of American Franciscan History, 1951.

Mumford, Lewis. *The City in History*. New York: Harcourt Brace Jovanovich, 1961.

Muriel, Josefina. Las cofradías hospitalarias en la formación de la conciencia comunitaria. In *La cultura purhé: Segundo coloquio de antropología e historia regionales*, edited by Francisco Miranda, 225–236. Zamora, Mexico: Colegio de Michoacán, 1980.

Navarrete, Nicolás P. *Historia de la Provincia Agustiniana de San Nicolás de Tolentino de Michoacán*. 2 vols. Mexico City: Editorial Porrúa, 1978.

Nutini, Hugo G. *Todos Santos in Rural Tlazcala: A Syncretic, Expressive, and Symbolic Analysis of the Cult of the Dead*. Princeton, N.J.: Princeton University Press, 1988.

Nutini, Hugo G., and Betty Bell. *Ritual Kinship: The Structure and Historical Development of the Compadrazgo System in Rural Tlazcala*. Princeton, N.J.: Princeton University Press, 1980.

O'Gorman, Edmundo. Introduction to *Evolución política del pueblo mexicano*, by Justo Sierra. Mexico City: Casa de España en México, 1940.

———. *La invención de América*. Mexico City: Fondo de Cultura Económica, 1958.

Olin, John C. *Christian Humanism and the Reformation: Selected Writings of Erasmus*. New York: Fordham University Press, 1975.

Osment, Steven. *The Age of Reform, 1250–1550: An Intellectual and Religious History of Late Medieval and Reform Europe*. New Haven, Conn.: Yale University Press, 1980.

Oviedo, Gonzalo Fernández de. *Historia general y natural de las Indias*. 4 vols. Edited by Juan Pérez de Tudela Bueso. Madrid, 1959.

Paden, William E. *Religious Worlds: The Comparative Study of Religions*. Boston: Beacon Press, 1988.

Pagden, Anthony R. *The Fall of Natural Man: The American Indian and the Origins of Comparative Ethnology*. Cambridge: Cambridge University Press, 1982.

———. The Humanism of Vasco de Quiroga's *Información en Derecho*. In *Humanismus und Neue Welt*, edited by Wolfgang Reinhard. Weinheim: Acta Humaniora, 1987.

———. ed. *The Languages of Political Theory in Early-Modern Europe*. Cambridge: Cambridge University Press, 1987.

Paredes Martínez, Carlos S., et al. *Michoacán en el siglo XVI*. Morelia, Mexico: Fimax Publicistas, 1984.

Payne, Stanley. *Spanish Catholicism: An Historical Overview.* Madison: University of Wisconsin Press, 1984.

Paz, Octavio. *Labyrinth of Solitude.* New York: Grove Press, 1985.

Peers, E. Allison. *Studies in the Spanish Mystics.* 3 vols. New York: Macmillan, 1951.

Pellicer, Carlos. *Don Vasco de Quiroga y los hospitales pueblos.* Coyoacán, Mexico: Ediciones Monroy Padilla, 1968.

Peters, Edwards. *Inquisition.* Berkeley: University of California Press, 1988.

Phelan, John Leddy. *The Millennial Kingdom of the Franciscans in the New World: A Study in the Writings of Gerónimo de Mendieta, 1525-1604.* Berkeley: University of California Press, 1956.

Pierce, Roy Harvey. *Savagism and Civilization: A Study of the Indian and the American Mind.* Berkeley: University of California Press, 1988.

Ponce, Manuel, ed. *Don Vasco de Quiroga y arzobispado de Morelia.* Mexico City: Editorial Jus, 1965.

Poole, Stafford. *Our Lady of Guadalupe: The Origins and Sources of a Mexican National Symbol, 1531-1797.* Tucson: University of Arizona Press, 1996.

———. *Pedro Moya de Contreras: Catholic Reform and Royal Power in New Spain, 1571-1591.* Berkeley: University of California Press, 1987.

Powell, Philip Wayne. *Soldiers, Indians, and Silver.* Tempe: Arizona State University Press, 1975.

Quiroga, Vasco de. *Información en derecho del licenciado Quiroga sobre algunas provisiones del Real Consejo de las Indias.* Edited by Paulino Castañeda Delgado. Madrid: Ediciones José Porrúa Turanzas, 1974.

Quiroga Fajardo, Francisca de. *Memorial genealógico del claro vetustísimo origen del apellido de Quiroga y su descendencia solariega ilustre.* N.p., n.d.

Ramírez, Susan Elizabeth. *The World Upside Down: Cross-Cultural Contact in Sixteenth Century Peru.* Stanford, Calif.: Stanford University Press, 1996.

Redfield, Robert. *The Primitive World and Its Transformation.* Ithaca, N.Y.: Cornell University Press, 1977.

Reeves, Marjorie, and Warwick Gould. *Joachim of Fiore and the Myth of the Eternal Evangel in the Nineteenth Century.* Oxford, England: Clarendon Press, 1987.

Ricard, Robert. *The Spiritual Conquest of Mexico: An Essay on the Apostolate and the Evangelizing Methods of the Mendicant Orders in New Spain.* Berkeley: University of California Press, 1966.

Ries, Julien. Cross. In *The Encyclopedia of Religion*, edited by Mircea Eliade. Vol. 4. New York: Macmillan, 1987.

Romero Flores, Jesús. *Estudios históricos.* 2 vols. Mexico City: Costa-Amic Editor, 1966.

Sahagún, Bernardino de. *Historia general de las cosas de Nueva España.* Edited by Ángel María Garibay K. Mexico City: Editorial Porrúa, 1982.

Salas Léon, Antonio. *Pátzcuaro: Cosas de antaño y de hogaño.* Morelia, Mexico: Editorial Cantera, 1956.

Sánchez-Albornoz, Nicolás. The Population of Colonial Spanish America. In *The Cambridge History of Latin America*, edited by Leslie Bethell. Vol. 21. Cambridge: Cambridge University Press, 1984.

Saunders, J. J. *A History of Medieval Islam.* London: Routledge and Kegan Paul, 1982.

Schoeck, R. J. *Erasmus Grandescens: The Growth of a Humanist's Mind and Spirituality.* Nieukoop: De Gaaf, 1988.

Scholes, France V., and Eleanor Adams, eds. *Proceso contra Tzintzicha Tangaxoan el Calzontzin formado por Nuño de Guzmán año de 1530.* Mexico City, 1952.

Schwaller, John Frederick. *The Church and Clergy in Sixteenth-Century Mexico.* Albuquerque: University of New Mexico Press, 1987.

Sejourné, Laurette. *Burning Water: Thought and Religion in Ancient Mexico.* Berkeley, Calif.: Shambala Press, 1976.

Shaffer, Ellen. *Fray Maturino Gilberti and His Books.* Los Angeles: Dawson's Book Shop, 1963.

Shields, W. Eugene. *King and Church: The Rise and Fall of the Patronato Real.* Chicago: Loyola University Press, 1961.

Sierra, Justo. *Evolución política del pueblo mexicano.* Mexico City: Casa de España en México, 1940.

Simpson, Lesley Byrd. *The Encomienda in New Spain: The Beginning of Spanish Mexico.* Berkeley: University of California Press, 1950.

Skinner, Quentin. Sir Thomas More's *Utopia* and the Language of Renaissance Humanism. Quoted in Anthony R. Pagden, *The Language of Political Theory in Early-Modern Europe* (Cambridge: Cambridge University Press, 1987), 128–129.

Soto González, Enrique. *Antología de Pátzcuaro.* Pátzcuaro: Impresos Hurtado, 1983.

Soustelle, Jacques. *The Olmecs: The Oldest Civilization in Mexico.* Norman: University of Oklahoma Press, 1985.

Spivakovsky, Erika. *Son of the Alhambra: Don Diego Hurtado de Mendoza, 1504–1575.* Austin: University of Texas Press, 1970.

Steinberg, Leo. *The Sexuality of Christ in Renaissance Art and in Modern Oblivion.* New York: Pantheon Books, 1983.

Taylor, William B. *Drinking, Homicide, and Rebellion in Colonial Mexican Villages.* Stanford, Calif.: Stanford University Press, 1979.

———. *Magistrates of the Sacred: Priests and Parishioners in Eighteenth-Century Mexico.* Stanford, Calif.: Stanford University Press, 1996.

Tellechea Idigoras, José Ignacio. *El arzobispo Carranza y su tiempo.* 2 vols. Madrid: Ediciones Guadarrama, 1968.

Tena Ramírez, Felipe. *Vasco de Quiroga y sus pueblos de Santa Fe en los Siglos XVIII y XIX.* Mexico City: Editorial Porrúa, 1977.

Toussaint, Manuel. *Pátzcuaro.* Mexico City, 1952.

Turner, Victor. *The Ritual Process.* Ithaca, N.Y.: Cornell University Press, 1969.

Turner, Victor, and Edith Turner. *Image and Pilgrimage in Christian Culture.* New York: Columbia University Press, 1978.

Urban, Greg, and Joel Sherzer, eds. *Nation-States and Indians in Latin America.* Austin: University of Texas Press, 1991.

Vaillant, George C. *The Aztecs of Mexico: Origin, Rise, and Fall of the Aztec Nation.* Harmondsworth, England: Penguin Books, 1950.

Van Zantwijk, R. A. M. *Servants of the Saints: The Social and Cultural Identity of a Tarascan Community in Mexico.* Assen, Netherlands: Royal Van Gorcum, 1967.

Varner, John, and Jeannette Varner. *The Dogs of the Conquest*. Norman: University of Oklahoma Press, 1983.

Velásquez Gallardo, Pablo. *Diccionario de la lengua phorhépecha*. Mexico City: Fondo de Cultura Económica, 1978.

Verástique, Bernardino. The Millennial Kingdom in Mexico. *Harvard Divinity Bulletin* 22, no. 1 (1992): 6–9.

Villaseñor, Raul. Luciano, Moro y el utopismo de Vasco de Quiroga. *Cuadernos Americanos* 68 (March–April 1953): 155–175.

Vives, Jaime Vicens. *Approaches to the History of Spain*. Translated by Joan Ullman. Berkeley: University of California Press, 1970.

Von Winning, Hasso. *Pre-Columbian Art of Mexico and Central America*. New York: Harry Abrams, 1968.

Warren, Fintan B. *Vasco de Quiroga and His Pueblo-Hospitals of Santa Fe*. Washington, D.C.: Academy of American Franciscan History, 1963.

Warren, J. Benedict. The Caravajal Visitation: First Spanish Survey of Michoacán. *Americas* 19 (April 1963): 404–412.

———. *The Conquest of Michoacán: The Spanish Domination of the Tarascan Kingdom in Western Mexico, 1521–1530*. Norman: University of Oklahoma Press, 1985.

———. Fray Jerónimo de Alcalá: Author of the *Relación de Michoacán? Americas* 27 (1970–1971): 307–327.

———. *La administración de los negocios de un encomendero en Michoacán*. Morelia, Mexico: SEP/UN SNH, 1984.

Watanabe, John M. *Maya Saints and Souls in a Changing World*. Austin: University of Texas Press, 1994.

West, Delno C., and Sandra Zimdars-Swartz. *Joachim of Fiore: A Study in Spiritual Perception and History*. Bloomington: University of Indiana Press, 1983.

West, Robert C. *Cultural Geography of the Modern Tarascan Area*. Washington, D.C.: Smithsonian Institute of Social Anthropology, 1948.

Wheatley, Paul. *The Pivot of the Four Quarters*. Chicago: Aldine, 1971.

Wilder Weisman, Elizabeth, and Hancock Sandoval, Judith. *Art and Time in Mexico: From the Conquest to the Revolution*. New York: Harper and Row, 1985.

Wolf, Eric. *Sons of the Shaking Earth*. Chicago: University of Chicago Press, 1959.

Zavala, Silvio Arturo. *Ideario de Vasco de Quiroga*. Mexico City: Colegio de México, 1941.

———. *La Utopía de Tomás en la Nueva España y otros estudios*. Mexico City: Antigua Librería Robredo, 1937.

———. La visión del mundo y de la vida entre los Purhépecha. Quoted in *La cultura purhé: Segundo coloquio de antropología e historia regionales*, edited by Francisco Miranda (Zamora, Mexico: Colegio de Michoacán, 1980), 143–158.

———. *Recuerdos de Vasco de Quiroga*. Mexico City: Editorial Porrúa, 1965.

———. *Sir Thomas More in New Spain: A Utopian Adventure of the Renaissance*. London: Hispanic and Luso-Brazilian Councils, 1955.

Zea, Leopoldo. *The Latin American Mind*. Norman: University of Oklahoma Press, 1963.

INDEX

abandonment movement (*abandono*), 58, 59–60
acháecha, 16
Acosta, Jorge, 8
Adams, Richard E. W., 5, 154
Agatha, Saint, 54
Aguayo Spencer, Rafael, xiv, 87, 110, 127, 132, 134, 165, 167
Agurto, López de, 130
Ahchuri-hierepe, 34
Al Andalus, 42
Albornoz, Juan de, 73
Albornoz, Rodrigo de, 73, 74
Alcalá, Alfonso de, 62
Alcalá, Jerónimo de, 9, 105–106, 148
Alcalá, University of, 62
alcaldes ordinario, 132
Alcántara, 48
Alexandrine Bulls of Donation, 120
Alfonso the Chaste, 47
Altamira, 38–39
Alumbrado movement, the. *See* Illuminist movement, the
Álvarez, Luis, 89
Amerindians: and Christianity, 126, 151, 152, 157, 168; and *cofradía* system, 139–140; culture of, xv–xvi, 115,

118, 151, 153, 164; mendicants and, 102, 150; religion of, 23–24; and Spanish conquest, xiv, xv, 145, 146, 149, 163, 171; in 20th Century, xvi. *See also* Aztecs; Chichimec; Mayans; Mesoamericans; naturales; Olmecs; Purhépecha; Purhépecha-Chichimec; Toltecs
Ancient Engenderer, The (Tharés Upeme), 10
Andalucía, Plain of, 38
Anderson, Benedict, 154
angatácui, 16
anti-Semitism, 160
Arab occupation in Spain, 40–42. *See also* Islam; Muslims
Arellano, Pedro de, 125, 126
Aryanism, 40
Asín Palacio, Miguel, 159
Atlas geográfico del estado de Michoacán, 154
Auándaro, 23, 26
Audiencia (first), 75, 78, 80, 86, 163
Audiencia (second), 86, 93, 125, 126, 128, 129, 130. *See also* Quiroga, Vasco de
Augustine, Saint, 42–43
Augustinians, 66, 79, 98, 99, 108, 147